P9-CQM-802

Students with Asperger Syndrome: A Guide for College Personnel

Lorraine E. Wolf, Ph.D.,
Jane Thierfeld Brown, Ed.D.,
and G. Ruth Kukiela Bork, M.Ed.

Foreword by Fred Volkmar, M.D., and Ami Klin, Ph.D.

APC

Autism Asperger Publishing Company
P.O. Box 23173
Shawnee Mission, Kansas 66283-0173
877-277-8254
www.asperger.net

© 2009 Autism Asperger Publishing Co.
P.O. Box 23173
Shawnee Mission, Kansas 66283-0173
www.asperger.net • 913.897.1004

All rights reserved. With the exception of Appendices C-G, no part of the material protected by this copyright notice may be reproduced or used in any form or by any means, electronic or mechanical, including photocopying, recording, or by any information storage and retrieval system, without the prior written permission of the copyright owner.

Publisher's Cataloging-in-Publication

Wolf, Lorraine E.

    Students with Asperger syndrome : a guide for college personnel / Lorraine E. Wolf, Jane Thierfeld Brown, and G. Ruth Kukiela Bork: foreword by Fred Volkmar, and Ami Klin. -- 1st ed. -- Shawnee Mission, Kan. : Autism Asperger Pub. Co., c2009.

        p. ; cm.

    ISBN: 978-1-934575-39-0
    LCCN: 2009900450
    Includes bibliographical references and index.

        1. Counseling in higher education--Handbooks, manuals, etc. 2. Student affairs services--Handbooks, manuals, etc. 3. Asperger's syndrome--Patients--Education (Higher) I. Brown, Jane Thierfeld. II. Bork, G. Ruth Kukiela. III. Title.

LB2343 .W65 2009
378.198--dc22   0902

This book is designed in Boton and Times New Roman.

Printed in the United States of America.

Acknowledgments

Thank you to all of the students we have worked with over the years who have educated us about Asperger Syndrome and the autism spectrum in general. We have learned more from our collective students than from anyone else.

Thank you also to our families for their unflagging support of our work and writing and to our own children on the spectrum, the inspiration for our work.

Thank you to Boston University, The University of Connecticut School of Law and The Center for Students with Disabilities, and Northeastern University for the support they offer to our students and for encouraging us to pursue our passions.

This book could not have been written without the support of our colleagues at the University of Minnesota, especially Lisa King, who contributed to this book, and Carrie Kelly. Thank you both. Also thanks to Brie Kluytenaar, Janice O'Leary, and Heather Carlson, who helped with editing. Finally, to our editor at AAPC, Kirsten McBride, who pushed us and greatly improved our book, our sincere thanks.

Lorraine Wolf
Jane Thierfeld Brown
G. Ruth Kukiela Bork

Table of Contents

Foreword

Sixty years after the original description of Asperger Syndrome (AS) (Asperger, 1944, see Asperger 1991 translation), there is still much debate as to whether it should be differentiated from autism and other clinical concepts (Klin, McPartland, & Volkmar, 2005). Despite these ongoing scholarly discussions, there is little doubt that the inclusion of AS in the American Psychiatric Association's *Diagnostic and Statistical Manual, 4th Edition* (DSM-IV; American Psychiatric Association [APA], 1994) has stimulated much research and interest in more able individuals with early emerging and longstanding social disability. While the finer points of nosology and validity may be of interest to some, this issue is much less relevant to the practical challenges that these individuals and their families face in their daily lives, which should therefore be a priority for discussion and action by the community as a whole.

Commensurate with the increase in knowledge, advances in treatment and other factors have led to a significantly improved outcome for many individuals with AS (Howlin, 2005; National Research Council, 2001). This has meant that a growing number of individuals are now able to lead productive lives, including enrolling in college. This wonderful development, in turn, has posed some important challenges for parents, the students themselves, as well as institutions of higher education. This volume provides a comprehensive approach to the issues related to including students with AS in college life. Here we establish the context making this book such an important resource.

In the past decade, many positive developments have impacted on the lives of individuals with AS. First, there is much greater recognition that their social and communicative difficulties are real, and not the result of willful transgressions of societal mores and regulations. This is critical because absence of this knowledge has been associated with unjust and unhelpful punishment, as these individuals were often ostracized and at times victimized by their peers and by the educational system. Indeed, this development has resulted in a legal mandate for provision of services that address their needs while capitalizing on their strengths.

Second, our view and adopted definitions of autism-related conditions have broadened considerably, with dramatic increase in prevalence rates that, at least partly, reflect the inclusion of a vast population that was previously invisible to all (at least until becoming the subjects of negative attention or disciplinary action). The recognition that these individuals require services is associated with greater understanding of their challenges and assets, making their welfare and success the province of discussion and action by a wide range of service providers and advocates, whereas previously they had been a private experience with which the individuals themselves and their families wrestled alone, in private and with no supports.

Third, while previously notions of the pervasive social disability often obfuscated the fact that these individuals have assets that may hold the key to better outcomes, there is now much more willingness to build, nurture, and channel their talents for the purpose of fostering independent living, vocational opportunities, and meaningful relationships.

Despite these positive developments, however, great challenges remain. While the K-12 system boasts noticeable improvements for students with Asperger Syndrome, there is an anachronistic disregard in society for what happens to these students as they transition into their adult lives. Thus, the lives of adults with AS often become the reality of only themselves and their families. This represents a tremendous missed opportunity for society at large, since relatively small supports might signify the difference between a self-satisfying and fulfilling life and one that is lived on the periphery of the mainstream where opportunities are meager and challenges are great.

This book is an important corrective step on this course. As more and more individuals with Asperger Syndrome become prospective college students, the system remains largely unprepared to receive them. While some students succeed as a testimony to their perseverance and resourcefulness, as well as their families' commitment and dedication, many do not. For those who succeed, the community is enriched by their talents and special perspectives, as prospective employers should be by their talents, reliability, and sense of loyalty.

What it takes is knowledge of what is needed to facilitate success in college and a strong conviction that these individuals should no longer be a ghost population, unknown by many and misunderstood by others.

This book spells out with clarity and practical good sense the range of steps that are needed to maximize success at this critical transition into adulthood. Colleges need to be prepared. The challenges faced by students with Asperger Syndrome are now well known. And so are effective remediating approaches and helpful resources and supports. The result to aim for is one of self-reinforcing success, when the students are valued for their unique contributions while being supported in areas that can derail the process of becoming self-reliant and productive members of the community.

To those who are not aware of Asperger Syndrome, the fact that great intellectual potential can co-exist with pronounced (at times profound) deficits in social and real-life skills, including "street smarts" (Klin, Saulnier, Sparrow et al., 2007), can be puzzling. Or that a great deal of factual knowledge (Klin, Danovitch, Merz, Dohrmann, & Volkmar, 2007) can co-exist with life-impairing organizational skills deficits and constraining routines (Ozonoff, 1997) is difficult to grasp. Knowledge of these common discrepancies and strategies to support and nurture the hearts and minds of individuals with Asperger Syndrome are exactly the tools that every college staff member should have in welcoming them to a promising adult life.

This is the message of this book. We congratulate Drs. Brown and Wolf and Dean Bork for compiling this comprehensive recipe for success. Our hope is that it will become a ubiquitous resource on the desks of faculty and support staff members in our colleges, and frequently used by clinicians and therapists who work with this population, in this and other countries. We can no longer pin the blame of the unacceptable status quo on lack of knowledge. This book is living proof of that. And it is also a recipe for action.

Fred R. Volkmar, M.D.
Director, Yale Child Study Center
Irving B. Harris Professor of Child Psychiatry,
Pediatrics and Psychology

Ami Klin, Ph.D.
Director, Autism Program, Yale Child Study Center
Harris Associate Professor of Child Psychology and Psychiatry

CHAPTER 1

Introduction

Students with Asperger Syndrome (AS)[1] are often very advanced in terms of intelligence and academic ability. Yet, these intellectually brilliant students often struggle in the realm of higher education. Despite intellectual and academic gifts, persons with AS have a decreased ability to decipher the intentions and actions of others, to integrate multiple streams of incoming information, and to navigate an increasingly complex social world. They may be rigid and perfectionistic and resist changing to meet the demands of their environment.

Students with AS are not like other groups of students with disabilities.

Students with AS are often naïve and, therefore, are easily victimized by others who possess more social savvy. As college students, they are challenged by deficits in social and interpersonal skills, organization, and self-advocacy, the very skills that are essential for success in college and beyond (Wolf, Thierfeld Brown, Bork, & Shore, 2004).

Many campuses are working to improve programming to support this very able yet challenging population of young people.

---

[1]While we use the term "Asperger Syndrome" in the title and generally throughout the book, we do not intend to be exclusive. We believe that this volume and the strategies presented are appropriate for most college students across the autism spectrum, including those who have high-functioning autism, Asperger Syndrome, pervasive developmental disorders-not otherwise specified, nonverbal learning disorders, and so on. We often use the abbreviation "ASD" (autism spectrum disorders) in the text to further that point.

Students with AS are not like other groups of students with disabilities. They experience pervasive difficulties in most aspects of the higher educational experience, including social as well as cognitive and academic domains. Accommodating students whose disabilities may very likely be in social and self-regulatory areas is a particular challenge for service providers who are not accustomed to reaching out into so many areas of student life.

Asperger Syndrome is a genetic neurodevelopmental disorder at the mildest end of the autism spectrum (American Psychiatric Association [APA], 1994; Asperger, 1991). It carries the best prognosis of all the spectrum disorders for independent functioning in adulthood, as many individuals complete high school and college and go on to successful careers. Recent coverage in the popular press and national talk shows has highlighted the surge in the diagnosis of autism and related disorders, often referring to it as having reached an "epidemic" level.

While the cause(s) remain unclear, there is no doubt that the public school system is facing increased numbers of students with AS and is making great efforts to deliver enhanced supports for these youngsters, enabling many to navigate their K-12 educational experience. Consequently, colleges and universities nationwide are also seeing a marked increase in the numbers of students who carry autism spectrum diagnoses such as Asperger Syndrome and are often unsure of the best way to respond to their needs (Wolf, Thierfeld Brown, & Bork, 2001).[2]

When the authors began talking to the disability service (DS) community about Asperger Syndrome eight years ago, the condition was

---

[2]Portions of the volume have been excerpted with permission from Thierfeld Brown, J. & Wolf, L. (in press). Transition to higher education for students with autism spectrum disorder. In A. Klin, F. Volkmar, & S. S. Sparrow (Eds.), *Asperger Syndrome* (2nd ed.). New York: Guilford Press.

largely unfamiliar to providers. A recent (2006) informal survey of 42 colleges by one of us (JTB) found an average of 4.28 students with AS at four-year institutions and 8.9 students at community and technical colleges. The recent prevalence estimate of 1:150 by the Centers for Disease Control and Prevention (CDC, 2007) predicts that the numbers will continue to grow. Many suspect that the increase in numbers reflects, in part, the inclusion of more individuals at the boundaries of autism (Rutter, 2005b) who would not have been previously diagnosed. It is these young people with milder symptoms who may well be our incoming population of college students in the future.

It is these young people with milder symptoms who may well be our incoming population of college students in the future.

Students with AS will continue to enter college in increasing numbers. While their needs differ from those of other populations seen by DS professionals and higher education administrators, the college environment can be uniquely equipped to help these students gain independence and become functional, gainfully employed adults. That said, most professionals and staff who will interact with students with AS know little about AS and how it affects daily life.

A bit of education and training can go a long way toward helping students have a successful college experience. To that end, we have written this book geared towards college administrators and DS professionals but also providing much-needed information to faculty, medical professionals, secondary school special educators, families, and students themselves.

Accommodating college students with AS involves a dynamic interplay between extrinsic and intrinsic variables. *Intrinsic variables* are those attributes that students with AS bring to campus. Intrinsically, each AS student varies from the "neurotypical" student in cognitive, behavioral, and/or social domains. We will discuss these in greater detail in Chapter 2. *Extrinsic variables* encompass the features that characterize each campus, such as size, location, campus culture (liberal, conservative, party school, Greek life, etc.), course and degree requirements, and so forth. Extrinsic variables may be relatively fixed within the individual institution or more malleable, depending on the campus.

The need to combine intrinsic student and extrinsic campus variables with changes experienced by all students entering postsecondary education (such as academics, classrooms, and housing) leaves some students with AS feeling totally overwhelmed. The more campus professionals understand how hard change is for students with AS and how different each case may be, the more we can do to help this population of bright and inquisitive students who have so much to offer.

The more campus professionals understand how hard change is for students with AS and how different each case may be, the more we can do to help this population of bright and inquisitive students who have so much to offer.

Why Should We Care?

Asperger Syndrome can have local impact on the individual's day-to-day functioning, but also has larger implications for a student's future. Consider employment, for example. According to 2004 U.S. Bureau of Labor Statistics (2004), the occupations with the largest anticipated job growth over the next decade are largely in service sectors.

10 Occupations with the Largest Job Growth, 2004-2014	
• Retail salespersons • Registered nurses • Postsecondary teachers • Customer service representatives • Janitors and cleaners, except maids & housekeeping cleaners • Waiters and waitresses	• Combined food preparation & serving workers, including fast food • Home health aides • Nursing aides, orderlies, attendants • General & operations managers (http://www.bls.gov)

Because of their interpersonal challenges, employment in the service sector is often the worst possible choice for those on the spectrum. Imagine an individual who does not make eye contact and speaks in a low voice functioning in food services as a waiter. However, detail-oriented people with AS might be very well suited to function in the postsecondary environment or in the high-tech fields as educators or researchers. College campuses are among the most tolerant cultures in the nation. Institutions of higher education encourage deep knowledge of one specific topic, something students with AS excel at before they even come to college. Whenever possible, university education is crucial for individuals with AS to succeed in later years.

From another perspective, along with the obvious high-tech and computer skills necessary in today's job market, the following attributes (Tan, 2007; workforce2.org) have been targeted as core assets employers look for in job candidates: (a) drive, (b) team orientation, (c) leadership, (d) enthusiasm and energy, (e) knowledge, (f) communication skills, (g) decision-making skills, (h) strategic thinking ability, (i) organizing and planning, and (j) ability to think outside the box.

While not every individual with AS possesses these qualities, many do. What employer would not value an honest, detail-oriented computer expert? Or one with a strong sense of right and wrong and a unique way of solving tricky analytical problems? Moving students into employment opportunities where these qualities can be coupled with an advanced knowledge base and nurtured in a supportive and accepting environment will be one of the challenges faced in higher education in the coming years.

The consequence of not creating an educated community prepared to accept students with AS is a society unprepared to support this large population with public assistance.

The consequence of not creating an educated community prepared to accept students with AS is a society unprepared to support this large population with public assistance. The 1-in-150 number of incidence cited by the CDC (www.cdc.gov) will begin to be realized when overeducated and under- or unemployed adults with AS are brought into the welfare and social service systems. Individuals without jobs will pose a burden on their families, on insurance companies, and on federal and state social services. This is not only unnecessary but also critically unfair to a large group of people in our society. To prevent this scenario, changes in educating the community must begin now.

A Favorable Prognosis

The good news is that Asperger Syndrome is a disorder that can and does change over time, as we will illustrate in this book. Studies have shown that three important variables characterize

Introduction

individuals with AS who have the best outcome – age, symptom level, and intelligence (Coplan, 2000). Thus, good outcome in AS may be associated with relatively higher intellect (Szatmari, Bryson, Boyle, Streiner, & Duku, 2003; Tantam, 1991). Therefore, intelligent young adults with AS whose symptom levels allow them to complete a college degree and enter the workforce may have the best prognosis for promising futures. This book is devoted to addressing the ways in which institutes of higher education can best foster this development.

There is a dearth of information available to professionals working with students with autism spectrum disorders preparing to go to college and to the colleges and universities preparing to receive them. This book will serve as a comprehensive resource for a wide range of individuals who work with college students with autism spectrum diagnoses, including postsecondary disability support personnel, college and university administrators, faculty, and staff.

This volume includes chapters and a detailed set of appendices (Appendices A and B for readers who wish to go into greater depth) on prevalence, history and definitions, clinical, cognitive and behavioral symptoms, biological and brain theories, and how to understand clinical information such as diagnostic evaluations and treatment reports. An emphasis is placed on understanding the challenges of Asperger Syndrome and how it manifests in young adults and how to recognize and accommodate symptoms and behaviors in the classroom, residence halls, and the campus at large. The appendices include useful intake and information forms, sample faculty letters and fact sheets, documentation guidelines, training modules, and more.

This book represents the combined efforts and expertise of three seasoned professionals who have been working together for nearly a decade. As experienced educators, clinicians, and DS providers with over 50 years' combined experience, we recognize what is necessary for students with autism spectrum disorders to be successful in college. We also fully appreciate the training necessary for administrators, faculty, and disability providers to accommodate students on the autism spectrum on their campuses. Further, as administrators, we are in tune with the policy and procedural challenges posed by the increasing numbers of students attending colleges and universities in this county. Finally, each of us is the parent of children with special needs (including several on the autism spectrum), which affords us an uncommon and exceptional perspective of this group of young adults.

CHAPTER 2

The Syndrome

The "Typical" Student with Asperger Syndrome

Imagine if you processed the pieces of the environment around you in the order in which they came and you could not organize the bits. Imagine if you then screened out some of the details because they confused or overwhelmed you. Imagine that you could not rely on consistency in your sensory environment and that light and sounds could be unpredictably painful. Imagine if you did not recognize people's faces at times or became easily lost in an otherwise familiar place. What if you could not conceive how or even the fact that other people process their environment any differently?

Now imagine that you are expected to comply with all of these things you don't understand, while also having to cope with confusion and fear.

This is a snapshot of how a brain wired with AS works. This is a person who can walk down a street on a city campus and notice orange cones, then yellow tape, then a backhoe nearby, but might screen out the gaping hole just to his right because it was not there yesterday. This individual is not adding up all of the sensory and environmental pieces that signal the presence of an active construction zone and possible danger. The same individual may not fathom that there is more than one way to interpret a passage of literature and may ignore the rules of the classroom because she doesn't understand them.

The typical AS college student is male, appears lumbering, clumsy, or physically rigid. He may appear "down" or depressed, and may even admit to sadness or loneliness. He may violate your personal space, standing too close or talking too loud. His vocal characteristics may be odd or somehow "off." He may use strange or stilted phrases or gestures, have singsong or monotonic speech, and not stop talking to check your reaction or listen to what you have to say. Alternately, he may say nothing at all, even with prompting, as he may be too socially inhibited to speak up.

He may have poor eye contact, looking off to your shoulder or behind you rather than looking at your eyes. Conversely, he may fix you with a stare that makes you uncomfortable. His dress and body habits may be slightly off; he may be wearing disheveled, dirty, or unfashionable clothes. He appears bright but may also appear vague and lost, seeming to follow what you say but not really understanding you. Most notably, he rarely comes to professional attention (such as the DS office on campus) on his own, particularly when he is younger. Rather, he comes under pressure from another office on campus or is brought to the attention of the disability office by his parents.

Understanding how students with AS comprehend the world is especially important for professionals working with this population.

Understanding how students with AS comprehend the world is especially important for professionals working with this population. It is also the most important aspect in developing effective accommodation plans for students with this disorder. People with AS perceive the world differently than most "neurotypicals" (a term often used to denote people who are not on the autism spectrum). Indeed, the environment we see as appropriate for learning is sometimes barely negotiable for students in this population, as illustrated in the following.

You have walked into a math class overcrowded with strangers whose language is too fast and too loud to decipher. The professor enters and conducts the class in a foreign language that you do not speak or understand. The lights in the room are so bright that they hurt your eyes and the hum of the air conditioner is at a frequency that makes you clench your teeth in pain.

Under these extreme conditions, you are expected to learn calculus.

This is an all-too-familiar scenario for many students with AS. If we do not understand these basic underpinnings, it may be nearly impossible to work with the student and the educational environment to foster success.

Definition and History

1943	Leo Kanner manuscript in United States
1944	Hans Asperger manuscript in Europe
1981	Lorna Wing describes "autistic triad"
1991	Uta Frith translation of Asperger monograph
1994	Asperger Syndrome coded into the *Diagnostic and Statistical Manual of Mental Disorders* (DSM-IV)

Asperger Syndrome gets its name from the work done by Austrian pediatrician Hans Asperger during World War II (Frith, 1991). Asperger described a group of boys with social, affective, and other disturbances that he termed "autistic psychopathy."

Around the same time, Leo Kanner, an Austrian psychiatrist who emigrated to the United States, published a description of autism after studying a group of children he diagnosed as having "autistic disturbances of affective contact" (Kanner, 1943). Kanner's manuscript attracted more attention from mainstream American child psychiatry by virtue of its publication in English.

In 1981 British psychiatrist Lorna Wing published a paper discussing the syndrome in 35 individuals (Wing, 1981). Wing first named the set of symptoms described by Kanner and Asperger as "Asperger Syndrome" and codified the "autistic triad" of deficits in social, behavioral, and language domains (Wing, 1981). Uta Frith's (1991) translation brought Asperger's original monograph to the attention of the wider English-speaking psychiatric community. Fifty years after its original publication, Hans Asperger was recognized by the American Psychiatric Association when the syndrome that bears his name was added to the fourth edition of the *Diagnostic and Statistical Manual of Mental Disorders*, known as the DSM (APA, 1994). This will be discussed in more detail below.

Incidence

The incidence rates of AS diagnoses have spiked in the last decade, as reported from multiple recent sources (Gillberg & Wing, 1999; Prior, 2003; Rutter, 2005b). Original incidence rates for autism hovered around 4 to 5 per 10,000 births (Lotter, 1966; also see review in Yeargin-Allsopp et al., 2003). A recent study reported that the increase in autism referrals in California has increased by 210% over the past 10 years (California Health and Human Services Agency, 1999; Croen, Grether, Hoogstrate, & Selvin, 2002).

As mentioned, in spring of 2008, the CDC revised its incidence estimates from 1:166 to as high as 1:150 for all disorders on the autism spectrum (www.cdc.gov). The CDC collected data from health care providers, hospitals, and school districts in six states. Certain states reported a higher prevalence than other states in the sample. New Jersey reported the highest prevalence, West Virginia the lowest. The reasons for the increase in identified children are unknown, although they are likely multifactorial. We will discuss some of the theories regarding prevalence below.

Increased awareness on the part of parents, medical professionals, and the educational system has resulted in an increased number of referrals of atypical children. Certainly, public awareness and recognition, formal codification of diagnostic criteria, and inclusion in the DSM has helped specialists identify children and adults with the syndrome. These individuals previously might have been thought to be eccentric or lumped in with a more general autism diagnosis. Thus, it has been asserted that the increase in prevalence is not actually a reflection of an increase in the actual numbers of autistic individuals, but rather reflects the broadening of the diagnostic categories coupled with increased awareness of the disorder (Rutter, 2005a, 2005b; Shattuck, 2006). Also, inconsistencies may reflect methodological differences between studies (i.e., some studies assess the base rates in non-clinical populations whereas others survey schools, clinics, or parents).

In a review of existing epidemiological studies, Rutter found that the prevalence rate had increased to 30-60/10,000, one quarter of whom were diagnosed with classic autism while the other 75% were diagnosed with another autism spectrum diagnosis. About half of the diagnosed individuals had mental retardation, ranging from mild to severe. This led him to conclude that the increase in prevalence is directly related to the broadening of the autism spectrum to include higher functioning individuals without mental retardation (Rutter, 2005a, 2005b). For example, the California study cited above found that the rise was greatest in children who had normal IQs. In other words, it is possible that we are diagnosing children today who would not have been diagnosed as autistic even 10 years ago (Rutter, 2005a). To determine whether this is the case, more sophisticated epidemiological studies are needed to look at base population rates in large numbers of children.

The CDC sample also documented that AS is three to seven times more prevalent in boys than in girls. This sort of gender distribution is not uncommon in neurodevelopmental disorders, which typically differentially affect boys. Interestingly, the rate is closer to three males to one female although there may be an increase in male prevalence with increasing intelligence (Fombonne, 2003).

Widening the diagnostic criteria to include milder cases has contributed to the observed increase in assigned diagnoses (Frith, 2004). This can be viewed as both positive and negative. On the positive side, increased awareness results in more children and adults being identified who are in need of interventions and services, and perhaps more tolerance on the part of educators, professionals, families, and peers. Public awareness also may result in a lessening of the stigma and fear involved in pursuing a diagnosis of an autism spectrum disorder. However, some fear that the use of the diagnosis for individuals who may be atypical but not autistic is too broad, threatening the diagnostic specificity of the condition (Frith, 2004). By making AS the "di-

Widening the diagnostic criteria to include milder cases has contributed to the observed increase in assigned diagnoses.

agnosis du jour," we risk trivializing what is often a devastating disability deserving of serious research and funding.

Symptoms of Asperger Syndrome

There are a host of excellent clinical references describing AS. However, clinical descriptions often do not capture the variable and heterogeneous nature of the disorder, which we will emphasize in our discussion below.

The DSM-IV (APA, 1994) compiled by the American Psychiatric Association is the diagnostic manual used by most psychiatrists and psychologists in the United States to assign official diagnoses of mental disorders. The DSM has its international parallel in the International Statistical Classification of Diseases and Related Health Problems (ICD-10 is the most current version; World Health Organization, 1992).

Asperger Syndrome is one of several disorders grouped by the DSM-IV as "Pervasive Developmental Disorders." This category also includes two other autistic disorders (autistic disorder and pervasive developmental disorder-not otherwise specified) and two rare degenerative disorders (Rett's disorder and childhood disintegrative disorder). The ICD-10 and the DSM-IV criteria for autistic disorders are nearly identical. The DSM-IV Pervasive Developmental Disorder category groups disorders that all share "impairment in reciprocal social interaction" as the core diagnostic feature. The diagnostic criteria for AS in DSM-IV include the following (APA, 1994, p. 77).

DSM-IV Diagnostic Criteria for Asperger Syndrome

A. Qualitative impairments in social interaction, as manifested by at least two of the following:
1) Marked impairments in the use of multiple nonverbal behaviors such as eye to eye gaze, facial expression, body postures, and gestures to regulate social interaction
2) Failure to develop peer relationships appropriate to developmental level
3) A lack of spontaneous seeking to share enjoyment, interests, or achievements with other people (e.g., by a lack of showing, bringing, or pointing out objects of interest to other people)
4) Lack of social or emotional reciprocity

B. Restricted repetitive and stereotyped patterns of a behavior, interest, and activities, as manifested by at least one of the following:
1) Encompassing preoccupation with one or more stereotyped and restricted patterns of interest that is either abnormal in intensity or focus.
2) Apparently inflexible adherence to specific, nonfunctional routines or rituals
3) Stereotyped and repetitive motor mannerisms (e.g., hand or finger flapping or twisting, or complex whole body movements)
4) Persistent preoccupation with parts of objects

C. The disturbance causes clinically significant impairment in social, occupational, or other important areas of functioning.

D. There is no clinically significant general delay in language (e.g., single words used by age 2 years, communicative phrases by age 3 years).

E. There is no clinically significant delay in cognitive development or in the development of age-appropriate self-help skills, adaptive behavior (other than in social interaction), and curiosity about the environment in childhood.

F. Criteria are not meant for another specific Pervasive Developmental Disorder or Schizophrenia.

(APA, 1994, pp. 75-77)

The clinical presentation of AS is variable, especially at the upper ranges of functioning. Asperger Syndrome appears to involve more of the social and behavioral domains with less involvement of the language domain. Recall that there must be no significant language delay for a child to be diagnosed with AS. However, most persons with AS do present with subtle language deficits, particularly in the areas of conversation and communication. This will be discussed later.

Social problems and AS. The social disability in AS involves core social skills that feel involuntary for most people, such as eye contact, starting and ending conversations, and regulating interpersonal distance. Social awareness is typically impaired, and persons appear naïve and lost. They have difficulty recognizing, interpreting, and responding to verbal and nonverbal cues sent by listeners or conversation partners, especially in unstructured social situations. This may affect their understanding of sarcasm and figures of speech.

As children and adolescents, they are easily bullied or victimized and must be protected in school settings. For example, they may be bullied to give up their lunch money or possessions as youngsters. In college students, this may translate into being coerced into doing the lion's share of work on a group project or being taken advantage of in social situations, such as being coerced to foot the bill for a large group of students. Alternately, they may be used as willing dupes in illegal or criminal activities.

The child or adult with AS desires contact but is typically socially awkward. Others see him as disinterested, withdrawn, avoidant, or odd. He has limited use of social language and poor understanding of nonverbal cues, whereas the typical individual has a natural understanding of social cues called "intuitive social knowledge" (Tanguay, 2000). For example, a student with AS meeting someone for the first time might not know to stand further away to catch a sense of the interaction and behave appropriately. She may approach and attempt to interact with roommates and professors the same way, unaware of important hierarchical, age, or social differences that call for different approaches. In contrast, the neurotypical student intuitively processes these hierarchies and knows to vary social approaches for parents, professors, and peers.

Behavioral problems and AS. The behavioral disability in AS may be seen as rigid, stereotyped behavior and/or mannerisms. A defining behavioral feature is an unusual preoccupation with specific objects or ideas, often to the exclusion of other activities. Pet interests are often mechanical in nature, such as maps, weather, trains, and schedules. These areas of special interest may become genuine talents and assets leading to a career and future success. However, they may also come to dominate all interactions and conversations as long-winded monologues that others find tiresome and that therefore are unproductive.

Children and adults with AS may also engage in repetitive behaviors such as flapping their hands or twisting their fingers, making faces, humming or muttering, or needing to constantly have objects to fiddle or twirl. Such mannerisms often increase in times of stress. We have encountered students who needed to pace (including one who had to be allowed to walk during exams) or who needed sensory fidgets (gadgets) in the classroom to enable them to sit still or focus on a lecture. We have seen children and adolescents who compulsively masturbate or pick at their skin as a repetitive behavior in times of stress. These mannerisms lead others to perceive the individual with AS as odd or unusual and, indeed, many of the mannerisms do look rather disturbed.

A Word About Eye Contact

Decreased eye contact is often seen in individuals with autism spectrum disorders. We bring it up here as a behavior that is off-putting to others who do not understand that the individual is not bored, but simply does not feel comfortable looking in others' eyes.

Interesting, one study found that eye gaze is diminished during conversations when the other person is talking (i.e., when listening to others) and when the topic of conversation is highly stimulating. However, gaze is normalized when the individual with AS is doing the talking (Tantam, Holmes, & Cordess, 1993).

Students may be taught tricks such as looking at a point on the speaker's forehead rather than meeting the eyes. However, they should never be forced to make eye contact, as that may make them acutely anxious.

Language problems and AS. The language disability in AS typically affects conversation and discourse. Despite a diagnostic schema that specifies the absence of significant language deficits, most practitioners and many neuropsychological studies find evidence of subtle language defects that may affect both expressive and receptive language (Szatmari et al., 1990, 1995; Wing, 1981). Expressive language is often superficially good, although there may be formal or pedantic phraseology with a narrow range of topic choice and use of peculiar phrases.

> *One of us worked with a student whose pet phrase was "funnily enough," which he inserted into every second or third sentence. Other students don't know how to begin, end, or join in a conversation, and are stymied by the dance of conversational pauses that regulates turn taking. These deficits lie chiefly in the area of social language, referred to by neuropsychologists and language pathologists as "pragmatics."*

- *Language pragmatics* are the rules for using language within a social context, including the nonlinguistic aspects of language such as tone of voice, gesture, and communicative intent. Pragmatics affect both the input (comprehension) and output (production) of speech and language. Further, pragmatics involve both a language-based system, which codes the rules for conversation, and an emotionally based system, which includes motivation to interact with others (Abele, 2006). There are also culturally relevant rules in all languages that govern listening, conversation, and discourse (Abele, 2006), and persons with AS are often impaired in these areas of language.

Children need to learn the language code for conversing with others, but also need to be emotionally motivated for social discourse. They need to appreciate that language can be used for many different functions and that we can change our use of language for different purposes and in different contexts (Abele, 2006).

This may be one of the most disabling and enduring symptoms in an adult with AS. Social language problems may give rise to anxiety, withdrawal, isolation, low self-esteem, and possibly depression.

This may be one of the most disabling and enduring symptoms in an adult with AS. Social language problems may give rise to anxiety, withdrawal, isolation, low self-esteem, and possibly depression. The specific language features may be subtle or pronounced.

Children with AS are often described as "little professors" due to pedantic speeches about their particular topic of interest that seem more like lectures than conversations. The volume of speech may be loud, with uneven or peculiar characteristics of pitch and prosody (can be monotonic or can be squealing or sing-songy). Individuals with AS may not take the listener's cues and conversational markers into account, failing to notice signs of disinterest or confusion such as rolling of the eyes, turning the head, or change of topic (Abele, 2006). Frequent violations of conversational rules signal to others that one is not really a partner in the language interaction. This can lead to rejection when the listener concludes the other is not interested, is rude, or self-centered. Adolescents in particular can be fierce in their rejection.

Language comprehension may tend to be inflexible, with particular difficulty in dealing with sarcasm, figurative language, jokes, and getting the gist of a conversation. Often the more emotional or interpersonal the tone of the conversation is, the less effectively the individual with AS processes the information (Tantam, Holmes, & Cordress, 1993). Finally, understanding and using language against a background of noise (such as in a bar, at a party, or even in a classroom), may be nearly impossible for the individual with AS.

We often notice that students with AS pay attention to the sequence of words rather than processing their meaning simultaneously. In other words, language is processed in the order in which it comes in, rather than reorganized and resynthesized. This may account for some of the over-literal features of AS we have noted.

In most spontaneous conversations (as opposed to lectures), words are not predictable or sequenced. It is for this reason that the language processing of individuals with AS tends to break down in unstructured social situations. This includes notable difficulty understanding jokes and sarcasm, idioms or figures of speech, which are nonlinear by definition and are important cultural references that mark one as "in" or "out." As a result, when verbally interacting with an individual with AS who has pragmatic language deficits, it is important to speak slowly and in an even tone (no shouting), avoid open-ended questions, which can easily be misinterpreted, avoid sarcasm, colloquialism, or figures of speech, and stick to a conversational agenda that includes cuing the listener to topic shifts. We also suggest keeping the emotional tone of the in-teraction neutral, if possible.

One of the authors fondly recalls a conversation with a stu-dent in which she commented that the student should avoid "putting his foot in his mouth" only to observe him – after a puzzled look – untying his laces so that he could examine his foot!

Other associated symptoms. Although not part of the formal diag-nostic schema, three notable features often accompany AS.

- ***Motor clumsiness*** is often present in children and adults with AS (Leary & Hill, 1996; Nayate, Bradshaw, & Rinehart, 2005), both for fine- and gross-motor functioning. This may be apparent as a general lack of graceful movement, stiff walking with a decreased arm swing, falling out of chairs (when younger), or bumping into things. Deficits may also be seen in motor planning (also known as "praxis"), which refers to coordinating the large and small movements for skilled, purposeful activity. This in turn may affect writing legibility, participation in sports or dancing, handling equipment in the lab, or even going in and out of rooms. We have seen one student whose notable dyspraxia (poor motor coordination) precluded her from acquiring sufficient sign language skills to meet her foreign language requirement.

- *Psychiatric symptoms* of depression and anxiety are commonly part of the diagnostic profile of individuals with AS (deBruin, Ferdinand, Meester, & De Nijs, 2007; Fitzgerald, 2007; Ghaziuddin, Ghaziuddin, & Greden, 2002; Tantam, 2000). The diagnostic scheme of the DSM allows for multiple diagnoses, when appropriate. Thus, individuals may be separately diagnosed with depression, anxiety, or some other psychiatric disorder. This is very useful to know and such information should be sought where appropriate. The presence of numerous psychiatric diagnoses may also be a clue to an undiagnosed autism spectrum disorder.

> *The presence of numerous psychiatric diagnoses may also be a clue to an undiagnosed autism spectrum disorder.*

> *One of us received documentation for a student that listed a compendium of separate diagnoses accompanying a clear nonverbal learning disorder (including separation anxiety, disorder of motor skills, and specific language impairment in childhood plus current diagnoses of social phobia, depression, and obsessive compulsive disorder) rather than entertaining an overarching diagnosis of a pervasive developmental disorder.*

- *Sensory dysfunction* is another common feature in AS (Dunn, Myles, & Orr, 2002; Rogers & Ozonoff, 2005). Individuals may be hyper-(over) or hypo-(under) sensitive to input from all of their senses. Sights, smells, sounds, and tastes may be extremely exaggerated and even painful, due to differences in processing information. These and other sensory issues, including clothing and tags of clothing, sounds of markers on a whiteboard or chalk on a blackboard, or the smells of other students' hair products, perfume, or aftershave, can interrupt the learning environment for the student with AS. Lights and classroom noise such as that from air conditioners and heaters, or fans on LCD projectors, can be physically painful. Students with severe sensory issues must work hard to keep control when their senses are bombarded.

In response to sensory overload, many students with AS engage in a behavior colloquially known as "stimming." "Stims" are repetitive, apparently purposeless behaviors or mannerisms that serve to reduce anxiety as well as to enhance focus for some students. Stims can include spinning or whirling, especially in young children, or repetitive finger flicking, mouth movements, chewing of nonfood items, or fiddling with objects. Stims serve an adaptive purpose

Stims serve an adaptive purpose and should not be forbidden.

and should not be forbidden. Rather, the student should be helped to develop stims that are not disruptive and do not call undue attention to the student. We have successfully advocated that students be allowed to bring sensory gadgets (such as a stress ball, sunglasses, straw to suck on, etc.) into a classroom rather than leaving their seat to wander around the room, for example.

Now that we have defined and described AS and its associated symptoms, let us move the discussion towards the impact that the symptoms of this disorder present in a college or university environment, in particular those faced by the office of Disability Services and Student Affairs.

CHAPTER 3

Asperger Syndrome and Issues for Disability Services

On most campuses, the office of Disability Services (variably named Disability Support Services, Student Services, Special Services, Access Services, etc.) is the authorizing body for students with disabilities. In other words, students must be cleared through this office to be recognized as students with disabilities for the purposes of receiving services and accommodations. Numerous lawsuits and complaints have turned on whether the student had properly self-identified to the appropriate body on campus. Failure to do so jeopardizes students' exercise of their legal rights under the Americans with Disabilities Act and Section 504 of the Rehabilitation Act of 1973.

In this chapter we discuss the role of Disability Services (DS) in the life of a student with AS, how the disability professional fits into the unique situation of the student in this population, and what issues may arise that are different from the usual workings of the office.

Roles of Disability Services

Roles of Campus Disability Services

- *Narrow Role:*
  - » Responsible for policy and eligibility determination
  - » Arrange for academic accommodations
  - » Deal with access issues

- *Broader Role:*
  - » Assess availability and student use of resources
  - » Refer student on and off campus
  - » Function as point person
  - » Educate campus community about AS
  - » Teach student skills to manage AS
  - » Offer technical assistance to faculty, staff, and administrators

---

Disability services offices are typically staffed with professional disability experts who may work with students with physical and medical, sensory, learning, cognitive, psychiatric and other disabilities. Few DS providers would consider themselves experts in working with AS, but over the past five years an increasing number of providers have sought special training in this area. Still, the student, the family, and the health providers (psychologists, psychiatrists, counselors, cognitive therapists, and clinicians) must be prepared to inquire, educate (when necessary), and fully disclose to the disability professionals who will be working with the student.

Each DS office must establish and follow policies and procedures. When working with students with AS who tend to be very literal and visual in their thinking, it is important that policies and procedures be presented in a clear and concrete way, often accompanied with a written list to refer to. For example, if your policy states that students must make appointments with a secretary before coming in for weekly meetings, make it clear to students with AS that they are not allowed to drop in whenever it is convenient for them. If you have a specialized program that requires students to meet with you once a week, decide how many meetings they can miss before there is a consequence and what the consequence is.

Each DS office must establish and follow policies and procedures.

Self-Advocacy

Learning to self-advocate is a crucial skill for being a successful adult. Students with AS must be taught to self-advocate to be independent. Learning this skill should begin in middle school with the student taking on increased responsibilities each year. For students whose parents and teachers have always taken on the advocacy role, their new-found independence must begin first semester freshman year with them assuming increased responsibility for their accommodations each semester.

Students may need assistance at first in negotiating their accommodations. Some students are not developmentally ready to negotiate on their own and may require a short period of "extra" assistance. For instance, it is permissible to have a representative from DS accompany the student to the professor's office to meet with the faculty member about accommodations for the first semester or two and model effective accommodation negotiation. This and other assistance should optimally be used sparingly and phased out quickly so as not to undermine the student's development of self-advocacy skills.

It is often incumbent on the DS office to teach students with disabilities to stand up for themselves, to be able to express their needs, and to know their rights. For students with AS, these skills are not just important; they can mean the difference between living as independent adults and as adults in need of supervision.

Working with the Family During Transition

Optimally, well before the student's arrival on campus, DS staff and relevant administrators should develop a healthy partnership with the parents of students with AS. This will be a tremendous asset when working with and learning about a new student. We suggest that providers learn about the ways in which the parents have supported their students and the types of transitional work the parents and the high school have done with students to prepare them for the transition from high school to college. For example, we find it useful to learn about the types of involvement the parents have had in the realm of social and self-care activities. Questions such as those below are pertinent to ask when getting to know a student.

For students with AS, these skills are not just important; they can mean the difference between living as independent adults and as adults in need of supervision.

Getting to Know the Student
- Has the student had experience doing laundry?
- Has he cooked and shopped?
- What kinds of friendships did the student establish in high school?

- How have decisions been made about how the student spends his time during the school week and on the weekends?
- Has the student held a job?
- If so, what types of work was the student engaged in, and how much training and supervision were provided?

Other areas to be reviewed with the family include the student's level of self-advocacy. Has he ever discussed his disability with anyone in the past? If not, the family and the relevant clinicians must review with the student his documentation, his functional limitations, and the accommodations and supports to be requested. The staff at the DS office should not be the first persons of authority to discuss with the student that he has been diagnosed with AS.

All of us have had this uncomfortable discussion with students who have repeatedly been told that they do not have AS, when it is abundantly clear from their documentation that they do – one of us even had an instance in which the diagnosis was never revealed to the student until after he was dropped off at school.

Some administrators insist that the student with a disability is now an adult who must learn to advocate for himself without parental intervention. This letter-of-the-law interpretation is correct; however, we believe that an active partnership between the campus, the family, and the student is a better practice for supporting students with AS. For example, preparing transition information based on questions such as those listed above can be a shared task between the DS office and the student's family (who usually know best what the student is most interested in learning about). In this way, the student is actively involved, the family feels supported and understood, and the DS officer does not feel overwhelmed by the small details. Strategies for managing this interaction so that it does not become intrusive will be discussed later in this chapter.

... an active partnership between the campus, the family, and the student is a better practice for supporting students with AS.

General discussions of this nature, specific responses, and the type of feedback received from the parents will provide excellent insights upon which to build a plan of action for working with each student. A private meeting between the parents and disabilities staff, another with staff, parents and the student, and a meeting alone with the student will help provide further insights about how best to work with each individual and determine what level of support the student will initially require.

Staying in Touch with Parents

Once the student has arrived on campus, support staff may wish to be in contact with parents or family members. For students with other disabilities, independence is encouraged, which means less contact with parents. However, we have found that for students with AS, parental involvement is sometimes essential to success.

We suggest that a designated point person be identified on campus that will be willing (with the student's permission) to have regular contact with the family or the student's therapist or other clinician regarding the student's progress. This can be a DS worker, a counselor, advisor, tutor, professor, resident advisor (RA), or even a dean. Many individuals on campus across disciplines and divisions can serve as effective, sensitive, and informed resources and point people for students with AS. We will discuss training these individuals in later chapters, but for now let us stress that whoever the designated point person is, he or she should not hesitate to inform parents when a health or safety issue arises.

We prefer to discuss the boundaries of contact with the family and indicate the number of times they may (or may not) call, write, or email about their son or daughter. This establishes a professional relationship that reassures the parents that the provider knows how to deal with the student on the spectrum and at the same time sets the tone for the emerging independence of the student.

We assure parents that we will call them if necessary (health or safety reasons most assuredly) but will not do so for trivial situations (such as loss of an accommodation letter or missed appointments) or day-to-day reasons (such as Kevin not handing in his assignment) and that they may not call for regular updates.

Transition ...
- Requires active collaboration between DS, student, and family
- Should create an explicit sets of rules, scripts, and expectations for student to follow
- Optimally happens prior to the start of the semester

Working with the Student During Transition

Throughout this book we will follow a beginning college student with AS, whom we will call Kevin, to illustrate some of the issues under discussion. While Kevin is not a real student, he is absolutely realistic. Kevin is a composite of some of the interactions and student experiences all three authors have encountered, and in

33

no way depicts any of the individual students with whom we have had the pleasure to work.

 Kevin goes to his summer orientation at college. He is put into a group for academic advising, a group that takes a tour of the campus, and a group intended for students to get to know each other. Kevin does not like groups and does not talk much around others. The groups are led by students who don't know what to do with Kevin's lack of participation and his avoidance of other group members.

As part of orientation, Kevin is shown the laundry facility and told how to work the machines. Kevin cannot concentrate with the group of students, and since he has never done laundry, none of the information makes sense. When he gets to school for the beginning of the semester, Kevin is clueless as to how to clean his clothes or who to ask.

We cannot emphasize enough that a well-managed transition often makes the difference between a successful and an unsuccessful first semester.

Once the student has arrived on campus for the semester, it is critical that she meet with a DS professional at least once, preferably twice, during the first week of classes. Students should be encouraged to talk about each class they attended and explain what they learned in the first class meetings. Disability specialists might also want to review syllabi and other handouts students received in class. Syllabi are foreign objects for most freshmen, but they can hold the keys to success in class. For example, many freshmen are accustomed to having parents and aides break their assignments down for them and may not understand how to use the syllabus to accomplish this task. Additionally, the rules and regulations contained in a syllabus can give students with AS, who are rigid thinkers, something to latch on to.

We cannot emphasize enough that a well-managed transition often makes the difference between a successful and an unsuccessful first semester.

Gathering further information. We have included sample intake and information-gathering materials, which may be found in Appendix C (i.e., Intake Questionnaire and My Areas of Difficulty Checklist). These forms may be used with the student and his or her family in the initial meetings and may be augmented with more information gathered from the documentation or any conversation with the student's clinical providers. Beginning students often need parental help to complete some of the history forms, but some enjoy using this opportunity to be a source of data without interference from a well-meaning parent.

Forms can also be sent home to the student and family to complete before their initial meeting. It seems like a lot of information, but we emphasize that the more understanding we can gather about a student at the outset, the better we can develop a preliminary plan and anticipate any pitfalls which might arise later.

Some students' perceptions of their ability to handle things independently may not be accurate, as they may approach their attempt to acclimate to a new environment and handle new situations with a great deal of naiveté. Ask students for specific examples of how they will undertake the task of learning to live and work within their new environment. Responses containing extremely broad generalizations are clues that the student may not have a clear idea of how to manage those tasks. If this is the case, engage in a discussion of case studies or role-plays to allow the student to explore different scenarios and how she might handle certain situations. Case studies might also be given to parents at the start of the summer to be used to help the student begin to acclimate to her new surroundings while she is comfortable at home. For example, a role-play might involve how to greet new roommates, how to negotiate which side of the room to claim, and so forth.

In addition to using the initial meetings to gather information and learn how the student thinks in general, such conversations can provide insights into what the student understands about how to use a syllabus and how she identifies the important aspects of being a student in each class. It is particularly helpful when DS specialists are familiar with the instructors and how they run their courses and can compare the student's perceptions of the class with their own knowledge. This strategy may work well on smaller campuses, but may not be realistic on larger campuses with many professors. On larger campuses, it is useful for DS specialists to gather similar information from other students and/ or faculty and professionals with whom they are familiar. Often someone in DS will know one person in a department to whom he or she can direct questions.

Upon acceptance to a university, a suggested transition sequence might appear as follows:

Family and student contact DS and disclose disability
- Family, student, and DS set up initial intake meeting (summer before entering; see Intake Questionnaire in Appendix C)

Family, student, and DS begin transition planning
- Housing, documentation, accommodations, orientation, and registration
- Family and student arrange campus visit(s) before move-in

Student and DS set up regular meetings in first weeks of semester
- Student provides Disability Services permission to contact parents, professors, and other personnel as needed
- Student and Disability Services determine level of further parental involvement

Clearly, through this transition, the leadership role shifts from being primarily parental to parental and student, and finally to student and DS, consistent with the goal of assisting the student in developing self-advocacy skills.

Registration and Course Selection

Information about how students selected their courses in high school and how they created each day's schedule can prepare disability specialists for how to work effectively with students. It is important for DS staff to be aware of what types of information are significant in helping the student become well established at the college. This may include breaking down the steps involved in making decisions and choices during the registration process, beginning with identifying the steps and

... through this transition, the leadership role shifts from being primarily parental to parental and student, and finally to student and DS, consistent with the goal of assisting the student in developing self-advocacy skills.

the timeline in which the process begins, such as the following: Where do students go to preregister for upcoming terms? Do they go to a central registration area? Do they go to their academic department to obtain the registration materials? Must they meet with an academic or faculty advisor first? Do they register online? Do they register via telephone? What is the timeframe of the pre-registration period?

We suggest that students be assisted in developing a tip sheet such as the one below to help them through the preregistration for upcoming terms. The tip sheet can include information about the process as well as information about how to make changes and corrections and handle situations where the student missed or skipped a step. Doing so can help reduce the level of anxiety a student might experience if he discovers he missed a deadline or failed to take care of one or several steps in the preregistration process. Due to the visual learning styles of many students with AS, frequent use of tip sheets is recommended.

Preregistration Tip Sheet

- Course level and prerequisites
- Placement tests needed
- Professor name and contact information
- Hours and location
- Dates for registration
- Last date to register
- Necessary signatures
- Online registration numbers

For the first few terms, it is useful for the student to review the process with a disability specialist before the semester begins and check in with him or her once she has completed the process. The specialist can then identify anything the student may have overlooked. If the school uses a telephone preregistration process, students should be introduced to these processes through the use of the tip sheet and modeling of the steps they will have to take on their own. Do not forget to include information about how to make changes and corrections later on, should that be necessary.

Some of these steps may be outside of the traditional purview of DS providers but can be accomplished through a cooperative partnership between the student, the family, and other resources such as counselors, advisors, and/or registrar's office staff on campus.

Some of these steps may be outside of the traditional purview of DS providers but can be accomplished through a cooperative partnership between the student, the family, and other resources such as counselors, advisors, and/or registrar's office staff on campus.

Scheduling Classes and Time Management

When discussing class schedules with students, DS professionals should ask them to explain their plan of action for completing assignments and homework. This will help shape an initial profile of each student's ability to apply what he learned in class and from the syllabus into a solid plan of action.

Disability professionals may consider keeping a copy of students' syllabi to be able to track the extent to which they are managing in each course (see Assignment and Grade Tracking form in Appendix D). This is particularly important in courses that require students to work on long-term projects. In general, the typical high school student has had a minimal amount of experience planning for long-term projects, and many students on the autism spectrum have particular difficulty with time management and, subsequently, with meeting deadlines for long-term projects that they must work on independently.

Students with AS tend to do better in courses that require students to submit drafts of papers or lab reports for instructor review, as they provide a structure to follow and an example to model in future courses. However, it is important not to be misled by the belief that a student is managing well based simply on a brief self-report. Students are often not reliable reporters, and sometimes DS providers must be prepared to do a little detective work to determine how the student is actually doing. Typically, it is not encouraged that DS staff be in regular contact with faculty, but in the case of students with AS, it may be both essential and enlightening for a designated member of the DS staff to check in periodically with faculty.

Disability specialists should offer students an example of a typical well-structured daily and weekly schedule, and, after learning more about students' courses through discussion and review of their syllabi, work with students to develop a basic schedule for the week during more "typical" weeks, with the caveat that this schedule will need to be adjusted before midterm and final exam times. An example of a daily schedule is found in Appendix D.

Daily Schedule

Time	Mon.	Tues.	Wed.	Thurs.	Fri.
9:00	History		History		History
9:30					
10:00	Study		Study		Study
10:30		Calculus		Calculus	
11:00					
11:30					
12:00	Lunch				Lunch
12:30		Lunch	Lunch	Lunch	
1:00	1:15 English	Study	1:15 English	Study	History Discussion
1:30					
2:00	Break				Study or Break
2:30		FYE	Break	FYE	
3:00					
3:30					
4:00	Work Out	Work Out	Work Out	Work Out	Work Out
4:30					
5:00	Shower	Shower	Shower	Shower	Shower
5:30					
6:00	Dinner	Dinner	Dinner	Dinner	Dinner
6:30					

Academic Challenges and Asperger Syndrome

Information gathered from discussions about students' experiences in class will provide insight into their note-taking challenges, learning style, ability to function successfully and independently in the classroom, and their sense of reality as a student. It will also provide a reality check for the students' self-assessments regarding the skills they bring to the university. This, too, should help staff develop a plan of action for each student on the spectrum.

The forms in Appendix D are designed to help you gather information about student strengths and weaknesses and to begin to develop an accommodation plan as well as conduct a resource assessment. In the sections below we will illustrate some of the more common domains in which we have found students with AS to struggle.

Writing papers. Many students on the spectrum experience difficulty meeting their professors' expectations for writing papers. Trouble can crop up in one or several aspects of the writing process, including content, parameters of the assignment, focus, and structure. Regarding content, often students with AS focus on a tangent that never returns to the assigned topic or subject matter, following a pet topic of interest instead. A disabilities professional, writing center tutor, or writing instructor can help refocus such a draft by pointing out where a student veers away from the main point and suggest other reminders to stay on topic, such as sticky notes on each page, timed computer pop-up messages, and the like.

Frequent Writing Challenges
- Producing text and narrative (instead of lists of facts or outlines)
- Analyzing or understanding plot and motivation when writing
- Essay questions (understanding what the question is asking, directing flow of ideas, writing enough)

- Term papers (planning, time management, focusing or reducing topic)
- Compare and contrast
- Using personal perspectives
- Managing long-term assignments (initiating and sustaining)

A review of the student's work in comparison with the paper's requirements and a discussion of the student's approach to writing the paper will help assess the student's writing strengths and weaknesses. When a DS professional engages a student in a discussion of the topic, taking notes of the discussion can provide the student with additional suggestions about developing his paper in a manner consistent with the instructor's expectations. This can also serve as an example to the student of how to write future papers.

Most DS professionals are competent writers who can assist with some analysis of students' writing challenges. However, we suggest that true writing instruction be provided by experts – another opportunity to recruit the partnership of the writing center or tutoring service on campus (see Chapter 9). Also, there are many online and commercially available manuals and style guides that are useful to keep in the office for student use. The writing centers on most campuses also maintain tip sheets and manuals for students to review.

Some students have difficulty expanding their papers because the process of typing or writing draws their attention away from the topic area. In cases such as these, we have found it useful to work with students to explore strategies of capturing the information pertinent to things other than writing or typing such as dictation software, audio recording with or without transcription, graphic organizers, outlining, or even drawing.

Other areas of difficulty for students faced with report or paper writing is the organization of material in the paper and transitions between paragraphs. As students' writing strengths and weaknesses become clear, DS professionals can consult with the writing center to help the student develop a tip sheet or templates on basic paragraph and term paper structure with concrete steps to follow when writing future papers and reports. Many DS offices have developed such sheets for students with learning and other disabilities, and those can easily be revised. Again, we strongly suggest that students be referred to the campus writing center for formal instruction in college-level writing.

We have found that a call to the writing center director or a senior staff member explaining the impact of a student's challenges on her writing often results in a hand-picked writing tutor who can be further trained to work with AS challenges. The student can then meet regularly with one individual who understands her issues, and the DS professional does not have to expend energy in an area in which he or she may not be an expert.

Taking exams. Students with AS may require some initial guidance in terms of how to prepare for exams. This may occur gradually, beginning weeks in advance of a known exam. Introduction of strategies to prepare for exams that loom immediately before them, while helpful, are not as effective, as this does not provide students with a template of guidelines to follow in similar future situations.

Common Exam Challenges
- Essay questions (ties into writing challenges)
- Following instructions
- Processing speed
- Managing distractions
- Sensory issues in the room

It is important to break down the student's exam-taking behavior into concrete steps. It is also critical to ascertain whether the student understands what type of exam she will be taking (multiple-choice, essay, short-answer, or some combination), for the student may need to use a different approach for each of these types. Disability services professionals should discuss strategies, planning week by week and day by day. They might also supply a worst-case scenario, in the event a student did not realize an exam was approaching and now has only two days to study. Avoiding this is ideal, but the reality is, it will happen.

If students have been granted accommodations for exams, it is imperative to review with them how and when to make arrangements for accommodations.

If students have been granted accommodations for exams, it is imperative to review with them how and when to make arrangements for accommodations. It may also be necessary to contact the professor of a given course to make sure the student has indeed taken these steps. If he has not, remind the student of his responsibility in this area. Some students may require review of how to use accommodations, where and when to obtain computers, or how to use their extra time. Many students will need additional information about why the particular accommodations have been suggested (in terms of their functional limitations) to assist them in more effectively negotiating the accommodations with the professor.

Role-playing and scripting are the two best methods we know for preparing a student to request an accommodation from a professor, including having a DS professional and the student act out scenarios in which an accommodation letter is refused, a professor is with a group of people when the accommodation request is presented, and so forth.

The following scenario illustrates a sample script that the DS provider can use to rehearse with the student how to deliver letters and arrange exam accommodations.

Sample Script

"O.K., these are your faculty accommodation letters. Please read them carefully so that I know you understand your accommodations. As we talked about, you are approved to receive an extra 50% time on exams in a separate, distraction-reduced room. You are also approved to circle your answers in the test booklet or on the answer sheet instead of filling in the bubbles.

Do you have any questions about your accommodations? Can you tell me in your own words what your accommodations are and a little about why you receive them? Good, now let's review what you are going to do with the letters. I want you to contact your professors by phone and by email to set up a private appointment to deliver your letters. You will give a letter to each professor, and then you are going to work with your professor to set up the accommodations. I know this is a little different from high school, and we are all going to work together to help it work for you. You need to ask some questions that we can list if you need to. For example, can you stay late to take the exam or do you have to come early? Do you have any other conflicts where you will have to ask the professor to reschedule your exam? Where will the exam take place? Who will be available to answer any questions you have during your exam?

O.K., good. Now let's talk about telling your professor about why you receive accommodations. Do you want your professors to know anything about your AS? If you want them to know a little more about your issues, we can work together to rehearse a few lines if you need to. If you give me permission, I would also be able to help you and your professor with the exam details."

Presentations and group projects. Presentations and group projects often require more attention from DS specialists, as addressing those goes beyond standard accommodations. In many instances, it is necessary to work directly with the student and the professor to address difficulties in this area. The list below highlights problems that may arise as a consequence of various functional impairments seen in students with AS. For example, anxiety and poor social skills may render a student speechless when asked to do a presentation in front of the class. In such a case, accommodations such as videotaping or close-caption TV may be helpful. At other times, working with a faculty member to address the functional requirements of the course and the necessity of such activities is the best course of action.

Common Presentation Challenges

- Social anxiety
- Language deficits
- Speed of processing
- Narrow or literal interest in topic

Kevin is taking Introduction to Rhetoric, where a presentation in front of the class is assigned. Kevin becomes paralyzed when speaking formally in front of a room of classmates and consequently stutters uncontrollably when giving a speech. The DS provider and

Kevin speak to his professor and learn that the presentation counts for 25% of the final grade.

Faced with the necessity of Kevin doing some sort of presentation, the DS provider begins to explore with the instructor what the fundamental and essential components of mastery are for the course and suggests alternatives such as allowing Kevin to give his speech in front of the instructor and one or two peers or videotaping the speech and playing it in front of the class.

For any of the options above, it is essential to engage in in-depth discussion with the instructor, keeping in mind that in some cases no alternative or a reasonable accommodation will meet the course requirements.

Group projects require that professors and other course personnel (teaching assistants or fellows) be aware of the dynamics in a group or a lab and address difficulties as they arise. For example, are other students leaving the student with AS out of important meetings or group social or team-building activities? Are they dividing the work equitably, or is the student with AS getting assigned the bulk of the unpleasant tasks? Lab partners and group members are usually keenly aware of differences in working smoothly with an individual on the spectrum; however, they are unlikely to articulate their reasons for not wanting to work with him or her.

A skilled intervention from the more experienced professor (often in consultation with DS) can go a long way in turning an unfortunate experience into a rewarding and positive student interaction. Monitoring and managing such difficulties requires that DS establish excellent working relationships with faculty who are teaching students with AS in lab or group related courses. This will be discussed in more detail in the next chapter.

Taking notes. As DS personnel (or tutors) meet with the student regularly, they should request to see class notes and ask the student questions about instructors' styles of teaching. Does the instructor tend to lecture for all or most of the class time? If so, and the student has either minimal notes or large gaps in notes, engage in a discussion of what it is like to take notes in that particular class.

Questions to students should elicit feedback about being a student in that class. Does the student feel he understands the material to the point that he does not need to take many notes? Does the student believe there is much "irrelevant" information in the class lecture? Does the student struggle to take down information verbatim, thereby losing out on many notes? Or are other, extrinsic barriers standing in the way, such as harsh lighting, seating arrangements, an open door, a bank of windows, or uncomfortable temperatures?

Students should understand that notes become the "textbook" of their professor's lecture and should be given strategies. For example, some students do well with a structured system such as the following three-column strategy to improve note-taking skills. In this form, one column is for vocabulary from the lecture, one column for information from the lecture and one column for questions.

Three-Column Strategy

Vocabulary	Information	Questions

Students may also be offered accommodations such as permission to audio tape lectures or use a note taker, or a smart pen, a device that writes like a typical pen but includes a computer chip that can record the professor's voice. The smart pen is used with special paper that allows the student to go back to parts of the notes to hear parts of the recorded lecture again.

If the student has been approved for a note taker, it is important to review with her the policies on your campus for arranging and using that individual, and to make sure that the student knows how to recruit a note taker. If she does not, permission should be sought to enlist the professor as a resource. The following is an example of a script for the student.

 DS Provider: O.K., Kevin, I will pretend to be a student in your class who you want to ask to be your note taker. Here is a card that you need to review to be sure that you give the note taker all the important information and that you get the information back. On the card you need to put your name, the class name and time, and your schedule so you can arrange to meet the note taker to get his notes as well as his email and phone number so you can contact him if you have questions. Be sure to give him your contact information, too. O.K., so let me pretend to be sitting here in class. What do you ask me?

Student: My name is Kevin, and I am in your Rhetoric 101 class. Professor Smith suggested you could be my peer note taker. Is that something you want to do?

DS Provider: I don't know what that is or how it works.

Kevin: Well, if you agree to become involved, the Disability Office will pay you to make a copy of your notes for me. You and I figure out when to meet so you can give me the copy of your notes [obviously the script will differ depending on the policies of the individual campus].

DS Provider: But I type my notes on my laptop.

Kevin: That's fine. Then you can email them to me; here is my email address. Here is the contact for DS so you can get paid.

(and so forth)

As pointed out at the beginning of this chapter, establishing a sound partnership with the student and his or her family is key to fostering success for students with AS in higher education. Having reviewed some of the more general issues that arise when working with students on the spectrum, in Chapter 4 we will turn to some of the legal underpinnings for accommodating students with disabilities and some specific suggestions about academic accommodations for students with AS.

Unique Challenges
for Disability Service Providers

In Chapter 3, we outlined some of the preliminary steps that DS professionals take to establish partnerships with students with AS and their families, including managing the transition, getting to know the student, beginning to develop a plan for accommodating the student, and setting boundaries for contact with the family. Many students and their families are good consumers – responsive to our interventions and suggestions with little drama and conflict. However, there are times when the DS provider is called on to manage a student or parent situation that requires a great deal of skill, sensitivity, and finesse. This chapter will examine some of these situations in detail.

Amount of Student Contact

Compared to other personnel on campus such as faculty and advisors, DS professionals often have the most individual contact with the student with AS on campus. Thus, we may spend several hours per week working with a needy student and fielding calls from other staff, faculty, parents, and clinical contacts.

The level of contact and assistance provided is based on a particular institution's philosophy and program for students with AS. We suggest that DS officers establish a level of programming that is appropriate for a given institution. Whatever model is chosen, it must be explained thoroughly to families and interested students before they come to campus. In an effort to recruit a student or impress a family, we strongly discourage institutions from exaggerating their level of programming or degree of expertise with students with AS (we are aware of many such instances). Families who are promised services rightfully expect services.

In the nearly 10 years we have been working together to bring our philosophy of working with AS to other campuses, many programs and models of service delivery have been developed. Some of these are outlined below.

Models of Service Delivery
Commonly Used for Students with AS

Disability Services	Accommodations plus regular meetings with student; other assistance as needed (no fee); may include peer mentoring
Augmented Services	Regular group or individual meetings for social and academic skills are added to above (often for a fee)
Clinical Model	Counseling, coaching, or therapy are added to above for a fee; often run out of counseling center on campus
Therapeutic Model	Special housing and monitoring added to above, often with medication monitoring; sometimes external to college campus, very costly

Once the institutional model has been determined, we suggest that the DS office develop expertise by attending courses, workshops, and other trainings; establish institutional alliances with other offices of support; and then stick to the model with which the college is comfortable. Some students and families ask more of DS than is reasonable (such as requesting social coaches and unlimited time on exams). It is up to DS to explain the program to the student again and set limits.

It is important to set guidelines and expectations for the level of contact the DS office will have with students.

We suggest that you let students and families know in advance what services your program provides and use reminders if necessary. Most families are looking for the same thing you are – successful students who become independent. At times, families of students with AS need to be reminded that what makes students successful may not make them independent (e.g., too many aides or too many accommodations). Some of this was discussed in Chapter 3. In the sections below, we offer suggestions for how to handle these situations.

Examples of Unreasonable Parental Requests

- Alter course requirements (papers in lieu of exams or vice versa)
- No sanctions for conduct code violations (plagiarism, cheating, stealing, etc.)
- Tolerating violent or abusive behaviors towards faculty, staff, peers
- Changing fundamental policies/procedures
- Personal services (wake-up calls, toileting, clothing, medications)
- Aides to keep student on task or monitor behaviors

Setting Boundaries

It is important to set guidelines and expectations for the level of contact the DS office will have with students. We strongly suggest that students meet with someone in the DS office on a regular basis (once or twice a week for as little as 10 minutes and up to no more than one hour) for at least the first two semesters. While this may be time-consuming in the beginning, it will save much effort and time later on, as it assists the student in the transition process, in developing a healthy working relationship with the DS officer, and in understanding when, where, and how to come for help when needed.

Some students are especially needy and will require multiple meetings per week (especially during periods of transition, change, or stress, such as the beginning of a new semester, or mid terms). There is nothing wrong with this unless (a) it becomes too burdensome for the DS office to handle; (b) there are concomitant signs of stress, depression, or high anxiety that would best be referred to a mental health professional; or (c) the student seems paralyzed and can only move forward with the support of DS.

A student who comes in several times a week and cannot make a decision without a DS professional is being enabled and is not being provided effective services. In cases like this, the DS professional has become the surrogate parent and has not assisted in the student's move to independence. It is up to DS to set and maintain boundaries with students and with parents.

We suggest that during weekly meetings you check in with the student to find out how classes are going, what assignments he may be having trouble with, how the residence hall situation is going, and what support he needs in negotiating that environment.

Armed with this information, you can help the student learn to make decisions on his own and ask for help when needed. There will be mistakes, and that is part of learning. Usually students with AS are doing better than they think they are and only need some validation of how well they are handling things.

To assist in developing these critical skills in communication and coping, we suggest using a strategy familiar to speech-language pathologists and others – scaffolding and scripting. Students with AS are typically good at following scripts and rules and can, therefore, use them to guide their interactions and communication with other key people on campus. You can develop sample scripts that can be adapted for use in a variety of situations in which the student needs to communicate specific information to another professional. With time, scripts can be phased out as the student learns to communicate more effectively on her own.

A student who comes in several times a week and cannot make a decision without a DS professional is being enabled and is not being provided effective services.

Developing scripts and scaffolding. The student who does not communicate or interact fully in class is not only missing out on opportunities to learn, she is also missing the opportunity to improve on those skills. Fortunately, students with AS are often very good at using scripts, templates, and scaffolds to compensate for weak interpersonal, language, and organization skills. Guided participation with classmates, professors, and peers will increase and enhance those competencies (Schuler & Wolfberg, 2000).

As the term implies, *scaffolding* provides predictable structure that gradually builds upon an individual's developing competency. Scaffolds are individually determined and must be adjustable to suit the student's changing needs and circumstances. As competency develops, supports are withdrawn until the student has mastered the task at hand.

Sample Scripts

- Being a good self-advocate
- Negotiating strategies
- Working with faculty on problem solving
- Getting a job on campus
- Working with peers
- Interacting with members of the opposite sex
- Getting started in organizations

Many students with AS have difficulty interacting with faculty members despite the mandate that they must do so to arrange their accommodations. In a scaffold scenario, the student and the DS professional meet to review accommodations and procedures. With the student's permission, DS contacts the professor as a heads-up that the professor will be hearing from the student and to discuss some of the particular AS issues that may come up. The student then outlines what she wishes to discuss with the professor, and the DS specialist and student prepare a script. The student first rehearses the script on her own and then practices with a staff member in DS. Additionally, the student emails the professor to set up an appointment. During the appointment, the student delivers his accommodation letter according to the script:

"Professor Smith, I am in your Rhetoric 100 class, Section 2. Here is my accommodation letter from DS. I would like to talk to you about extra time, a separate room, and

a note taker. I am free the hour before class to begin the exam, but I can't stay late. Would that work for you? I also need to find a note taker but I don't know anyone in the class. Can you suggest a student I could ask? If you want to know anything more about my disability, feel free to call DS."

Following the appointment, the student and the DS specialist meet to review the interaction and to modify it (if needed) for other professors. The next time, the student takes more initiative in carrying out some of the steps as she has developed a more solid comfort level with the process. Once she feels fully comfortable in the practiced situation, the scaffold is no longer needed.

It is helpful if the DS professional creates multiple scripts with the student to ease the anxiety of different kinds of interactions. Creating multiple scripts for issues on campus can build an arsenal of confidence for the student who cannot comfortably speak to other students, staff, or faculty. With practice, the student should be able to utilize multiple levels of scripting to move through more and more complex situations (what to say if the professor denies the accommodation, and so forth).

We acknowledge that this will be time-consuming for DS professionals; however, it is time well spent, for it will increase the student's confidence in making individual arrangements.

Amount of Parent Contact

Students with AS come to higher education with parents who often have very different expectations for the relationship that will emerge between the student, the college, and the family. Parents of students with disabilities are accustomed to attending all meetings and being consulted every time a change is made to their child's educational plan (as per special education law). Thus, they may expect (even demand) an open line of communication between the university, the DS office, and the home. They may not be familiar with the laws governing family contact on an individual campus (these are not uniform between campuses) and find it difficult to let go. Further, one or both parents may exhibit signs of the broader autism phenotype themselves. Consequently, their behavior may reflect deficits in self-regulation and interpersonal and communication skills. With your assistance, the parent will give the student greater opportunity for independence and growth.

Creating Effective Partnerships with the Family

Due to most college and university policies as well as legal restrictions, such as the Federal Education Right to Privacy Act (FERPA), which will be discussed at length in the next chapter, there are mandated limits on the involvement of families in the college life of the student with AS. Disability services staff, with the student's permission, may speak to or work with a parent or family member. However, without a student's permission, no communication may take place. Most DS offices are accustomed to informing parents of the limits of confidentiality and in easing the parent out of the relationship.

Disability services staff, with the student's permission, may speak to or work with a parent or family member. However, without a student's permission, no communication may take place.

We advocate that the relationship with the family of a student with AS be handled rather differently. This is especially important because parents of students with disabilities have different rights vis á vis their child. For example, parents may disclose the nature of a student's disability to the office of Residence Life in situations where the DS office would be prohibited from doing so. Families are the experts on their child's disability and the child's reactions to changes and stresses, which is important to anticipate in working with a student with AS. For these and many other reasons, we advocate forging a respectful partnership with the parents of spectrum students.

Information Families Should Provide
About Their Son or Daugher

- Routines and interests
- Likes and dislikes
- Previous school experiences
- Relationships with peers
- Relationships with teachers
- Types of support services received in the past
- Challenges and/or problems (especially psychiatric)

Parents of students with disabilities are accustomed to being in charge. Therefore, it is difficult to tell them they have to back off and let the student learn to succeed, or fail. Starting with what is best for fostering the student's independence is often a successful way to begin this discussion.

The intrusive parent. Some parents do not take no for an answer. These are parents, often termed "helicopter" parents, who are involved in every aspect of their child's life. They call, text, or email their children constantly and want to speak directly with professors, administrators, deans, and even college presidents. They receive, edit, and red-line term papers and homework. They may call DS several times per week and expect an immediate call-back. Many students with AS do not object to this level of intrusion from their parents even in college. Yet, it undermines the goals of fostering independence and self-advocacy.

One of us has termed the parents of children with developmental disabilities "commando parents," who elevate the concept of the helicopter parent to a new level. These parents have found that this mode of interaction was necessary to get the services during the school years that enabled their offspring to make it to college. It is terrifying to send a young person with a disability off to school, especially if the school is far from home and the student is not a great communicator. It is not easy to challenge such parents' authority and command of their child's disability but the following may prove useful.

How to Handle Commando Parents
Remind them ...
- Their goal is to have an independent, functional son or daughter
- Frequent intervention sends their son or daughter the message that he or she needs rescuing
- Parental interference in solving issues results in students who resist independence
- Despite having a disability, students with AS want independence
- To recall the level of parental help they would tolerate when they went off to college
- To trust that by sending their offspring to college they have sent a strong message about their belief in his or her capability
- Mistakes will be made, but without mistakes there is no learning or growth

Parents who are intrusive and controlling must be told that college offers the opportunity to teach their child to be independent to help ensure he will be able to handle his own finances and live on his own. Parents usually see the value a good program of services can offer their child, and DS staff can assist them in stepping back and letting their child go out a little more on his or her own. Thus, the relationship of sharing information and working out issues with the student, with the parent playing only the role of consultant, may begin.

If a partnership has been developed that respects parents' expertise about their child, coupled with a sense that the DS office has expertise in working with students with disabilities (AS in particular), the groundwork is in place for a frank discussion about the limits on contacting the DS office.

While every family is different, it is necessary to establish a contract that sets guidelines about the frequency and duration of calls or emails. For example, something like "barring emergencies, you may call me once per week for a 5-minute chat and email me not more than twice per week. You may provide me with any information you feel might impact your child's academic experience, and I will update you on his or her general status only if your son or

If a partnership has been developed that respects parents' expertise about their child, coupled with a sense that the DS office has expertise in working with students with disabilities (AS in particular), the groundwork is in place for a frank discussion about the limits on contacting the DS office.

daughter has given me permission to do so" (see Release Form in Appendix E). We insist that students are told about such guidelines (which is often enough to limit the parent who begins a call with the words "I don't want him to know that I am calling you but …"). Explaining to such parents that their son or daughter has a right to know is a direct reminder that the child is now an adult with rights of his or her own.

The "absent" parent. In some situations, after dropping the student with AS on campus, the parents are absent. These parents refuse to engage with the DS office in making any arrangements for their child with AS. Some parents are exhausted. Others may not have worked through their feelings about their child's diagnosis, such as mourning the lost ideal of a perfect child.

Still others are new to the diagnosis and may not understand the level of interaction and commitment necessary for the partnership with DS to work on behalf of their son or daughter. The latter type of parents is easier to work with, as they can be helped to understand that their student can succeed on campus with support from home. To do so, provide education about the nature of their child's condition and its likely impact on his college experience. Also, point them to literature or helpful websites. Contacting the evaluator, with the student's permission, to let him know what is going on has also been successful, as it enables him to reach out to the parent to provide more information as needed.

It is vital to remind yourself that DS cannot necessarily effect change within the parents. You are there to provide accommodation and services for the student but not for the parents. As tempting as it may be, resist the urge to counsel or advise the parent unless you are specifically trained or mandated to do this. We have suggested that parents find support groups (online or in their local area) to find other parents who are working through similar issues.

In rare cases, the student and his (often recent) documentation of AS arrive on campus without any advance notification of the diagnosis or need for services. No one has worked with the student or his family to understand anything about AS or college. There is no good way to engage parents who have signaled their unwillingness to support the student with AS.

There is no good way to engage parents who have signaled their unwillingness to support the student with AS.

In such situations, our first suggestion is to direct attention toward the student by helping him find support *in loco parentis* (in place of the parent) on campus as soon as possible. This means finding a counselor or similar person on campus who will help guide and support the student in the way a parent would. We also suggest that the level of support to the student be increased and that efforts be made to locate surrogate resources on campus for the student (perhaps a residence assistant, a faculty in residence, or a counselor).

This level of support is typically beyond the scope of most DS offices, and it runs the risk of the student turning to DS for all of his or her needs, decisions, and other worldly advice. Students in this situation may need to explore other educational options with the help of DS professionals. If students are capable of remaining on campus, a support network must be built of others besides DS staff.

The angry parent. Some parents remain angry at having a child with a developmental disability and take their anger out on the college personnel. Other parents may be angry at the college for not communicating with them or asking for their input. As parents of children on the spectrum themselves, the authors are very familiar with the range of feelings associated with developmentally disabled children and understand how the parents of college students are feeling (one of us has a child who just entered college).

Again, in these cases we suggest communicating to the parents that you value their input and working with the family to establish guidelines for managing the flow of information. Often giving the parent a concrete and important task, such as speaking to the hall director or lining up a psychiatrist to manage medication, is useful. Some parents have to be told directly that they may not take their anger out on office personnel. Understanding that these reactions most often stem from fear, frustration, and misunderstanding can help diffuse such situations.

Guardianship

For students who have guardians, the guardian relationship should be treated differently than that with a parent. Guardians or, in some instances, conservators are "in the shoes of" the student legally. (In some states these terms have specific meanings. Sometimes *guardian* is only used for people with intellectual and cognitive disabilities. Check the meaning in your state.) This means that a guardian or *conservator* (a legal process approved by a probate judge where a parent or guardian is declared "responsible for the care " of an adult 18 or older) may assist the student in choosing classes, see the student's grades, etc. However, a guardian or conservator may not attend class with the student or do his work. For these reasons, there is much more interaction between a DS office and a guardian or conservator than with a parent.

The parent falls under FERPA rules, and permission must be signed by the student in order for DS to speak to or get information from the parent. This is not the case with the guardian or conservator. Disability service providers should request the legal paperwork that establishes the guardian's relationship with the student before they interact with the guardian. The paperwork varies state by state.

Service Provider vs. Clinician

We struggle against this tendency constantly and must remind ourselves that no one on campus can be everything to any one student.

It is easy for DS professionals to cross the line between providing good academic services and becoming clinical providers when working with students with AS, because their needs may be compelling, because the students are endearing and interesting, or because the provider feels that she is the only person on campus who understands the disorder and the student. This may particularly be the case on smaller campuses where there is one DS worker for all students. In addition, some DS providers have clinical training, which would give them the skill to go beyond the structure of their jobs.

We struggle against this tendency constantly and must remind ourselves that no one on campus can be everything to any one student. With the AS population, it is especially important to keep this in mind, as it can easily become the case that the student uses only the DS professional for all of his social contact, guidance, and access to information. Recalling that these students like predictability and routine, stopping by the DS office every day to check on email, for a chat, or to ask for a favor can quickly become a familiar pattern that the student will not likely change. This is bad for all concerned as the student becomes stuck and the DS professional becomes burned out by feeling so responsible for the student.

It is vital that all resources on campus be explored for sharing the student and sharing the work (see My Campus Resource Assessment in Appendix D). Counseling and student mental health centers are main resources, particularly for students with co-morbid psychiatric diagnoses. Residence Life and Housing are important resources in negotiating with roommates and other conflicts. Sororities and fraternities may be interested in sponsoring mentorship programs for students. Tutoring services may be called on to work with the student in developing executive strategies. Faculty and academic advising might be willing to provide extra assistance with registration and course selection.

Off-campus resources are also important. If the student has an outside mental health professional, it is vital to seek permission from the student to contact that individual on an as-needed basis. Speech-language pathologists, coaches, cognitive remediation specialists, and so on, are examples of allied health professionals with whom the student may be involved. If they are not, it may be prudent to consider whether such professionals can address some of the student's difficulties.

Universities that have or are partnered with education training programs (especially special education), allied health professional training (such as special education or occupational therapy programs), and clinical psychology or counseling may be interested in working with students with AS. Graduate students, in particular, may be recruited to serve as mentors or to assist with campus orientation, transportation, and so on. Also, faculty in those schools may be more knowledgeable about AS than you know.

The take-home message is that an entire campus can be involved in addressing some of the student's widespread issues rather than the DS office feeling solely responsible for managing the student on campus.

The take-home message is that an entire campus can be involved in addressing some of the student's widespread issues rather than the DS office feeling solely responsible for managing the student on campus.

Special Considerations for Graduate and Professional Students

So far we have discussed mainly issues related to undergraduate students. However, many students with AS are entering graduate and professional programs, including medicine, dentistry, law, and various research-oriented fields in sciences and social sciences. We have worked with medical, law, and other professionals and students with AS, many of whom have been quite successful in undergraduate settings. This reminds us every day that the work we do with an undergraduate with AS may be preparing him or her for a graduate or professional career.

Issues pertaining to housing, residence life, and faculty may be less problematic for these older students (although we have encountered many notable exceptions). More compelling issues usually revolve around fundamental requirements for professional programs.

Graduate and professional programs are more rigorous in terms of their professional competencies and less willing to make accommodations that do not follow these closely. Students in medical school, for example, must often sign a statement of technical standards indicating that they possess a set of fundamental attributes that include communication (written, oral, and listening), sensory and motor coordination, integrative ability, capacity for critical thought, and behavioral and social attributes, which include empathy. Students with AS must be aware that they are expected to demonstrate that they either possess these attributes or are able to demonstrate them with reasonable accommodations.

In addition, accommodating students in graduate programs may require more non-standard accommodations (given that many graduate students do not take exams but work independently on individual research projects), field placements, and clinics (especially for medicine and law). Interpersonal and professional issues may include sensitivity to others with whom the student is working as a trainee, or cultivating a professional appearance or demeanor.

We have stressed throughout this volume that the needs of students with AS are wide ranging, affecting both academic and non-academic areas. Let us now turn to the legal underpinnings and academic accommodation needs of students with AS.

CHAPTER 5

Legal Issues and Academic Accommodations

Colleges have become proficient at working with many students with disabilities in recent years. However, the needs of students with AS are different from those of students who struggle only academically. As mentioned, students with AS have pervasive difficulties throughout all aspects of their higher education experience, including social domains, cognitive domains, and executive functioning.

For most college service providers, the challenges lie in the social and executive areas, as they are used to helping students with cognitive deficits and sensory or physical impairments. Social skills deficits especially affect students in college, a time of independence for most peers. Specifically, students with AS find it hard to make friends in the residence halls; indeed, living with a roommate can be very difficult – for both parties. Some of the same things that keep them from making friends – lack of eye contact or lack of understanding of unwritten social codes – can also be a challenge for students with AS in the classroom. These factors make the college student with an autism spectrum disorder unfamiliar and often difficult to fathom and to work with. Successfully accommodating this student requires a thorough grounding in what makes a student with AS "tick."

In this chapter, we will review the laws pertaining to students with AS in higher education. We will review the concept of accommodation under the law and define what is reasonable and unreasonable in terms of accommodation. Finally, we will make some suggestions with regard to accommodations. Since academic accommodations are so entwined with the law, we have combined them in this chapter.

Pertinent Legislation

When students with disabilities are in K-12, the law considers them *entitled* to special education by virtue of being diagnosed with specific medical, learning, or other health impairment. Thus, special education laws guarantee evaluation, remediation, and accommodation of impairments. Parental permission and participation is, of course, guaranteed.

As students move forward to higher education, however, the legal focus shifts from entitlement and remediation to *protection from discrimination and equal access*. Increasingly, the student must be able to self-identify as a person with a disability and demonstrate that she is qualified as a member of a protected group. In other words, adult students must take charge of their education and their disability. This comes as a shock to many families, who find their involvement limited by the policies of the university. Families discover that documentation guidelines and the review processes for eligibility have become more stringent. Students may for the first time face a rejection for accommodations and services. Even when approved, families discover that services and accommodations are usually more limited than what they enjoyed in high school.

The principal laws that govern access to institutions of higher education include Section 504 of the Rehabilitation Act of 1973,

72

the Americans with Disabilities Act (ADA), and the Federal Educational Rights and Privacy Act (FERPA). We will review these individually. Section 504 of the Rehabilitation Act and the ADA prohibit discrimination solely on the basis of disability in employment, education, and physical plant (see below), and thus protect individuals

In other words, adult students must take charge of their education and their disability.

with disabilities from discrimination. FERPA guarantees access to educational records as well as student privacy. There are many key differences between the special education laws and the disability statutes that protect college students with disabilities. We will summarize some of these below.

Section 504 of the Rehabilitation Act of 1973 (http://www.hhs. gov/ocr/504.pdf). While less well known than its younger cousin, the ADA, Section 504 is the a key civil rights law that prohibits discrimination on the basis of disability in programs and activities, public and private, that receive federal financial assistance, including federal grant monies, or that provide federal financial aid to their students. Most colleges and universities in the United States fall within this category, with the exception of a few religious colleges that do not accept federal aid. Section 504 is the law that mandates accommodations in higher education, for the most part.

According to Section 504,

> No otherwise qualified individual with a disability in the United States, as defined in section 7(20), shall, solely by reason of her or his disability, be excluded from the participation in, be denied the benefits of, or be subjected to discrimination under any program or activity receiv-

ing Federal financial assistance or under any program or
activity conducted by any Executive agency or by the
United States Postal Service. (Sec 504, a; Wrightslaw)

The Americans with Disabilities Act (ADA; www.ada.gov). The
ADA was enacted in 1990 as a federal civil rights law that ex-
tends Section 504 to protect against discrimination for reasons
related to disabilities in employment, education, and accommodations, and to provide program and facility access to public facilities. It too applies to public and private entities that receive federal funds, and thus covers access in most places of employment,
colleges, and universities. Titles II and III of the ADA prohibit
discrimination on the basis of disability in employment, government, public accommodations, commercial facilities, and transportation. It includes building and facilities access, employment
practices, self-evaluation of the services provided, and grievances.

*Federal Educational Rights and Privacy Act (FERPA; www.
ferpa.gov).* FERPA was enacted as a revision of the laws that
were established to allow adult students to access and amend their
educational records. Prior to FERPA, student records were sealed
and could not be viewed or changed by the individual (recall
your "permanent record"). Under FERPA, a college student can
request to see his or her record, including all relevant information
pertaining to her education and contest any inaccuracies or disclosure of sensitive information without consent.

While FERPA does not strictly prohibit parents of dependent students from viewing educational records, different campuses adhere to different legal interpretations. Along with medical privacy
regulations, many disability offices use FERPA as the justification
for controlling access to disability information and maintaining

student privacy. With this reasoning, most offices (a) mandate that the adult student make and control all disability requests (rather than their parents), (b) limit parent access to and involvement with disability information and files, and (c) limit campus personnel access to disability information (including clinical records) without student written permission.

University Rights and Responsibilities

Under Section 504/ADA, a college or university must provide the qualified student with a disability equal access to all educational programs, services, facilities, and activities. The university must also provide reasonable accommodations, academic adjustments, and/or auxiliary aids and services to eligible persons with disabilities. The university or college is also responsible for maintaining student confidentiality as far as their disability is concerned, and must establish and maintain written policies and procedures (including procedures for filing grievances).

University Rights

- Maintain academic standards, integrity, and freedom
- Determine fundamental requirements of courses and programs
- Maintain and enforce conduct codes

With regard to the last bullet, students with disabilities must also be able to maintain appropriate behavioral standards in class. No exceptions are made to conduct codes for students with AS. For example, a student who has an outburst in class and argues with a professor, thereby intimidating the class and the instructor, may be subject to conduct code charges. The fact that the student has AS may be brought up and could be part of determining any sanctions. However, the presence of any disability does not excuse the student's behavior or eliminate the prohibition on disruption of the educational environment.

University Responsibilities

Universities must ensure the following for qualified students with disabilities:

- Equal access to all educational programs, services, facilities, and activities
- Reasonable accommodations, academic adjustments and/or auxiliary aids and services
- Student confidentiality
- Written policies and procedures (including grievance)

Disclosure and Confidentiality

As college students are typically legally adults, they have full access to their files and full protection of confidentiality. However, different campuses have different attitudes toward disclosure. As discussed above, some institutions maintain a strict interpretation of FERPA and do not share any information with anyone without the student's written permission. Other campuses share certain information such as grade reports, judicial sanctions, and health information with professionals at the college.

Schools should take into consideration what information students are comfortable sharing and with whom. Questions arise when trying to determine what information can be shared with parents. For example, it is often useful for schools and parents to work together to identify a safe place to which a student can retreat (such as a dorm room or resident advisor's [RA] room) and establish back-up systems for students when stressed; however, it is up to the student to determine what and how much clinical information may be disclosed.

Kevin is not used to so many individuals being involved in a single course (professor, teaching assistant, lab coordinator, recitation instructor). While he was unaware of the amount of information being shared when he was in high school, Kevin benefitted from his teachers getting information about his

... it is up to the student to determine what and how much clinical information may be disclosed.

AS from the resource room. Now that he is in college, Kevin does not know to whom he should address his questions. Of all of them, the lab instructor is the most accessible. However, he has a thick foreign accent making it difficult for Kevin to understand him.

Eventually, Kevin gives up trying. Never having used a syllabus before, Kevin does not realize the weight it carries and its relevance at the college level. While he did pay attention to the sections of the syllabus that his teachers referenced in class, he did not take any initiative to look at the other sections of the syllabus. One course had a 12-page syllabus, written with care and in great detail, clearly outlining students' responsibilities and the professor's expectations and course requirements. Kevin barely looked at the syllabus with predictable consequences. He did not hand in his work and is failing two courses. The disabilities office thinks Kevin should disclose his AS to the course instructors and ask for extra help and some more accommodations, but Kevin is reluctant to do so.

Students' Rights and Responsibilities

Under the law, students with disabilities have the right to equal access to all university programs and activities. Rights that the universities must recognize include the right to receive effective, appropriate, and reasonable accommodations. This is often the first point of intersection between the student with AS and the university, as the student and/or his family contacts the university to arrange accommodations for tests or in residence halls. Unlike high school, students must engage in an interactive process with the DS office in requesting and monitoring their accommodations.

Unlike high school, students must engage in an interactive process with the DS office in requesting and monitoring their accommodations.

Student Rights

- Equal access to all university programs and activities
- Equal access to all educational activities
- Reasonable and appropriate accommodations
- Privacy and confidentiality

Along with student rights come student responsibilities. Students are ultimately responsible for disclosing their disability to a designated entity on campus. Failure to do so means that the university is not obligated to recognize the student as having a disability or offer the legal protection that affords. Self-disclosure also includes providing documentation of disability in compliance with campus policy. The student is responsible for requesting her own accommodations and monitoring their effectiveness. Finally, the student must follow reasonable established policies and procedures with regard to disabilities accommodations and must meet required academic and behavioral standards (e.g., be otherwise qualified).

Student Responsibilities

- Self-disclose to designated entity on campus
- Provide reasonable documentation of disability in compliance with campus policy
- Request accommodations and monitor effectiveness
- Follow reasonable policies and procedures
- Meet required academic and behavioral standards

What Are Accommodations?

Accommodations are defined as adjustments to an academic program or environment intended to mitigate the impact of the functional limitations of a disability on participation in that environment. Adjusting academic assignments, changing classrooms to enable physical access, and using alternate-format books (audio or computer discs rather than print) are all examples of accommodations commonly provided on college campuses. Known for "leveling the playing field," accommodations make the academic environment manageable without fundamentally altering the curriculum.

Students who qualify for accommodations must be able to attend classes and complete the required work – academic standards don't change. For example, students with AS are expected to complete the same assignments and are evaluated using the same academic standards as students without disabilities. Students are not excused from reading the same books, writing the same term papers, and attending the same classes simply by virtue of their classification as a student with a disability. However, certain modifications may be necessary, which will be discussed at greater length, such as extended time or a lighter course load.

Universities have the right to maintain academic standards, integrity, and freedom, and to determine the fundamental requirements of their individual courses and programs. Fundamental requirements are essential aspects of a course or program that do not need to be altered or modified for a student with a disability.

An example might be a math or foreign language requirement in a liberal arts course of study. Just because a student is an Engineering major who never intends to read a non-technical book or travel abroad, he or she is still expected to meet the same foreign language or general education requirements as other students if it has been determined that these are essential to the Engineering education.

Fundamental requirements are essential aspects of a course or program that do not need to be altered or modified for a student with a disability.

Accommodations must not provide students with AS an unfair advantage over other students. ADA Title II defines an accommodation as a modification of the institution's rules, policies, or practices; environmental adjustments, such as the removal of architectural or communicative barriers; or auxiliary aids and services (Macurdy & Geetter, 2008). While, by definition, accommodations may be either reasonable or unreasonable, the interpretation of this distinction is far from simple. The university may determine what is reasonable and appropriate and select among effective alternatives. This means that despite the student's request for a note-taker, for example, the university may determine that another alternative is reasonable and appropriate (such as audio taping lectures).

Reasonable vs. unreasonable. Reasonable accommodations are guaranteed under the law to level the playing field for a person with a disability. Reasonable accommodations for students with AS require careful planning and dialogue. Many accommodations are straightforward and flow directly from the student's functional limitations and the provider's understanding of the essentials of AS. On the other hand, unreasonable accommodations are adjustments that could (a) confer an unfair advantage to the recipient; (b) compromise the fundamental requirements, technical standards, or essential functions of a course program or position; (c) pose an undue burden to the provider; or (d) be inappropriate per the diagnosed condition and its functional limitations. (See *Southeastern Community College v. Davis,* 442 U.S. 397, 423 [1979], where the Supreme Court determined that colleges and universities are not required to make changes to program standards that can be demonstrated to be fundamental or essential to the program of study; also see Macurdy & Geetter, 2008.)

For example, it would be reasonable for a student on the spectrum to take an exam in a separate room with extended time to control anxiety. An unreasonable request for an accommodation would be to provide an aide to accompany the student to all exams and classes and to clarify all of the student's answers to his professor. The first accommodation levels the playing field and allows the student to demonstrate his knowledge. The second request is outside the scope of higher education, which expects students to be independent. A personal aide for a person with a physical disability is a different request since that person may need help turning a page or getting a book. As an accommodation, the student with AS may need extra time on an exam, a room changed for sensory issues, or a single room in the residence hall.

Other examples of unreasonable academic accommodations (all of which the authors have individually or collectively encountered) include waiving required courses that are deemed fundamental to the course of study (such as the English requirements for the student who struggles with composition), permitting papers in lieu of exams for the student with test anxiety, assigning a tutor to attend class and prepare individualized study guides, permitting independent or directed studies for courses with attendance requirements, assigning fewer readings or less homework, waiving lab attendance, unlimited time for exams, and unlimited extensions for homework, papers, or out-of-class assignments.

Institutions of higher education are not required to make accommodations that would have the effect of altering fundamental aspects of a course or degree program. Thus, colleges and universities are permitted under the law to determine which aspects of their educational programs are essential. Once these fundamental requirements have been established (following the legal guidelines for such determination, *Wynne v. Tufts Univ. School of Medicine*, 932 F.2d 19, 26, 1st Cir. 1991; also see Macurdy & Geetter, 2008), the college or university would not need to waive or modify the requirement as an accommodation for a student with a disability even if the student had demonstrated that she would benefit from such an adjustment. As mentioned, universities also have the right to maintain and enforce conduct codes without regard to a student's disability as a mitigating factor (unlike public schools that often cannot discipline a student unless disability is taken into account).

Institutions of higher education are not required to make accommodations that would have the effect of altering fundamental aspects of a course or degree program.

Accommodation Basics

According to the ADA, students with disabilities have the right to receive accommodations to mitigate the impact of their disability on their academic performance as part of "leveling the playing field" to be commensurate with that of students without disabilities. In essence, this is the same as an accessible entrance or a ramp for someone in a wheelchair. That is, for students with AS, accommodations allow them to better learn and demonstrate proficiencies in an educational environment, preventing them from drowning in an atmosphere that is far too social for most students with AS to survive in.

Students with AS often need academic support in subjects that are not their strength. For example, a student who is strong in math and science but weak in English and humanities may require extended time for tests in the weaker areas and no accommodations in their strength subjects.

Are there typical accommodations for AS? Every student with AS is different; therefore, it is impossible to offer a laundry list of reasonable and unreasonable accommodations. We firmly believe that successful accommodations stem from understanding the diagnosis, the way it affects an individual student, and the fundamental requirements of a course or program. Further, accommodations must be individualized for the student and not "prescribed" per any particular diagnosis. One does not "accommodate AS," but rather accommodates a student with an autism spectrum diagnosis that affects him or her in a uniquely individual manner.

In theory ...
- Academic difficulties in AS are related to deficits in integration, executive function, and self-regulation
- If we understand why, we can figure out when and how to best accommodate

---

While we are reluctant to offer a list of recommended accommodations for the reasons outlined above, we have provided some of the more common adjustments with which DS providers and faculty are generally familiar and comfortable.

Common Academic Accommodations

- **Exams:**
  - » Extra time
  - » Reduction of distractions
  - » Use of computer
  - » Clarification of questions or answers (written or oral)
  - » Separate room for major exams
  - » Breaks as needed
  - » Oral supplement to essay exams
  - » No use of scantron forms

- **Presentations:**
  - » Webcast or videotape presentation
  - » Present to professor only
  - » Alternate assignments (if allowable)

- **Classroom:**
  - » No cold-calling in class (call on student and return later)
  - » Permission to bring sensory objects
  - » Permission to bring drinks or food
  - » Breaks as needed
  - » Note taker/audiotape
  - » Laptop for note taking

We encourage providers to consider requests that may be somewhat unfamiliar. For example, while a student who struggles with writing essays analyzing personal motivations of a character in a Shakespeare play should not be offered a waiver on his literature requirement, he might be permitted to substitute a paper on the historical or sociological factors operating in Elizabethan England, which may include the author. We encourage providers to consider how unreasonable requests might be changed into reasonable accommodations. For example, can the student who requests not to be required to do class presentations due to social anxiety be permitted to deliver her presentation via webcam from the comfort of the residence hall?

Specific Academic Accommodations for Students with Asperger Syndrome

As we have emphasized repeatedly, we believe that the cornerstone of successfully accommodating a student with AS is to understand the nature of the student's functional impairment, the demands of his or her course of study, and the requirements of the program. The intake forms in Appendix C are constructed so that the information gathered about student challenges, strengths, and weaknesses translates into accommodation needs, resources, intrinsic and extrinsic factors, and an actual accommodation plan. In addition, the following section

We encourage providers to consider how unreasonable requests might be changed into reasonable accommodations.

helps DS providers better understand the particular challenges of the student with AS in cognitive, interpersonal, social, and behavioral domains in the academic sphere of the university.

Recall that the major domains of AS discussed in Chapter 2 include social (including language), cognitive, and behavioral. Each of these may have an impact on the educational experience for the college student. Thus, all may be subject to accommodation. We will now briefly review them in the context of accommodations.

Cognitive Challenges, Related Academic Domains, and Appropriate Accommodations

The cognitive disability in AS has been explored in many excellent references (Minshew, 2001; Russell, 1997; Schopler, Mesibov, & Kunce, 1998; Wetherby & Prizant, 2004). We will distill it very briefly here. Because of widespread integrative and regulatory deficits, the cognitive domains impacted by AS are also discussed at length in Appendices A and B.

Students with AS have difficulty understanding the bigger picture of assignments, tests, and reading. The organization of writing is typically problematic, as are managing long-range projects, time management, planning, and maintaining momentum. With regard to the student's academic needs, DS providers might be called upon to accommodate such basic academic venues as writing, reading, integrating, test taking, and organizing. We will review some of these areas below.

Exam accommodations. The content of exams is often not problematic for students with AS in that they are good at memorizing large amounts of information and regurgitating it on demand. However, the format, including physical settings, can pose challenges. Some students who have AS have a nonverbal learning disability profile of reduced visual and visual-perceptual skills (see Appendix A for details). Such students might have difficulty answering exams with a scantron-type format due to reduced visual scanning ability. Others may not fully read test instructions or listen for additional instructions in the exam room. Still other students on the spectrum may have such overarching anxiety as to undermine any exam setting. Additionally, essay-format exams may be problematic because of the demand for organized, concise writing.

Disability services staff should inquire (e.g., by using the intake form in Appendix C) about distraction and sensory issues in an exam setting so that any accommodations that might be directed towards those factors can be in place. Professors may be asked to monitor such things as excessive ambient noise (construction noise, machinery or air conditioners, even traffic) if they know that one of their students is sensitive. Rectifying these issues may be the difference between good and abysmal exam performance for the student with AS.

Common exam accommodations were presented in the table earlier in this chapter. Typical examples of reasonable accommodations for exams would be extended time (time and one half to double is typical, as unlimited time tends to prolong inertia and is not recommended for students with AS). Testing in a separate, distraction-reduced environment is appropriate for many students, especially those with distractibility or social anxiety.

Less Familiar Exam Accommodations

- Allow sensory toys
- Reduce ambient conditions
- Relocate exam
- Provide alternate format of exam
- Substitute alternate assignment (used very sparingly)

More creative accommodations might include reduction of ambient distraction such as air conditioning or heating vents, street noise, or flickering lights. Reduction of ambient smells may be necessary for some students. It is also important to ask the student whether there are sensory issues in the testing environment that are disruptive. Some students may be allowed to bring sensory fidgets into exam situations (see section on sensory dysfunction and integration in Chapter 2 and in Appendix A).

Some exams may require an alternate format, although this is not an adjustment to offer lightly. That is, if all else fails with the standard format, it is sometimes useful for the student and DS provider to explore with a professor whether an alternate is available that would still fulfill the course objectives and demonstrate that the student has attained all of the course benchmarks. For example, permitting the student to meet with the professor after the exam to orally clarify his answers or to be graded on lists of relevant facts rather than written essays are adjustments that we have successfully brokered.

... permitting the student to meet with the professor after the exam to orally clarify his answers or to be graded on lists of relevant facts rather than written essays are adjustments that we have successfully brokered.

All students should be afforded an opportunity to clarify test questions. The student who is taking his exams in a separate location may not understand that he must ask how and if he has permission to leave the room to seek clarification or assistance during the exam. Professors typically do not anticipate this need.

Assistance of any kind during an exam is typically a compromise of test security and academic conduct codes. Students must understand that such help must come from the professor or designated proctor and should be discussed in advance. Aides or coaches during exams are not consistent with the goals of higher education.

Accommodations for writing. While many students with AS are proficient writers, others struggle with writing tasks. Weaknesses in this area relate to executive functioning deficits and integration and synthesis difficulties; that is, students struggle with organizing their thoughts into a cohesive paper and understanding how the details or evidence accumulate to prove a thesis. Also, due to language-based confusion, the issue of plagiarism can come up.

Some students may struggle with essay questions on exams, while others encounter difficulty with term papers because long-range planning and organizing is challenging. Still others may have difficulty writing creatively or succinctly, preferring to write lengthy essays that contain facts but no interpretation or synthesis of ideas. Some students even submit lists and outlines in lieu of essays. In some instances, we have asked that professors consider this as an adjunct to a written assignment, although we do not often recommend that students be able to substitute such work for written assignments. Many students with AS require direct interventions such as a writing coach or tutor to teach them better written organizational skills. In some cases, students may require special accommodations to allow them to demonstrate their course mastery in an alternate manner.

Note-taking accommodations. Due to attention difficulties and problems sorting out important concepts during lectures, many students with AS need note takers in classes. The sheer demand of sitting in lengthy lectures with many other people may be over-stimulating. In addition, the student may be disrupted by sensitivity to ambient conditions such as lights, sounds, or classroom smells such as chalk or dry erase markers, making it challenging to focus on taking good notes. In such a scenario, a student may need to exert so much energy to maintain attention and control behaviors that they are unable to take in and process information from the lecture.

A note taker, at least during the transition to college, may be an excellent idea. We also recommend that when a student is authorized the use of a note taker, she receive training from the academic support center or from a tutor on how to take notes herself in the event a note taker is not available, and that she understands strategies she can use to offset sensory sensitivities (see Low Tech Accommodations on page 100).

> *A note taker, at least during the transition to college, may be an excellent idea.*

Clarification. Due to difficulties in attention and integration, or due to rigid processing style, some students with AS need a professor or tutor to assist in clarifying assignments, test questions, or paper topics. Students should know how and where to access individuals (such as the professor and the teaching assistant or tutoring center) if they have questions about an assignment. Part of transitioning the student might involve DS or a tutor scripting a scenario with the student. For example, if the student is confused about a term paper assignment on the syllabus, how might he or she ask the professor for assistance?

Integration. Because students with AS tend to see only one perspective (i.e., cannot see the forest for the trees), they often miss the connections that make up the whole. Mis-integrating details can potentially impact many aspects of a student's college trajectory. For example, a student may not realize that receiving a poor grade because of not attending class can have ramifications for future scholarship money, eligibility to take other classes, or timely graduation. It would be impossible to anticipate and address in advance each situation where a student might misunderstand information. However, all personnel working with the student should be aware that such misunderstandings can and do occur and that the solution may require both understanding and flexibility.

Reading. Students with AS are often characterized as early and strong readers. However, in college reading comprehension may be problematic as a result of impairments in integration and synthesis. That is, a student may well understand the words she reads but not be able to form a cohesive picture of how all the details and individual sections add up to one greater lesson. This may be related to the difficulties in integration discussed above.

> *... in college reading comprehension may be problematic as a result of impairments in integration and synthesis.*

Reading comprehension can also suffer as a result of not being able to take multiple perspectives into account at once. Reading accommodations might include extra time for reading demanding exams, extension on deadlines in certain courses with extensive reading demands, or use of auxiliary aids such as digital or recorded books for certain texts. When reading comprehension interferes with taking exams or writing essays, we suggest accommodating the reading deficit first, then addressing the exam or writing issue second.

Executive functioning. Executive functioning refers to a set of skills commonly associated with planning and foresight, organization, synthesizing information, delaying, and initiating activity (see Appendix A for more detail). Deficits in executive functioning are common in individuals with AS. While such deficits may have a tremendous impact on academic functioning, they are often straightforward to mitigate. For example, the student with AS and executive deficits may have trouble organizing his schedule. This student may forget where and when he has class or not plan enough time to shower, eat, and walk to class in time. Or he might tackle three chemistry problems due at the end of the week instead of the paper due the next day because of difficulties with prioritization.

There are no accommodations per se for executive dysfunction, but we believe that it can and should be addressed through teaching the student important skills and using available tutoring resources on campus. Some students will never master some of these domains and will require assistance from the DS staff and some consideration from their professors in order to demonstrate they have mastered their course objectives.

Academic Domains That Tax Executive Function
- Translating a syllabus to an academic game plan for the semester
- Breaking assignments down to small chunks
- Organizing and regulating flow of ideas
- Multi-tasking determined by the timing of exams and papers
- Knowing how and when to begin semester-long projects and papers
- Maintaining organization for semester-long projects
- Prioritizing and managing time for short- and long-range work

Many students struggle with time management issues, including reducing a syllabus into a semester game plan. Many cannot surmount the demands of an academic calendar that insist they be able to multi-task, study for several exams at one time, or have several long-range projects on the table at the same time. Others struggle with task initiation and maintaining motivation, and require external assistance to "keep their eye on the prize."

Direct instruction in time management (use of a date book, whiteboards, "to do list," colored sticky notes, interim deadlines, etc.) is strongly recommended for students with AS. These tools can often be provided by DS or by the academic tutoring support center on campus. In some instances, students and families must locate and pay for an outside professional to provide this service.

Social Challenges, Related Academic Domains, and Appropriate Accommodations

The social disability of college students with AS includes development of self-awareness and sense of self, as well as core social skills such as social perception, reading social cues, and social language. Obviously, such challenges have implications for academic functioning. This becomes particularly problematic when students are required to negotiate with faculty, staff, and administrators as they try to arrange accommodations or register for classes. Asking a professor who may have written the textbook used in the class for an accommodation is a daunting task for many entering, and even more senior, students. A student with a core social skills disorder may simply not know the rules to approach such a person with the proper degree of respect and decorum.

The social disability of college students with AS includes development of self-awareness and sense of self, as well as core social skills such as social perception, reading social cues, and social language.

Other classroom interactions such as forming study groups or working on group projects require particular attention, as students are prone to being taken advantage of in a group setting (if indeed they are willing to enter into the group at all). We will return to this in the section on group projects.

Social Issues in Academic Areas
- Social anxiety and phobia
- Public speaking and answering in class
- Working in groups, choosing lab partners or study groups
- Speaking to the professor, asking for help

Social anxiety. The behavioral manifestations of social anxiety are apparent in the academic setting. Some students may be unable to participate in study groups or work with lab partners due to extreme social discomfort. It may be feasible in such cases to videotape ahead of time in-class presentations and play them to the class rather than asking the student to present "live." In other cases, professors may be amenable to rethinking whether their requirement for public speaking is fundamental to the course (in which case they may be subject to little if any modification) or whether the professor might consider an alternate activity for the student with AS who has severe social anxiety. Along the same lines, professors might be asked for additional time in answering in-class questions (especially in law school, where the Socratic method is strictly applied).

... professors might be asked for additional time in answering in-class questions (especially in law school, where the Socratic method is strictly applied).

- *Presentations.* Presentations are often difficult for students with AS because of deficits in organizing and struggling to synthesize details as well as social anxiety. For example, one student might present her ideas systematically as a list without adding the details up to a greater whole. Another student might ramble on and on, including every arcane detail he knows rather than filtering out the salient details. Some students tend to be pedantic on a special interest and have trouble reading social cues of boredom or impatience. They may simply be too anxious to stand up in front of the class to present even a well-organized project or paper. Such students may require some assistance from DS as well as from the professor in order to meet the course demands.

- *Working in groups.* Because of their social disability, students with AS often do not work well in groups. Types of problems associated with group activities include perfectionism, inability to negotiate, and difficulty interacting with partners. Often labeled as odd, students with AS may not know how to initiate a conversation or insert their own thoughts or contributions into a project or discussion. Thus, many remain observers on the sidelines, causing resentment in group members and poor marks from professors.

Also, often the student with AS feels that all his work must be perfect, whereas the same may not be so for the other group members. In fact, some of the other group members may not be capable of perfect work, or they may be more interested in the other group members than in the work. This is incomprehensible for students with AS who cannot function with this work ethic.

We will discuss this in detail in the Faculty section in Chapter 9 because these interactions often require that faculty be approached to form groups rather than allowing students to choose partners. Faculty may also be asked to monitor group interactions more actively when a student with AS is involved than they might do otherwise.

Negotiating, or give-and-take, is part of the process of working with a group. It is also an important skill for employment. All professional work requires some negotiation and work with others. The art of negotiation is usually underdeveloped in students with AS, and thus group work is problematic for them. Students with AS cannot figure out the total task, see the strengths of others and assign tasks based on those strengths and complete the work. Further, problems with executive function and organizational management may interfere with the student with AS carrying out their end of the group project, and problems with social skills will certainly interfere with their ability to resolve it with group members. For example, can this student skillfully apologize for missing a deadline or meeting?

Barriers to Working in Groups

- Anxiety
- Perfectionism
- Rigidity
- Poor social skills and communication
- Coercion or being taken advantage of
- Preference for solitary activities

Working with a group requires interaction with peers and faculty, progress checks, renegotiating based on time and assignments, and so on. All of these tasks are socially oriented and problematic for most students with AS. For all the above reasons, most academic group work is appropriate for accommodations. Direct intervention in the form of formal training in social skills is not recommended. DS personnel are not required to do social skills training. Given the short time frame, time would be better spent addressing the issue with the faculty member either as an accommodation or an area to monitor, while working with the student to script and rehearse a few different negotiating scenarios.

Behavioral Challenges, Related Academic Domains, and Appropriate Accommodations

The behavioral disability in AS is often difficult to separate from the social disability discussed above. It usually involves rigid, stereotyped behaviors such as needing to sit in the same seat (with concomitant anxiety if the seat is taken), to eat certain textured or colored food, or to wear the same clothes because they are comfortable and familiar. Behavioral difficulties often escalate during times of transition or change as the student no longer can count on being able to integrate in the new environment.

Behavioral difficulties often escalate during times of transition or change as the student no longer can count on being able to integrate in the new environment.

At these times, we may see the emergence of new behaviors (or "stereotypes" in clinical parlance) or worsening of certain behaviors such as chewing on non-food items, waving or flapping hands, or withdrawal and flight from a situation, if particularly stressed or overwhelmed.

In most cases, the behavior itself serves to calm the student and should not be discouraged or interrupted (unless it disrupts the educational environment or poses a danger to self or others). Extreme behaviors typically communicate that there is something bothersome either in the environment or that the student does not understand what is being asked or expected.

The student may be taken aside to find out whether he or she is aware of something in the environment that is triggering the behavior. Are there sensory irritants? Are people sitting too close? Has the student been asked to do something such as speak in front of the class that is overwhelming? This sort of intervention is often a useful way to address the situation before it escalates into an outburst.

 Kevin is enrolled in Chemistry 101, which is a lab science requirement. He was waived from this requirement in high school due to his extreme sensory sensitivities to smell. The DS office was not aware of how extreme his sensitivity or his reactions are. During the first lab session, Kevin sat far from the demonstration table and was O.K. However, when lab partners and tables were assigned, Kevin was placed close to the lab instructor. When the lab was being demonstrated, Kevin began to feel sick and panicked at the smell of the chemicals and the gas burner. He grabbed his backpack and fled the room.

He has been barred from returning to class. The DS office suggests a meeting between the student and the lab instructor to develop a plan of action that might include using a respirator or a mask when Kevin is in a lab setting.

Interrupting or disrupting class. It is not uncommon for professors to call DS regarding the behavior of a student with AS who does not adhere to the rules of classroom conduct. Students need to understand that interruptions and speaking out of turn, correcting the instructor, walking out of the classroom, or eating and drinking in class are usually not permitted. Some students require sensory integration materials such as squeeze balls to remain focused in the classroom (see section on Low-Tech Accommodations). Disability services staff (with the student's assistance) should be prepared to explain these sorts of interventions in such a manner that a professor understands that the student is not being disrespectful. The reactions of other students to the student with AS may also need to be monitored and the student made to understand the impact of her behaviors on her peers.

Disrupting the educational setting is a breach of the conduct code at the majority of institutions of higher education in this country. This is a situation where both accommodations and working actively with the professor and the student can be brought to bear.

Strategies for Making the Classroom Environment More Tolerable for All

1. Have professor and DS staff inform student that he may only ask a question or speak when called on twice per class.
2. Ask professor to allow 5 minutes after each class to speak with student and clear up unresolved questions or comments.
3. Have student use a whiteboard where he can write down all comments during class that are not spoken out loud and then review them with professor.
4. Ensure accommodation that allows student to get up and leave only once during each class.
5. Allow the student to use sensory gadgets that do not disrupt the environment.

6. Just as you would for access, move classes for students with AS to accommodate sensory issues (e.g., if light flickering or sound such as fans set the student off).

7. Suggest the student take notes with one sheet of paper on a clip board covered with sandpaper using a fine marker instead of a pen (this is for sensory feedback).

8. Allow the student to wear sunglasses in class if lights are disturbing.

Several of these strategies involve very simple low-tech adjustments, such as those discussed at more length below.

Low-Tech Accommodations

Not all solutions are technological in nature. Very effective "low-tech" solutions to assist students with AS in the classroom and beyond include permitting students to use stress fidgets in class and during exams or meetings to help them stay attentive and calm. The range of low-tech accommodations is diverse and limited only by the student's needs and the practicality of the solution. Disability providers may have creative ideas of their own and also consult closely with the student in crafting low-tech solutions. For example, the authors have had success with students using all of the following to modulate extreme sensory reactions that caused difficulties in the classroom:

- Rubber squeeze balls and heavy rubber bands to provide sensory input during lectures and exams
- Quiet foot massagers on the floor under desk during long classes
- Permission to write exams in pencil to add resistance to writing and to allow erasure of mistakes for the anxious individual

- Clipboards covered with sandpaper and single sheets of paper to take notes on rather than a pad of paper to provide more sensory feedback to the hand
- Fine-tip markers on covered clipboard to provide more stimuli than ballpoint pens
- Sunglasses of different colors and baseball caps to help deal with offensive lighting in classroom or lecture hall
- Bike shorts for compression, similar to deep compression
- Placing a heavy backpack on lap to provide sensory input

High-Tech Accommodations

While some issues can be resolved using little technology, others call for more sophisticated adjustments. Computers and other technological advances have greatly improved the ability of many people with disabilities to function in the academic and work environment. Referred to as assistive or adaptive technology, these may include computers that read, write, scan, organize, and/or take notes for students.

Assistive and adaptive technology solutions can be particularly useful for some (but not all) students with AS. Certain tech accommodations such as voice input on the computer may help alleviate anxiety, and voice output for long reading assignments and personal digital organizers (PDAs) may help with organization. Earphones of different types can also be helpful; some eliminate high frequencies, and others eliminate all but middle frequencies for voices.

Access to adaptive and assistive technology is governed by Section 508 of the Rehabilitation Act (see www.section508.gov for details). Section 508 mandates that persons with disabilities have access to electronic and information technology (such as course websites or online library catalogs). However, some of these devices will not be provided by the university or college, as they are considered personal equipment that the student is responsible for providing and funding herself (such as computers, calculators, PDAs, and much computer hardware). Disability providers working with families during the transition should ask whether the student has used adaptive technology and should specifically inquire what hardware and software solutions they have explored. If they have not used such devices, it is worth considering whether high-tech solutions may be useful.

Summing It Up: How Do You Deal with the Big Challenges Asperger Syndrome Presents to a Successful College Experience?

In summary, the "big" challenges that impact academics for students with AS may involve overall faulty integration and synthesis. Students tend to miss the big picture and process the "forest for the trees." Students may become anxious and rigid in the face of this confusion. As well as being a core feature of the diagnosis, rigidity serves the additional function of helping to cope with the anxiety aroused by novel situations and change (Rosenn, 1999). Planning, shifting, prioritizing, and other aspects of executive and regulatory control also may be affected (Happe, Booth, Charlton, & Hughes, 2006; Hill, 2004; Joseph & Tager-Flusberg, 2004; also see Thierfeld Brown & Wolf, in press, for review). Finally, deficits in the social arena, including being an effective social agent and being able to take the perspective of another (theory of mind; Baron-Cohen, 1989, 1999), may be problematic in a university environment.

We know from experience that these domains of functioning can have different impacts in and out of the classroom environment.

Thus, difficulties in the areas of cognition, behavioral, and interpersonal/social skills can be felt in the classroom, on exams, in the residence halls, and in student activities (to name but a few areas of campus life). In order to handle all of these challenges, it is important for DS professionals to develop a systematic understanding of the issues and the impact these issues pose in different arenas.

... difficulties in the areas of cognition, behavioral, and interpersonal/social skills can be felt in the class-room, on exams, in the residence halls, and in student activities.

We conceptualize this as follows.

Academic and Classroom	Co-Curricular
Cognitive	Cognitive
Behavioral	Behavioral
Interpersonal	Interpersonal

The two columns (Academic and Co-Curricular) correspond to the major facets of the college experience. Academic activities are those that occur within the academic and classroom domains, whereas co-curricular refers to such areas as residence life, student activities, and the like (to be discussed further in Chapter 6). The rows correspond to the three major areas of function that might require accommodation or attention: cognitive, behavioral, or interpersonal.

The following chart was developed to assist the DS provider in conceptualizing these challenges (the examples refer to some of Kevin's experiences):

DOMAINS	Cognitive	Behavioral	Interpersonal
Academic	*Slow processing, poor executive functioning; writing issues; note taking*	*Blurts out in class, scratches self, comes late, complains of smell in lab, runs out of lab*	*Isolates self in class; no study partners; group presentations hard*
Co-Curricular	*Poor self-organization in residence hall; can't study in room; easily overwhelmed with too much information*	*Melt downs when challenged or overwhelmed in residence hall and during student activities*	*Roommates complain about mess; sensory issues with smells in room; needs help finding student groups and activities of interest*
Other	*Does not want to disclose to faculty; accepts accommodations*	*Sees therapist for behavioral coaching; DS support to professors regarding limiting behavior in class; explore mask for smells in labs*	*Find social skills group. Speak to parents about hygiene issues in room*

As illustrated, many of Kevin's major challenges can be summarized in a way that makes it clearer how best to design accommodations and other interventions to assist him in being more successful on campus. The format of this chart can be adjusted to suit the areas of interest (for example, making it more specific with regard to academic areas rather than general as above so that more detail can be captured).

Now that we have discussed legal underpinnings and academic accommodations in detail, let us turn to nonacademic (or co-curricular) activities in the next chapter – typically a significant area of challenge for students with AS.

CHAPTER 6

Co-Curricular Needs and Accommodations

In this chapter, we turn to the non-academic aspects of college life. These involve experiences that occur outside the classroom and outside the strict academic environment of the college or university, such as in residence halls, student activities, clubs and groups, Greek life, athletics, and so on. They are termed "co-curricular" activities because they are seen as complementing the student's academic life.

Consistent with our thesis in the previous chapter that the three major symptom domains of Asperger Syndrome impinge on academic life, we will use the same format in our discussion of co-curricular needs. Thus, we can apply the chart as used in the academic realm; that is, parsing out the student's needs, which might be attributable to cognitive, behavioral, and interpersonal deficits.

Cognitive

Cognitive challenges such as faulty integration, executive problems, or being literal-minded (see Appendices A & B for more information) impact the student with AS as he or she attempts to navigate the residence hall and the social climate of the college or university. The student may have difficulty organizing her room, keeping track of her belongings, or even remembering the routes between classroom buildings, residence halls, and dining halls. The student may not comprehend instructions given orally by the residence hall director or the RA and may need to receive instructions in written format (such as safety drills). He or she may require additional assistance in navigating the card swipe systems most campuses use to access campus buildings and to pay for meals in the dining hall or to do laundry.

Multiple repetitions to capture routines other students may grasp in one or two reviews may be necessary for the student with AS.

Multiple repetitions to capture routines other students may grasp in one or two reviews may be necessary for the student with AS. Students with AS may over-think the new routines and ask unanswerable questions of why. Such questions may be compared to the constant questions from a 2-year-old, but on an adult, often genius level.

Behavioral

In order to gain the most from the college experience, students are encouraged to get involved with life outside the classroom, which includes student organizations, the campus community, and so on. Challenges in this area for students with AS often come from "odd" or unusual behaviors that put people off and can, at times, even be frightening. Self-comforting techniques like rocking, flapping, or self-injury may assist the student with AS but sometimes make others very uncomfortable, as illustrated in the following quotes.

> *"A student was not passing most of his classes, and we decided to have a meeting with his parents to assist him in discussing his problems. When the issue came out that he had not attended any of his classes in over a month, the student*

began to bang his head on the table, then his father began to bang his head on the table. I felt I had lost total control of the meeting and did not know how to intervene."
– A disability support services provider

At times when behavior is unacceptable, students must be informed of such and instructed on how to better meet their own needs for calming or expressing frustration in higher education and also for the future in the workplace.

"I once asked a student what he did when he became upset. He replied that he fled or ran away. When asked for more information, he stated the following 'Once when I was leaving school and had my driver's license for about a month. I backed up and then pulled forward, thought I had enough room, but I didn't and hit the car in front of me. I didn't know what to do, I panicked and drove home. When I got there I told my mom what happened, she called the police and we all went back to the high school parking lot. The car I hit was still there. The police asked why I had fled the scene. I told them I didn't know what to do and I was scared.' So now this student says that when he is stressed he 'flees the scene.'"
– A disability service provider

Social-Interpersonal

Social disability is one of the major hallmarks of AS, and social interactions govern the residential realm. Students with AS may alienate roommates or suitemates with poor grooming habits, piled-up laundry, or stereotypical behaviors. They often do not understand the rules of behavior – informal and formal – that can lead to judicial affairs confusion. Often referred to as the "hidden curriculum," these are rules we all seem to know without being told. We observe, we model, we learn. But students on the spectrum don't learn the "hidden curriculum" without direct instruction. Without assistance they may remain unaware of networks and channels in which to seek friends. Let's look in on Kevin to see how he is doing on the campus at large.

 Kevin has some specific issues he must resolve. He does not know which courses he should take next semester or how to decide on a major. He is doing poorly in his math class but cannot seem to find a tutor. His work-study award requires him to find a job, but he does not know how or where to go. He cannot find his meds in the mess of his room. He thinks maybe his roommate stole them but is afraid to report it because he thinks he may get in trouble. Most professors have agreed to his accommodations, but one refused, and Kevin failed the test in that class. He has not told his parents because he knows they will interfere.

Worrying about all of this has made Kevin sick to his stomach, and he has not been able to eat or sleep well all week. There are so many offices at college, and Kevin does not know who to talk to for what. A counselor or a DS staff member? A professor, teaching assistant, or lab instructor? And what is a bursar? A provost? This is way too confusing.

As we discussed when we introduced him earlier in the book, Kevin is typical for a student with AS, thus illustrating that his challenges cross into all spheres of his college experience. He finds that there is too much required of his executive functioning, so at some point he shuts down. Much of this is due to social skills (or lack of). Developing better social skills and using them in non-academic areas can be key to much of the difficulty in college.

Developing better social skills and using them in non-academic areas can be key to much of the difficulty in college.

What Are Non-Academic Accommodations?

Non-academic accommodations cover activities that fall outside of the classroom and academic environment such as housing or dining and other areas of student support such as community service and student activities. Students may request special accommodated housing such as a single room or a private bathroom. These may be appropriate for some students but we do not assume that all students will require this adjustment. Many students with AS want a roommate and do well in such a setting.

Many DS providers and campuses wonder whether the student's social life is an appropriate domain to accommodate, and if so where the limits are. Do we have to help the student make friends? What is our role in helping students deal with a roommate issue? Join a club?

We offer the assurance that it is not the role of the campus DS office to teach social skills (unless yours is a program that offers that specifically by trained professionals). However, we can and should help to mitigate the impact of social skills deficits on the student's academic and program access.

Typical Questions DS Providers Ask About
Co-Curricular Accommodations

- Do we have to accommodate social skills deficits? If so, how?
- Do we have to provide social skills training or aides in higher education?
- Should we find activities or clubs for students with AS?
- Are these appropriate areas to accommodate? If so, which ones?
- Who decides the accommodations: Students? DS? Activity organizers?
- If the experience doesn't work, who intervenes? DS? Counseling? Activities?

Student Activities

While it is not the responsibility of the DS office to provide formal social skills training or to find suitable activities for students with AS to engage in, these students may need a little guidance in how to navigate the social nature of student activities. Having one or two activities outside the classroom will help add structure to the student's weekly schedule and increase social opportunities.

Clubs such as the chess club, fantasy gaming, or animé are often inviting because they tend to attract quiet, like-minded individuals. A Dungeons and Dragons group or a film group may also be popular. These activities use intelligence and gaming in ways that highly intellectual minds enjoy. Students with AS explain that they enjoy animé since the drawings are simple, yet explain emotion in straightforward ways not seen in typical animation.

A successful co-curricular life enhances the academic and overall college life of all students, and those with an autism spectrum disorder are no different. With some coaxing, encouragement, and support, such activities may well assist students to become better adapted socially and academically.

 Kevin has been coaxed to join the role-playing club. There are students in the club he knows slightly from his Chemistry and Rhetoric classes and his residence hall. He has talked with his DS provider about the importance of balancing academic and social life, and making new friends. The DS provider suggested that maybe he could ask one or two of the guys if they would like to meet for a study session in the coffee shop in the student union before or after the meeting. Kevin replies, "Oh, that won't work. I only drink tea."

The vignette above illustrates how students with AS may think about social activities in a very different manner than typical students and how their social skills are often colored (indeed blunted) by their rigidity or literal mindedness.

Some Student Activities Issues

- Social and interpersonal (finding, joining, managing groups)
- Navigating and negotiating with peers
- Off-campus activities (novel situations)

We suggest that DS consider locating a peer mentor, fellow student, or a student worker who is willing to act as a social facilitator and attend one or two meetings with the student on the spectrum. Alternately, we have found it helpful to call or meet with the director of the office of Student Activities (with the student's permission) to discuss some of the student's social issues. All sanctioned student activities on campus have a faculty advisor who can also be recruited to monitor the student with AS as he or she gets used to a club or activity. Relatively structured activities (political clubs, religious affiliations, community service outings) may be good first steps for a student learning to navigate the social life of campus.

Peer Mentoring

Peer mentoring is increasingly being offered on many campuses as a support for students with AS. A mentor is defined as a wise and trusted counselor or teacher. Mentors are used in many colleges and universities for students with AS as models of good behavior, teachers, and guides to the campus and spoken and unspoken (hidden curriculum) social rules. Some schools provide a social skills group for students with AS where members may meet other students with AS or other similar challenges. Other schools have social mentors who meet students once a week or more to have a meal or do something social together. As the student becomes more comfortable with the mentor and looks forward to their meetings, they may be more likely to venture out in the social world of college on his own. This is the best possible scenario.

Once the first steps have been taken, the DS provider can solicit a counselor or advisor to help the student learn better strategies for negotiating with peers, through role-plays or scripts as discussed previously. Finally, it is important to remember that novel situations are often stressful for students with AS and, therefore, can be expected to provoke anxiety and (perhaps) some escalation of atypical behaviors such as withdrawal, use of stims, or flight. A peer mentor, fellow student, or counselor may be needed to role-play these scenarios.

Dating

Dating is an intricate social interaction often not mastered by typical college students. Not surprisingly, it is a huge challenge for students with AS. Disability services professionals do not have to act as support in this area but may encourage the student to consult a counselor, therapist, or other professional for assistance in learning appropriate dating etiquette.

As in many other areas of life, students with AS need clear rules and information about dating and how to interact. This can be taught through a social skills group and, ideally, is learned before the student attends college. However, this is not usually the case, as the student is not developmentally ready for dating before college.

As in many other areas of life, students with AS need clear rules and information about dating and how to interact.

> *The authors have had some degree of success with role-play with a graduate assistant and with showing videotaped segments of TV shows with young people interacting (OC, One Tree Hill, Dawson's Creek, etc.). The program is viewed in a group with the sound turned off. Then the facilitator stops the video and asks the group (or the student) what the person's body language or facial expression is saying. This technique can assist with dating etiquette, dining etiquette, and social interaction.*

The "Two-Card Strategy" for students. For students who have difficulty with unspoken dating rules, we suggest a variation of the 2-Card Strategy for Faculty, which will be discussed in the next chapter. In brief, the DS professional and the student prepare a set of two cards and laminate them (so that they hold up over time).

One card lists three or four things that the student must do on a date (recall that individuals with AS usually appreciate rules and "musts"):

1. I must talk to my date.
2. I must be respectful and polite.
3. I must ask what she/he wants to do and where he/she wants to go.

The second card lists some things the student must NOT do on a date:

1. I must not touch my date or kiss him/her without asking first.
2. I must not be rude, such as only doing what I want or eating and leaving food on my face.
3. I must not leave my date alone somewhere just because I am ready to go home.

The cards are reviewed with the student, who is trained (usually though role-play with the DS professional or some other individual) to refer to the cards whenever there is a question regarding a particular behavior or incident. The specifics on the cards can change with each person and his or her circumstance.

For all college students with AS (and for many college students in general), having a girlfriend or a boyfriend is desirable, yet the reality for many students is that the social behavior necessary to maintain a relationship is too stressful during the college years. For others, however, a successful relationship with a boyfriend or girlfriend helps the stress of college.

Putting It All Together

As we did with the chart of academic accommodations above, let us use the same system to problem solve some of Kevin's co-curricular challenges.

DOMAINS	Cognitive	Behavioral	Interpersonal
Academic			
Co-Curricular	*Literal-minded, rigid; does not communicate well with peers in groups; dominates conversations*	*Blurts out of turn; complains about smells (cologne, smoke); flaps when stressed*	*Does not try making friends with others in group*
Other	*Talk to faculty advisor and group leader about using an agenda statement for each meeting*	*Move to nonsmoking location; ask others not to wear scent; discuss with Kevin and family strategies to reduce stims*	*Peer mentor to accompany Kevin to groups and invite some kids for coffee later; role-plays with Kevin*

As illustrated, Kevin's challenges in his group activities cross all domains of difficulty and require a creative approach that involves recruiting the assistance of other offices on campus. Chapter 8 will address the importance of developing partnerships with offices on campus to achieve an integrated approach to dealing with these challenges.

Involvement in co-curricular activities is what makes college enjoyable, develops friendships, and helps retain students in college. For students with AS, finding other students who enjoy the same pursuits and at the same deep, intense level as they do can be an awesome and life-changing experience. One important co-curricular challenge for students with AS is housing and residential life. We turn to those issues in the next chapter.

CHAPTER 7
Housing and Residential Life

Living on campus is an integral part of the college experience. Many students with AS want this experience and are eager to leave home. Living with other young people can be challenging for students who do not have disability-related challenges, so it is not surprising that students with AS often meet with even greater obstacles in the residence halls. On some campuses, residence halls house hundreds of students, all of whom seem – at least for the socially challenged student – to be paragons of social success. They know where to sit, whom to eat with, and what to wear.

Some students with AS do unexpectedly well in residence, discovering their social talents and niche for the first time. For others, dormitory life is akin to 24/7 of the worst aspects of high school. In this chapter we explore some of these challenges and suggest ways to address them in the residence halls

Residence Hall Issues

- Orientation to residence life
  - » Student safety
  - » Fire drills, etc.

- Room selection

- Roommates
  - » Conflict resolution
  - » Disclosure of AS

- Sharing space and belongings
  - » Cleanliness and order

- Socializing, free time, making friends
  - » Bullying

- Personal care
  - » Laundry and personal hygiene
  - » Sleep/wake cycles

- Sensory issues

Orientation to Residence Life

We need to be sure that students demonstrate effective daily living skills before adding the other complex social interactions involved in living on campus. Students with AS must be specifically oriented to what to expect when they move into a residence hall to reduce the often negative impact of unexpected novel experiences. We suggest that this be done in the summer prior to matriculation, when campuses are typically quiet and staff has more time to devote to special populations.

Orienting Students to Residence Life

- Introductions to staff and their roles
  (RA, RD [residence hall director])
- Understanding residence procedures (key cards, security, overnight policy, etc.)
- Point people/buddy system (peer advisor, freshman advisor, RA)
- Explanations of social programming (freshman events, study areas, socials, etc.)
- Expectations for student behavior in residence
- Tour of residence hall
- Safe spaces
- Best if done as part of transition planning

Student Safety in Residence Halls

Part of the orientation to residence life for the student with AS must include safety issues. For example, students may need specific instructions on how to keep safe and how to protect their belongings (including medications), as most students will not have had to lock the door to their rooms at home. It may be helpful to explain that locking their room is like locking a house in a city. There are many people around, and you do not know everyone. Safety and/or locks for laptops may also need to be explained.

Part of the orientation to residence life for the student with AS must include safety issues.

Letting strangers into locked residence halls, propping open fire doors, talking to strangers, and attending parties in houses where no one is known are risks that all undergraduates must be cautioned against. However, these situations are even more risky for the student with AS.

121

Fire alarms and safety drills. Fire drills are another unfamiliar experience for all students new to residence hall living. It is important to provide information about safety drills, including routes to get out of the building, in direct and explicit terms, and to point out to the student that he must comply with all fire or safety drills.

It is important to be sure the student knows what to do if the fire alarm goes off. A visual reminder (similar to what is found in hotel rooms) that clarifies emergency procedures is helpful. A card with information or even pictures should be attached near the door with Velcro.

Sample Fire Alarm Card

1. When alarm rings, take room key or card and leave immediately.

2. In cold weather, bring your coat.

3. Leave the rest of your belongings in your room.

4. Go to _____ location as designated by your RA.

5. Do not go back to the building until told to do so by someone in authority.

Ask the student and her family whether fire alarm sounds are so disturbing to the student that it would cause her to hide or tantrum. If so, DS and residence life must plan an alternate strategy such as assigning a buddy to be responsible for helping the student out of the building or finding a safe place where she may go in case of an emergency. Again, it is important that residence hall staff understand that they must make a plan with the student and practice the plan.

We have heard of an area high school where simply changing the fire alarms to bells instead of sirens all but eliminated one student's meltdowns during this important safety drill.

Room Selection: Is a Single Room the Best Solution?

Many parents and residence directors believe that the best way to avoid roommate conflicts is to assign the student with AS a single room. We agree that this is often a good solution; however, it is not always necessary. In some cases, it may isolate the student further from the mainstream of dormitory life. We are aware of many students who never left their single rooms except to go to class and meals and had no friends at all. On some campuses, single rooms are located in smaller or specialty houses that are full of upperclassmen. In such cases, a young student with AS would be in a particular difficult situation and such an arrangement would be a mistake.

When possible, a single room in a suite may be the best arrangement. In these situations, the student has her own space but shares bathrooms and has suitemates with whom to interact. Even so there are always exceptions. One of us monitored a student who went an entire semester without ever meeting his suite mates!

Many students with AS do not want to be singled out as being different among their new peers and, thus, will not accept any special housing accommodations. They want the full college experience even if it

When possible, a single room in a suite may be the best arrangement.

involves sharing a small room. We respect this choice and would want permission from the student to have an open discussion with Housing to ensure that the student is placed carefully in a residence hall with a strong RA or RD who can monitor potential roommate conflicts carefully. Even if the student does not wish to accept housing accommodations such as a single or a quiet floor, we strongly suggest that all options be reviewed with the student and her family during the transition meetings and that the student meet with a member of the housing assignment staff to review the available housing options on campus.

We have all experienced situations where the family did not seek DS assistance in the room selection process and the student was placed in an unfortunate residence situation (such as a quad room with bunks beds for a student who is afraid of heights, or a smoking floor for a student with sensory sensitivities).

Roommates

Living with a roommate is difficult or even impossible for some students with AS. Students may need to move into the dorm early to adjust to the environment, get used to the sounds and smells, and set up new routines. Getting accustomed to the shared bathrooms in a residence hall also takes time. Many students choose to attend a summer school before their freshman year to experiment with living in the residence hall and begin to adjust.

 Kevin is anxious about starting college. He has packed and tried to do some of the things his parents asked, and is planning and shopping. He just wants to get started or make this process stop and go back to his old life. Kevin does not like change, and this is a huge change!

The day finally comes when they drive to school. The car is packed; Mom is anxious, Dad is driving. Kevin has not talked the entire trip. They get to the college, find the

dorm, and meet the hall director, who gives them keys. Kevin shakes hands but does not talk. They find the room, open the door, and see that one of Kevin's roommates, Joe, has already arrived and set up his side of the room. There are sports and music posters everywhere, and music is blaring. Joe approaches Kevin, shakes his hand and pats him on the back saying, "Yo, dude, we're going to be roommates!"

Considering Kevin's sensory sensitivities, this was less than an auspicious beginning. Read on to learn more about Kevin's roommate experiences.

Conflict resolution. Resolving roommate issues is difficult for all students, especially if they have never lived in a shared space outside their family before. Ordinarily, residence life issues are not addressed by DS unless the student has made an accommodation request or there is a problem. We encourage RAs to pursue additional training and work with their hall directors to be alert to the fact that most students with AS do not complain about a roommate situation. A history of bullying may have taught them it does no good to turn to anyone for help. Consequently, there may not be any red flags that they are having problems until a crisis point is reached. Meltdowns over room issues can and do result in students being brought to the attention of the campus safety office, judicial affairs, and even end up in the hospital. We have provided a sample training module for RAs in Appendix F.

 Kevin was assigned a triple room with two roommates. He arrived on campus after the other two fellows had moved in and found he had been relegated to a low bed and a desk in a dark corner of the room while the others claimed loft beds positioned near the windows.

125

Although he thought the use of space was not fair, Kevin did not feel he could protest or ask to move the furniture. He endured this arrangement until one evening when the roommates had a party and Kevin returned to find strangers sprawled on his bed. He began to shake with anger and shouted at the other students to get out of the room. The students began to laugh at Kevin as this display grew more dramatic. The RAs were called when Kevin began to scream and throw objects around the room.

Difficulties easily occur in residence halls where trying to manage roommate conflicts (never easy for any student) can quickly become a full-blown AS meltdown. An easily resolved issue such as noise levels can get out of hand. We emphasize the importance of preventing such blowups whenever possible, which often requires a cooperative effort by DS, a hall director, faculty in residence, or an RA, to check in with the student that all is well. The individual who will be checking on the student depends on the model your campus uses.

Disclosure to Roommates

In our experience, parents of prospective college students on the spectrum desire to disclose to their son or daughter's roommates in the hopes that it will help them deal with any "unusual" behaviors the student witnesses. However, most students with AS emphatically do not want the peers to know about their disability for fear of being stigmatized.

We must respect this need for privacy and control over access to their status as a student with a disability. As discussed above, we encourage students to disclose to their RAs or at least to the hall or area directors for their residence in the event of any emergencies.

Sharing Space and Belongings

Cleanliness and order. Many students with AS require order and need their rooms arranged in such a way that it makes sense for their world. For these students, it is inconceivable to have belongings out of place or to leave their room a mess. As this is not the way most college students live, there is a strong disconnect between the student with AS and other students and possible roommates in that respect. Some students with AS on the other extreme live in disorganized or even filthy rooms and fail to understand why their roommates complain. Often these are students whose symptoms include deficits in executive function and organization.

Many students with AS require order and need their rooms arranged in such a way that it makes sense for their world.

Rigidity is one of the ways that students with AS control their environment as it allows them to better understand and structure their everyday activities. The interaction with roommates may be too complicated for them to manage in addition to the other new social interactions that occur on a college campus. We suggest that the student and her family be asked specific information about how she arranged her room and managed her belongings when living at home. The aim is to be clear about the issues the student has had before so that you can either make an alternate suggestion about a room selection (e.g., recommend a single for a student who is seriously disrupted by having his stuff moved) or alert the student to what she can expect when she moves into shared space.

Some Sources of Overstimulation

- Lights (especially fluorescent or flashing)
- Loud or dissonant music
- Crowds, parties
- Disruption of private areas or belongings
- Smells (body odors, toiletries, smoke, incense, etc.)
- Fire alarms/lock-downs
- Arrangement of beds and furniture
- General residence hall noise

In some cases, the DS provider may recommend that a student is not ready to live on campus.

Socializing and Managing Free Time

One of the most difficult challenges for any student is to have 12-15 hours per week structured with class time and having to figure out how to spend the rest of the hours of the week. When to study, eat, sleep, and socialize are all left to the student's judgment. This is usually the most trying area for any student transitioning from high school to college. For students with AS who struggle with executive functioning, this can make or break their college experience. Most of these non-classroom hours are usually spent in the residence halls, making the college living situation a crucial part of success for the student.

To help address this area of campus life, DS or some other academic counselor can help the student develop a schedule. Giving the student a structure to the week and helping her stick to the structure is often the best support one can offer. Agendas, hanging white boards, computer schedules, or PDAs are all options for helping to structure the week.

Any structure to help students disengage from their preferred free time activity (computer games, TV, etc.) should be given first priority in the transition. For students without AS, socializing is a huge deterrent to studying. Regardless of the nature of the deterrent for the student with AS, structure can help balance life in the residence halls. We use the sample schedule below to illustrate how busy one day can be.

Sample Daily Schedule	
Monday	
9:00-10:40	History
11:00-12:15	Math
12:15	Lunch
1:00	Study history
3:00	Study math
4:30	Go to the gym
5:30	Shower
6:00	Dinner
7:00	Car Club mtg
8:30	Read for tomorrow's classes
10:00	Play on the computer
11:30	Go to sleep

Schedules of this level of detail often help students who need imposed structure and cannot determine what to do when in a schedule that may only dictate 12 to 15 hours of their week. A blank daily schedule is provided in Appendix D.

Making Friends

Many of us made our best and most lasting friendships during college. This can also be the experience of young persons on the autism spectrum if they have developed friendship skills. In order to facilitate this, most residence halls provide a considerable amount of social programming, especially in the first few weeks of the semester. These arrangements are designed as ice breakers, to let new students meet and mingle outside of the classroom as well as opportunities for students to meet their hall staff and review safety procedures and residence rules.

Many of us made our best and most lasting friendships during college. This can also be the experience of young persons on the autism spectrum if they have developed friendship skills.

Unfortunately, activities that can lead other students to bond are often lost on the student with AS. Typical games used for ice breaking are fast moving with idiosyncratic or confusing rules. Dance or physical activity is often included, as getting up and moving around is a social facilitator for most young people (unless they are on the autism spectrum).

If the RA and hall director have been informed of the presence of a student on the spectrum (and they need not know who it is), they can be aware of the issues when planning ice breaking and other social activities. Likewise, a sensitive and well-trained RA can look out for the student to make sure he is not left out of the group (which can happen when social contacts are made during meals or in the bathroom). Some of the strategies reviewed in the section on co-curricular accommodations in the previous chapter may be useful to review with RAs during their training (see specific suggestions for RA training in Appendix F).

Bullying

Many students with AS do not dress, act, or talk like their peers, and they are often emotionally and verbally attacked as others discover power only by teasing. Such behavior must be stopped when noticed by any college staff or administrator, and interventions and sanctions must be imposed on the bully immediately.

Bullying incidents must be handled very delicately with the student with AS, who may want to drop out of school and may experience severe depression from the bullying. Disability services should discuss with the office of Residential Life how to watch for this type of inexcusable conduct and what to do when it is detected. Further, Judicial Affairs and Residence Life directors should be consulted about potential violations of the student conduct code on the part of the bully. All residents of a hall where bullying has been reported can benefit from a reminder that student life on campus operates on a written code of behavior and community standards, violations of which can result in severe sanctions.

Complicating matters is the fact that the student with AS may not disclose information about a bullying incident freely – sometimes the information is shared in an off-had manner (if at all). It is important that the student trusts the DS provider so he feels comfortable disclosing victimization. To foster trust and communication, we suggest that the point person (be it DS, the RA, the student's advisor, etc.) shows interest in the non-academic life of the student. This may involve taking time at each meeting to casually inquire whether the student has had any negative experiences such as teasing, negative peer pressure, or coercion. Students should be reassured that disclosing this sort of incident will not typically result in any sanction against the reporter (unless they have also violated a community standard either through their behavior or in retaliation).

Personal Care: Laundry, Hygiene, and Sleep Issues

Many students arrive at college with minimal self-care skills such as doing their own laundry and buying personal care items such as shampoo or deodorant. Students' parents may have provided cues for when it was time to shower or change clothes and may have done all of the student's laundry prior to him moving away to college. Few things are more stigmatizing in a group living environment such as a residence hall than to be known as the student with poor hygiene.

In the interest of providing the student with AS with the best chance of social success possible, we strongly suggest having a discussion with the student and his or her parents during the initial transition appointments (see Chapter 3). Disability services and residence hall staff are not there to remind students when it is time to bathe. However, many have been called on to mediate a roommate conflict, dorm infraction, or even insect or vermin infestation, which can result if a student does not know how to take care of himself or herself.

Sleep disorders are common among individuals on the autism spectrum (see Appendices A and B). Students may require more or less sleep than their roommates or may be accustomed to very cold or very warm rooms. They may be used to wandering the halls or even the streets at night without regard for personal safety. Personal safety must always be reviewed with a student who has these habits. (Depending on the environment in which you are located, this may be more or less vital.)

Students should be assisted in discussing their personal sleep needs with their roommates so the group can assist in making a contract about noise, lights out, and overnight guests. Residence hall staff is specifically trained and skilled at negotiating such arrangements and should be made aware (optimally) of the spectrum-related sleep issues to the extent that they interfere with the student's overall functioning on campus.

Sensory Issues

Sensory issues can be especially problematic in a shared living space where the student must deal with the sounds, smells, and presence of others in close proximity. We suggest that this information be gathered as part of the initial intake (the forms in Appendix C are cued to ask students and their families about sensory sensitivities). Special attention must be paid to how sensory issues might present in the residence hall. For example, are there sensitivities to temperature necessitating housing the student in a room with an air conditioner or windows that open? Can the student live in a room near a common area? Does he need to be away from the smells of food? Are there issues in the residence halls or dining hall that are causing problems?

There are ways to desensitize students or to accommodate when necessary. Some of the suggestions for low-tech sensory modifications in Chapter 3 can be adapted for use in residence halls. To illustrate, let us return to Kevin.

 The director of DS is notified on a Monday that Kevin was taken to the hospital by ambulance on Saturday evening. He had an outburst in the residence hall that involved shouting at his roommates, throwing a computer, and running down the hall yelling that he was going to hurt himself. This outburst was apparently triggered by his extreme reaction to the smell of burning popcorn. This sensory overload, however, was

the culmination of a very contentious housing situation with three boys in one small room. Kevin had not been able to communicate his discomfort over sharing such close quarters, so the situation could not be anticipated or averted.

With the help of his parents and his psychiatrist, Kevin was cleared by the emergency room staff as not being a threat to himself, and Student Safety and Student Mental Health deemed that he could return to the residence hall. However, following his return to campus, Kevin was moved to a single room where he could be monitored more closely by residence hall staff and disability service.

It is important to understand that the student with AS may need to be left alone at these times or be put in contact with someone who knows how to de-escalate the situation. Often DS can negotiate a "safe space" with an established protocol for what the student can do and whom to contact if stressed. When the student has recuperated, it is important for DS or a counselor to review the situation with the student to assess the events leading up to the outburst (was the student pacing, muttering, or indicating that she was escalating) and look for possible triggers for the reaction in an attempt to put some safeguards in place to prevent similar outburst from recurring.

A Word About Parties

Because many students with AS do not understand or enjoy the social nature of residence halls, the noise and partying may be disruptive and overwhelming to them. For this reason many students opt for an honors dorm, a substance-free dorm (no alcohol, no drugs), or a dorm with enforced quiet hours, if such choices are available.

We believe that a carefully managed transition, orientation, and attention to staff training in residence halls can help a student with AS to thrive in a communal living space such as a residence hall. We also believe that it is important to review the requirements for residence life with the family so that a realistic decision can be made about the readiness of their son or daughter. Students who are unable to manage this stressor should be encouraged to consider other options before moving onto campus.

Now that we understand many of the academic, nonacademic, and residential challenges faced by students with AS, let us turn to the need to build effective partnerships with other offices on campus – particularly other divisions within student affairs.

CHAPTER 8

Partners on Campus

One of the most important things a DS office can do for students with AS is to increase awareness on campus about AS and its effects on college students. Without such training, all the work that DS offices do will be fruitless. Bring the issue of autism spectrum disorders up frequently when meeting with nondisability services staff on campus. Take a few minutes at a faculty or administrative meeting, participate in campus safety panels, or get yourself invited to attend department meetings. Provide training and information to dining hall staff on sensory and food issues for students with AS. All parts of campus should be educated in some way or the student with AS will feel like (and appear to be) an alien on campus.

In this chapter, we will highlight some of the offices most in need of training but also potentially of great use to DS staff in managing the wide-ranging needs of students with autism spectrum disorders. As appropriate, use inservice trainings, one-on-one, "teachable moments," workshops, etc., to share information.

Community Education

- Student Life
  - » Housing and Residence Life
  - » Tutoring and Academic Support
  - » Student Activities and Community Service
  - » Multicultural Affairs
  - » Dining Services

- Career Services
- Judicial Affairs
- Campus Police and Public Safety Officers
- Student Health and Counseling
- Academics Affairs (faculty, advising, and administration)
- Business Affairs (registrar, financial assistance, admissions, enrollment, and retention)
- Upper Administration

Housing and Residence Staff Training

We discussed housing and residence life extensively in Chapter 7. One of the most important residence hall issues is the training of staff. Though residence hall staff cannot be informed about specific students without these students' expressed consent, training can and should be provided with specific focus on the difficulties of residence hall and community living and how to assist students with AS. RAs and front-line resident directors especially need to be trained. Many students with AS exhibit most of their unique behaviors in the residence halls (see Overstimulation) and need some guidance. We have provided a sample training agenda for RAs and other Residence Life staff in Appendix F.

Topics for Training RAs and Residence Hall Staff

- Campus resources
- Security issues and emergency plans
- Conduct code/discipline
- Involving parents and families (disclosure vs. privacy)

The residence hall becomes a second home for students. We all present our public and our private persona differently. For example, most people are much more formal and polite in public and may let their guard down in private at home. This may be exaggerated for students with AS who work hard to keep symptoms at bay in public. When in the residence hall, their college home, students with AS often let go and appear more symptomatic than in public. Even very high-functioning students may look more autistic when tired, stressed, or both.

Students need to be told when they are exhibiting inappropriate behaviors and must have models of correct behavior. Many staff avoid addressing this directly for fear of being rude to the student and must be trained on how to most effectively communicate with a student with AS. For fear of breaking confidentiality, DS staff often avoids conversations with Residence Life staff. However, these are the people who work with students 24 hours a day. They must be informed, even if limited to AS in general and not one student in particular. Parents can be very helpful in this regard, as they may discuss their son or daughter's disability directly with Residence Life staff without fear of breaking confidentiality.

Students need to be told when they are exhibiting inappropriate behaviors and must have models of correct behavior.

Tutoring and Academic Support

We discussed recruiting the services of the writing center on campus in Chapter 5. Many students with AS do not require academic (subject-specific) tutoring, although it is often useful for them to go over course material with a tutor to work on integrating information from multiple sources (lecture, text, etc.).

Different from academic tutoring, strategy tutoring can be invaluable in teaching the student with AS to manage time, write clearly and concisely, break assignments down into manageable units, and then organize them. In other words, this intervention is targeted at the deficits attendant with the syndrome.

> *... many fee-for-service programs are being developed that aim to provide this targeted strategy intervention for college students with AS.*

A partnership with tutoring services is a great way to provide this level of service as well as to lessen the burden for direct intervention on a busy DS provider. Indeed, many fee-for-service programs are being developed that aim to provide targeted strategy intervention for college students with AS.

Students with AS may require direct academic assistance in some subject areas. This is sometimes difficult to believe when a student is otherwise brilliant in a particular area of study. When needing tutoring or any type of academic support, the main issue is how the support is delivered. We have found that students often do not think they need any support, so getting them to attend tutoring sessions can be a battle. One way to get around this is to arrange for support to be delivered by a graduate student whom the student with AS admires for his or her accomplishments in an academic area. To add further motivation, it can be set up so that the student engages in tutoring for one hour and then spends an hour on a favored activity with the graduate student.

Student Activities and Community Service

We discussed the importance of the Student Activities office in Chapter 6. It is important to develop a strong relationship with this office to ensure that there are appropriate activities for students with social skills deficiencies to engage in to increase their ability to make friends and function on campus. Many of these students' demands for interpersonal contact vary. The directors are in the best position to know which groups to recommend and may be asked to assist in facilitating a student's entry into a group.

Multicultural Affairs and Diversity

Most campuses have some office or designated entity that deals with issues of diversity, whether that is defined as multicultural or based on specific religious or cultural identification. Like their peers, students with AS may also be members of a separate cultural group, and belonging to a campus organization is an excellent way to foster social connectedness on a diverse campus. In addition, these offices sponsor events where students can learn about their own culture or language group as well as others represented on campus. This is often an area of great interest to individuals on the spectrum. If specialty housing based on cultural group is available, this is a good way for a student with AS to find a small, tight-knit living situation. Finally, group travel opportunities may be a great way for students to bond out of the classroom.

 Kevin has come to the DS office in a state of excitement. He is about to travel to a student conference in the state capital with his new student group.

141

Everyone will be wearing the same T-shirt, which the group designed and had printed. Kevin was volunteered by another group member to be in charge of the music for the bus ride (he has an extensive and well-organized CD collection). He is a bit leery of divulging the nature of the student group, as it is a religiously based political event and he does not want to offend the DS provider. She praises him on his group affiliation and his sensitivity to her views. They review how he is going to handle meals and the shared hotel room. He is off to have a great time.

Food and Dietary Issues

Some students have difficulty with the food available in the residence halls. Students with sensory sensitivities may not like spicy or ethnic foods (staples in some dining halls). Others have stringent dietary requirements or preferences (such as casein-/gluten-free foods, all white foods, or all bland foods). Fortunately, most medium and large campuses offer a plethora of dining options, including fast foods and national chains. Dietary preference should not prevent a student from enjoying his or her meals.

Some students have difficulty with the food available in the residence halls.

In some schools, dining hall services personnel are able to accommodate the dietary needs of a broad range of students, including students with food allergies and religion-based or dietary restrictions. While discussion of this is best handled prior to a student's arrival on campus, at schools that provide this type of flexibility, it may be possible to negotiate options consistent with the dietary preferences and needs of a student on the spectrum as the need arises.

Career Services

This is a very important office, which deals not just with employment after graduation. Career Services offices provide interest and aptitude testing, advice about selecting a major, and are the key to finding an internship in a chosen area. They can be especially helpful to students with AS, who need work experiences under supervision before they are ready to enter the workforce.

Employment issues will be discussed in more detail in Chapter 10; the office of Career Services can be a helpful ally in working with students on the spectrum at earlier points in their college careers. For example, career counselors are often skilled at conducting interest and vocational assessments, which may help a student clarify a course of study. They are experts in working with students on self-presentation skills for job interviews and may be amenable to coach a spectrum student on how to dress, speak, or behave in different social situations (even table manners). Further, they are skilled at helping students prepare résumés, regardless of their place on the job search ladder. The act of preparing a résumé for an on- or off-campus interview can help students clarify their interests and goals, which is especially useful for spectrum students, who may not be skilled at identifying their internal and external sources of motivation or their goals.

 In the spring semester of his third year of school, Kevin's parents ask what he plans to do when he graduates. Kevin has no idea. His parents suggest he make an appointment with Career Services on campus. Kevin makes an appointment and is told to bring his résumé and additional information about his work history. He has neither, and does not show up for the appointment.

It is fairly common for students with AS to have no résumé or work history. The world of work is very social, especially service jobs that teenagers generally have. We encourage all students to work in the summer and have some internships during college.

We encourage all students to work in the summer and have some internships during college.

Judicial Affairs and Safety

Disability is never an excuse for unacceptable or inappropriate behavior. A breach of conduct codes is just that – no matter what the student's diagnosis or disability. As students with AS usually appreciate having rules and guidelines, they may benefit from working with someone on understanding the rules of academic conduct prior to matriculating. This can be conducted by a transition counselor, college counselor, or a staff person from DS who specializes in transitions for students with AS (usually available only in specialized programs).

If the student's behavior rises to the level of becoming a problem for classroom, residence hall, or any campus environment, often Public Safety is brought in first. As a result, it is essential that Public Safety staff be trained and gain awareness of the typical symptoms of AS. Without such training, simple interactions can escalate in intensity to become conduct code violations. For example, being grabbed by police can make some students lash out, thus causing a much larger problem than the initial infraction may have been.

A trainer with experience and knowledge about AS and Public Safety can get information across and sensitize participants to this specialized topic. A sample agenda might look as follows:

Training for Public Safety
(10-15 minutes alone or as part of larger training
of Student Affairs staff)

- Explain and define AS
- Give examples of behaviors officers may see on campus
- Describe differences in how students with AS should be approached (e.g., do not grab students unless professionally necessary; talk calmly rather than yelling)
- Encourage contact with the DS office for information on particular incidents
- Close by presenting several examples where Public Safety was involved, as in the following example

 Kevin liked to study in the library computer lab where it is quiet and no one bothers him. He does not like his room in the residence hall, so he stayed in the library until closing. Kevin usually did not hear the announcements in preparation for the library closing. There would be three announcements, 30, 15, and 5 minutes before closing. Every night, library staff would have to tell Kevin it was time to leave as they were locking the computer lab. They would have to wait until he shut down his computer, gathered his belongings, and walked out of the library. Complaints were made by staff to the library administration that the library lock-up was 15 minutes late every night due to this student. Administration directed staff to call Security the next time the student was not out of the computer lab on time.

Security was called the next night as Kevin was still in the lab. A campus police officer walked up to Kevin and calmly placed his hand on his shoulder, asking him why

*he had not responded to the announcements. Due to
sensory issues, Kevin was very averse to being touched,
so his response was to jump up and flail his arms in an
attempt to get the sensation off of his shoulder. In the
process, he inadvertently hit the police officer, at which
point the officer restrained Kevin on the floor, called for
back-up of other officers, and took Kevin to the campus
police station.*

This extremely disturbing incident could have been avoided with
some prior training of both the library and police staffs.

Dangerous behavior. Self-injurious behavior is well documented
in autism spectrum disorders, although it tends to be more prominent in lower functioning individuals. A few studies have documented violent and aggressive behavior in AS, including murder
(see review in Schwartz-Watts, 2005), but these situations are not
common on college campuses.

Aggressive behavior may be seen in the context of sensory defensiveness or a reaction to being overwhelmed or bullied (Schwartz-
Watts, 2005). Such behaviors can also follow interruptions of
routines, especially when under stress. A full-blown AS meltdown
is a dramatic event to witness, as the individual may be temporar-
ily unable to respond rationally to any attempt to calm him down.
Campus police, residence hall staff, and medical personnel should
be familiar with the manifestations of such behaviors (such as
covering one's ears or eyes, running away, yelling or screaming,
or striking out when touched) so as to be able to respond appropriately to keep the student and the community safe. Training
should be conducted by a knowledgeable trainer.

Topics Related to Campus Public Safety
- Conduct codes
- Stalking
- Personal safety
- Emergency procedures (fire drills, etc.)

There have been cases in which the individual's area of special interest has included weapons, which potentially creates considerable alarm (Schwartz-Watts, 2005). Stalking behavior is also not unknown in this population, often due to misunderstanding of social behavior norms (Stokes, Nauton, & Kaur, 2007). Several excellent websites provide information for law enforcement about handling persons with autism spectrum disorders (e.g., www.policeandautism.cjb.net; www. autismriskmanagement.com). DS providers should become familiar with these and make them available to their campus police and Judicial Affairs personnel. For example, touching, yelling at, or restraining a person with AS can cause a sensory defensive reaction that can include hitting or running away (Debbaudt & Rothman, 2001). We caution DS professionals and others not to touch students (including seemingly benign gestures such as an encouraging pat or a brief hug) without the student's direct permission.

While we do not condone conduct violations on the part of individuals with disabilities, we encourage disability providers and Judicial Affairs personnel to be aware that individuals with an autism spectrum disorder may not understand the charges they are facing, and thus may not respond appropriately in the judicial

We caution DS professionals and others not to touch students (including seemingly benign gestures such as an encouraging pat or a brief hug) without the student's direct permission.

process. Several excellent documents (Debbaudt, 2006; Doyle, 2004) underscore the importance of ensuring that the individual understands her rights and that a lack of typical responses, aberrant communication, stiff facial expression, slow response time, inappropriate affect, or unusual behaviors not be interpreted as indications of guilt, lack of remorse, or lack of caring.

Student Health Services and Other Health Issues

Health Services is an essential partner on any campus with a large number of students with AS. Many campuses are now incorporating services for students with AS within their counseling and mental health centers, sometimes even offering academic support along with clinical treatment. Such campuses can expect their mental health allies to have a high degree of knowledge about and comfort with AS. On the other hand, many generic campus counseling centers do not have this special level of expertise and, therefore, require additional information and training from DS.

Roles of Typical Counseling Center
- Important resource for DS staff
- Important clinical back-up
- Referral network

Medical leave of absence. The authors have learned from working with many college students with AS that once a medical or mental health problem keeps the student from classes for several weeks or is unresolved despite doctor visits, medications, or therapy, a medical leave of absence is often the best choice. A medical leave of absence can prevent the student's grade-point average (GPA) from plummeting from a semester of bad grades due to illness and missed classes.

In this connection, it is extremely important that medical leaves of absence be handled officially, as the student's health insurance may be tied to his status as a full-time student. A letter to the insurance company explaining that the student is on an official medical leave of absence may be necessary. Such a letter can come from DS, the registrar, or the Dean of Students, depending on the institution.

... once a medical or mental health problem keeps the student from classes for several weeks or is unresolved despite doctor visits, medications, or therapy, a medical leave of absence is often the best choice.

Emotional and psychiatric issues. Concurrent psychiatric diagnoses are common in AS, especially anxiety disorders, such as OCD, social phobias, panic disorder, and depression. Individuals with AS may become easily overwhelmed and may have low frustration tolerance. Furthermore, internalizing psychopathology, depression, and even suicide, have been reported in this group, particularly in adolescents and young adults (Tantam, 2000). We believe DS offices should refer these issues to student counseling, even if the DS provider is a trained counselor or therapist. It is too risky to manage such an issue within the mandates of DS.

Optimally, DS should have all relevant medical and psychiatric information about a student with AS. The forms included in the intake section in Appendix C cue to gather this information. Students must be reassured that clinical and diagnostic information is not shared with anyone on campus without their direct permission and that it is possible to disclose the presence of AS to professors or others on a "need to know" basis without discussing co-morbid psychiatric issues. Families must also be assured that this information does not get into the student's academic file and will not follow the student beyond the college. Most families are willing to disclose psychiatric information when they understand how important such information becomes in assisting their student in managing successfully on campus. Students in this category must be connected with appropriate clinicians on and/or off campus.

Crisis management. For students with AS, crisis behavior may include not going to class, not leaving her room, or having outbursts. When the student is experiencing a crisis, ideally a staff member or DS professional is notified by the student or another staff or faculty member. Having an established relationship with a counselor on or off campus is very helpful at these times.

It is important to determine what precipitated the crisis, as it is often a key in assisting the student and averting future crises. Parents may be helpful in providing background information and interpreting the student's behaviors. Sometimes a break from school such as a long weekend at home is enough to help. At other times, a leave of absence may be required until the student's condition stabilizes.

The Stress Thermometer and 20 Questions Stress Test in Appendix C cue to gather information about how the student has handled stress in the past. This information may be supplemented by direct interview with the student and his family. Such tools will help to identify what behaviors or acts the student engages in when he becomes overly stressed (please note that it is not a standardized clinical instrument).

Stress Management

- Identify potentially stressful situations
- Determine what precipitates crises
- Identify how stress manifests itself (e.g., what behaviors are demonstrated?)
- Identify calming methods
- Determine medications used in past with medical/clinical support

Stress management. In our experience with students on college campuses, we have found that students with AS who are very affected by stress and anxiety need continued counseling support from the outset of their college career. Students who become depressed or over-anxious must be treated quickly and aggressively with therapy, and often medication. We have found that students who try to recoup from severe depression or anxiety on their own usually do not catch up academically (or socially) and lose the semester. Often they go deeper into depression or heighten their level of anxiety by attempting to continue in school and stay on campus.

... we have found that students with AS who are very affected by stress and anxiety need continued counseling support from the outset of their college career.

Several standard stress management techniques work well for students with AS. The first is regular exercise. A classic stress reducer, exercise not only increases the chemicals that battle anxiety and depression, it also strengthens the immune system. Exercise can be an excellent study break and can be accomplished more regularly when built into the student's schedule.

Social activity is another good stress management technique. On a college campus even eating meals can be social. Though students with AS have difficulty with social activities, there is still a great desire for companionship. Breaks from studying and lessened anxiety about social interaction can be a great way to reduce stress.

Stress-Busting Activities on Campus

- Regular exercise
- Outings with peers, friends, or family
- Maintaining a healthy eating and sleeping schedule
- Scheduled downtime every day and during each study period (see Daily Schedule)
- Structured time for TV, movies, or video games (with an alarm to end time)
- Yoga or meditation (also a good group activity)
- Listening to music

Medications. There is no single medication for symptoms related to AS. Many students with AS are on medications for diagnoses such as anxiety, depression, OCD, attention deficit disorder (ADD), and attention deficit-hyperactivity disorder (ADHD). Students must have a medical contact in the area where they attend college so that a health professional has their full history and can prescribe and refill medications. This is especially important in case of emergencies (e.g., while adjusting to a new routine, the student takes his medication in the bathroom and accidentally drops the bottle filled with medication down the sink). Students must know how to take their medications responsibly without adult supervision.

Academic Affairs and Advising

From their entry into college, students must understand the course requirements for their major and all core requirements for the college or university. We have found that many students with AS have little trouble being admitted to a university but encounter problems completing graduation requirements once they arrive. Some schools have rigid graduation requirements that cannot be waived or modified, which might pose a problem for the student who feels he cannot (or will not) be able to succeed in a given course. Students must be carefully advised regarding their options for courses as well as those that are nonnegotiable so that they can best plan for meeting them.

Let us see how Kevin is facing these challenges.

 Kevin likes math and science but does not do very well in his English classes. He avoided taking them for most of college, then took his first required English class his senior year and flunked. The creativity required was not in Kevin's realm of thinking. English composition is a requirement for his degree program, as is one additional writing or literature course. Kevin now has to figure out how to pass two English classes in order to graduate.

Kevin's situation is common, as many students with AS choose schools based on proximity to home and major, never looking at course requirements and graduation criteria. We strongly recommend choosing a college based on all of these, especially course requirements, to improve the student's success.

Academic advising is a crucial element to a successful college experience for any student. We believe that advising is best left to professional advisors rather than DS providers. However, on some campuses, students never see their advisors except when they need them to sign their registration cards. Indeed, many programs do not assign individual advisors until students have declared a major. In order for the advisor to get to know a student, the student has to be willing to meet multiple times. This may be in addition to meetings with DS, tutor, counselors, and so on. Some students avoid meeting with yet another professional and do not even try to find their advisors. We strongly suggest that DS providers ask students who their advisor is and get their permission to at least partially disclose the student's status. This can be enormously beneficial in advising the student about which, or how many, courses to take.

We suggest that advisors attempt to combine advising with a professor the student is comfortable with or make another qualified staff person their advisor. On small campuses, some DS professionals are also advisors. We strongly suggest that advisors and deans of advising be included in the campus-wide training for awareness about AS.

> *We strongly suggest that advisors and deans of advising be included in the campus-wide training for awareness about AS.*

Administrative Offices

Business affairs, enrollment and retention, registrar, financial assistance – all of these are the business-related offices on most campuses. Some staff in these divisions may be involved in student service, while others are not. To the extent that they are involved with students and their families, we suggest that these offices be included in a tailored version of campus-wide training so that the issues are not unfamiliar to them. For example, what does one do when a student with AS has lost his financial aid and health insurance because he did not know about the minimal residency requirements and dropped too many classes to maintain active enrollment?

Academic Administration

Academic institutions are strongly hierarchical organizations. In the academic sphere, the provost is the chief educational officer. Provosts are administratively over deans (dean, associate dean, assistant dean), who are over department heads (also known as "chairs"), who are over professors (full, associate, assistant, instructor), who are either full or part time, tenured or non-tenured. Professors, in turn, are over graduate students (often serving as teaching or research assistants or fellows), who are over undergraduate students.

We cannot emphasize enough that the route to faculty cooperation is through their department heads. Establishing cordial relationships with these individuals will be of great service when an issue arises with a professor who is reluctant to provide an accommodation or when a question about fundamental requirements arises. Busy senior administrators and deans are often not available for trainings and may be best reached through phone calls, memos, or invitations to staff meetings and new faculty orientations. This is further discussed in Chapter 9.

Upper Administration

The offices of the president, vice presidents, and the provost may be unaware of the issues posed by students with AS on their campuses. We suggest that these officials be made aware of the efforts your office is making in working with these students and the nature of the collaborative trainings you have arranged. Upper-administrative support (even if not in a dollar fashion) is vital to anything that goes above and beyond the literal interpretation of the DS office's mission. Sending white papers, recent journal articles, anything you have published or presented on the subject, makes these offices aware of the innovative things your office is doing to serve this population of students.

Now that we understand many of the academic, nonacademic, and residential challenges faced by students with AS and have explored the need to build effective partnerships with other offices on campus, let us turn to another key partner on campus and a major area of training need – professors and faculty.

Faculty Matters

In the previous chapter we touched on reaching faculty through their department heads and deans. We now turn to some specific issues that faculty is called upon to deal with on the front lines and offer suggestions and strategies for developing alliances with these important individuals in students' lives.

Many classroom and academic issues encountered by students with AS are best resolved directly between the student and the professor (sometimes with a little assistance from DS). For this reason, we strongly suggest ongoing faculty training and cultivation of a strong and respectful relationship between faculty and DS providers. This chapter deals with some of the elements of forging such a partnership.

Working with Faculty and Administration

It is imperative to get faculty and academic administrators (e.g., department heads, deans, provosts) on board as part of a complete campus transformation. These individuals will intersect with the students with AS in all arenas of their academic lives. Moreover, their support is essential for engaging faculty in the mandate to meet the needs of students with AS and encouraging them to devote some of their busy academic time to learning about this growing population of university students. Faculty discerns when a particular student group is embraced by the administrative layer on their campus and can be expected to alter their behavior accordingly (when necessary).

Some Pointers to Reach Faculty

- Use teachable moments with faculty when the need arises, sometimes immediately following an incident with a student
- Develop letters and fact sheets to help convey information (see samples in Appendix F)
- Seek upper-administrative support from department chairs and academic deans (not Dean of Students)

It is important to remember that, in many situations, faculty are being asked to think of creative accommodations or to learn to live with student behaviors that might at first seem unusual or even disrespectful until they better understand the underlying issues. The following outlines some problematic behaviors and misinterpretation on the part of faculty that might be resolved without incident if the faculty member can be helped to understand the individual student rather than to look at the behavior in isolation. Let's start with Kevin.

 Kevin is having a problem with his math professor. Kevin's professor complains that Kevin puts his head down on the desk during lectures and appears to be sleeping. He does not take notes or ask questions.

The professor asked Kevin to meet with him and was annoyed when he found that every time he made a statement, Kevin repeated it back verbatim. He finds Kevin's mannerisms odd and thinks he is rude and scary. He wants Kevin out of his class and has brought the matter up to his department chair, his dean, and the Dean of Students who has contacted DS for resolution.

Cleary, some intervention is warranted or a student like Kevin might find himself administratively withdrawn from the course (or worse). In a scenario like this, the DS provider might meet with the student to explore what is going on in the class. Once an understanding has been established, we suggest that the DS provider contact the faculty member to try to explain some of Kevin's behaviors and the underlying causes. We also would insist that the student begin to work on a plan to reduce the level of behaviors that the professor finds annoying.

Behavior	Possible Cause	Faculty (Mis) Interpretation
Mimics or recites back what professor says	Needs time and repetition to process information	Not taking speaker seriously
Talks too much	Compensates for receptive skills	Overestimation of functioning
Has odd speaking habits	Pragmatic language deficits	Inappropriate or rude
Does not respond to facial expressions, tone	Difficulty with processing nonverbal signals	Leads to miscues in meetings and assignments
Does not recognize you	Limited facial recognition	Aloof, rude
Does not shift topics on cue	Does not automatically catch on	Self-absorbed, uninterested
Lays head on desk	Sensory overload	Rude, sleeping

Once faculty members are helped to understand that the student who keeps her head down on the desk is not sleeping or being rude but is screening out intolerable sensory overload, they may be more tolerant of such behaviors in their classroom. On a more meta level, establishing a good understanding of one student with AS enables many professors to better understand other students with similar problems.

> *We have met many professors who have confided to us that working with a student with AS led them to a better understanding of a member of their own family. (Studies have shown that the incidence of AS in academia may be higher than in the general population.) In this way, faculty members may be educated (sensitized) for all students with disabilities.*

Disclosure to Professors

In most circumstances, students with disabilities do not need to disclose the nature of their disability to faculty. As we have seen earlier, there is no requirement that they do so under the law. However, we have found that when a student with AS struggles in the classroom or when the accommodations he needs are somewhat unusual, it can be important for the faculty to have some understanding of what the student copes with.

Many students are uncomfortable with the idea of disclosing the nature of their disability to their professors. This is understandable, as adolescents desire to be seen as one of the group, rather than risk being singled out as "different" or even "damaged." We believe that in many cases the faculty does not need to know about a student's AS as long as that student's behavior and interactions in the classroom are within the expected range for the other students. In other words, if the student is behaving within acceptable limits, doing his work, and has relatively mild manifestations of his condition, it may not be necessary to disclose any details to the professor.

Many students are uncomfortable with the idea of disclosing the nature of their disability to their professors

For other students, we strongly suggest disclosing to the faculty member. This is especially important when the student engages in odd behaviors or mannerisms, has had classroom issues in the past (such as interrupting professors), or requests unusual accommodations that the professor may need assistance in arranging. It is also important for students to know that professors belong to a group of peers and that students who have posed faculty issues in other classes are usually known within a close-knit department or college. In those instances, we believe it is by far in the student's best interest to provide the professor with a context for understanding the behavior than risking him or her drawing conclusions based on word of mouth and rumor.

How to disclose to faculty. As discussed earlier, disclosure of any student's disability requires permission and a signed release from the student. Sometimes an additional discussion between DS, faculty members, and the student is in order to elaborate on the disclosure. When the student has agreed to disclose to his or her professors, we suggest both a phone call and a letter, followed up with a visit for some cases. We have prepared a fact sheet (see Appendix E) that is useful to provide to professors. We also suggest a personalized letter that introduces the student and discusses some of his or her issues (phrased as situations that might occur) be prepared. We have provided a sample of one such letter in

Appendix E. Some students have been able to write personal narratives describing their disability and issues that they are comfortable providing to faculty, but this is rare.

It is often useful to send the student with the letter so that it can serve as an icebreaker. Most students require some scripting and rehearsal before they are comfortable discussing their symptoms of AS directly with their professors. It is perfectly permissible to for a mentor or a DS staff member to accompany the student if necessary. (The scaffolding section in Chapter 6 is useful in helping to prepare the student to deliver this letter.)

Pros and cons of faculty disclosure. The pros of disclosing to faculty include the overall goal of assisting the student in functioning better in class. If the student forges a relationship with a faculty member, the student may feel better supported and understood in class. Such relationships can turn into important mentorship opportunities, and even offers of jobs and internships. We are aware of students who have gone on to work in the labs of professors with whom they have established such bonds.

Disclosing also permits a faculty member to understand unusual behaviors or mannerisms. For example, a student who puts his head on the desk as a strategy to deal with flickering fluorescent lights would appear to a professor to be napping. Understanding the student's sensory sensitivities assists the professor in interpreting the behavior correctly. Similarly, interrupting the professor routinely might necessitate negotiating a contract between a student and the professor. This would not be possible if the professor did not have some understanding of the issues at hand.

Kevin has agreed to disclose his disability to his pro-
fessor. He has worked with DS to prepare a letter and
has sent an email setting up appointments to deliver
the letter. He has also developed a few scripts that he can
use, depending on how the meeting progresses.

The meeting goes fairly well, and the professor now un-
derstands that when Kevin puts his head down it is not
rudeness. But one area on which his professor will not
budge is Kevin's habit of interrupting during lectures,
which he finds challenging and disrespectful. They agree
that Kevin can write his questions down on an index card
and have 10 minutes with the professor after each class
to ask his question or make his point.

Provision of academic accommodations is often easier when the
professor understands the context in which it is sought, although
the law does not require the student to disclose his diagnosis to
receive accommodations. We suggest that, at a minimum, the
professor is made aware of some of the student's functional limitations; for example, "I receive extended time and use of a computer because I write slowly" will suffice for "I receive extended
time because I have dysgraphia."

On the negative side, uninformed or insensitive faculty members
have been known to single out a student with AS, even asking the
student to withdraw from class, because they feared the student
would be too much to handle. We have seen this scenario in some
cases where students have disclosed major psychiatric disorders such
as schizophrenia. In most instances, such behavior on the part of faculty members is blatantly illegal, but the student with AS may not be
able to advocate for herself and, thus, becomes the victim.

We encourage DS staff to intercede in situations where it appears that the professor is acting on prejudice and fear. If the student is disruptive and cannot be worked with, a case can be made that she is not otherwise qualified to be in class. However, the professor must be able to present his or her case with evidence that the issue is the student's behavior and not the professor's own fears.

The following letter is an example of one of the ways in which a frustrated faculty member might prepare a case against a disruptive student in his or her class.

Dear Deans:

I write regarding a student issue. After noting in my syllabus at the start of the semester that students with documented disabilities should contact me, Kevin presented me with a letter describing his accommodations. He also gave me a letter and some sort of fact sheet describing a condition called Asperger's Disorder. I understand that he has been working with DS throughout the semester. Kevin is doing fine academically, but I have problems with his behavior for which I ask your assistance and advice.

My experience of Kevin throughout the semester has been alternately one of "ups and downs." His behavior is very unpredictable. Some days he comes to class and is very relaxed, participates respectfully and acts appropriately towards his peers and me. Other days, he is extremely anxious and lashes out, shouting loudly, speaking disrespectfully, and keeping me after class with a litany of demands and complaints. I have documented these interactions throughout the semester, keeping DS apprised, but the behaviors keep getting worse. I have been receiving complaints from other students.

I have copied the Dean of Students and the director of Judicial Affairs; please advise regarding next steps.

A scenario like this may culminate in a formal judicial hearing against the student for creating a climate that interferes with the rights of the other students to learn. This is a very delicate situation in which all parties can easily become entrenched and, thus, be unwilling to compromise with anything short of sanction against the student and removal from the class. In some cases, the Dean of Students' office or the office of DS might broker a deal such as discussed above, where the professor tries to understand the student better and the student pledges to work on the unacceptable behaviors. Parents may be brought in as needed.

Less overtly, a professor might deem the student with AS incapable of keeping up with the class work and grade him unfairly. A professor may interpret some of the more creative accommodations (note takers, computers with voice input, clarification of exam answers) as conferring an unfair advantage on the student with AS and assume that the student must be graded more harshly (or conversely, graded more leniently).

It is important to assure professors that students with AS must be evaluated by the same standard as other students in the class and that accommodations (even unusual ones) do not mean that the course standards should be changed.

It is important to assure professors that students with AS must be evaluated by the same standard as other students in the class and that accommodations (even unusual ones) do not mean that the course standards should be changed. Optimally, such a discussion would occur at the start of the semester before the student has encountered a negative reaction from a professor in one of the venues suggested above.

If the student is unwilling to disclose his or her condition, it is possible to provide faculty with information in the abstract and let them infer about a student. The fact sheet in Appendix F is a good way to start, with an open invitation to the professor to contact you if he or she has a question about a student or a student issue. In that way, when and if a classroom problem arises, the professor is more likely to feel that he can call on someone for assistance. While DS may not be able to divulge the exact nature of a student's disability, information and support can be conveyed.

Reaching Faculty – "Teachable Moments"

Faculty time and access are at a premium. Arranging meetings between DS and a faculty member, or sending articles or fact sheets for faculty to read may be met with resentment. Some professors feel burdened already by being asked to assist in arranging accommodations.

As mentioned, if faculty is to be reached, support is often required from higher levels such as department heads, academic deans, provosts, and even the college president. If a campus is committed to supporting students with disabilities, a word from above may be necessary to remind faculty of their responsibility.

It is important to explore various venues by which faculty can be reached. We encourage use of FAQ sections on websites, articles in faculty/staff newsletters, blogs, or journal club as venues to provide information on campus. Cold calls to academic deans can result in an invitation to address various faculty groups, including department meetings and new-faculty orientations. The time-honored direct phone call and meeting for coffee tend to be the best, immediate means by which to engage a faculty member in a particular student's issues, as well as to impart more general information about AS. Often faculty members share that they are familiar with other individuals (sometimes other faculty, sometimes children, grandchildren, or neighbors) with AS and have a genuine interest in the condition. This delightful turn of events results in a faculty member who may take a real interest in mentoring an individual student.

In our experience, faculty cooperation in making adjustments, accommodating, and supporting a student with AS in class is enhanced when the professor is given information about the condition in general, and (if the student agrees) the student in particular, in a collegial and non-authoritative manner. It is important to acknowledge that in many cases we are asking professors to go above and beyond the minimum accommodation level (such as monitoring group or lab work closely, or negotiating out-of-seat breaks during class).

... faculty cooperation in making adjustments, accommodating and supporting a student with AS in class is enhanced when the professor is given information about the condition in general, and (if the student agrees) the student in particular, in a collegial and non-authoritative manner.

Disability professionals and staff who are not faculty level must also appreciate the fact that we are sometimes asking faculty to understand unusual, even disruptive, behavior from a student who may appear odd or even frightening. Professors must be reassured that they are still the ultimate authority in their classes and that the DS office wishes to assist in managing a student in their class (not mandate exactly how they must do it).

It is possible to alienate faculty members by demanding or insinuating that if they do not do things a particular way they are violating the university policy or even the law. Clearly, this is a bad approach. Professors work most effectively with students with AS when they are respected as colleagues, and not when they feel that they are being given commands about how to run their classrooms.

Many DS officers have not had the experience of teaching in a college classroom and do not understand the politics of university teaching. It may be worthwhile or even necessary to have a discussion with a sympathetic department head or a dean if a particular professor is resistant to working with the DS office beyond the minimum level.

Many DS officers have not had the experience of teaching in a college classroom and do not understand the politics of university teaching.

The concept of a "teachable moment" may be particularly useful in working with faculty who encounter a problem with a student. Such professors are often looking for guidance and assistance, although their contact may come across as irritation or resistance. For example, a student who constantly interrupts a professor has gotten on the professor's nerves, and the professor feels that the disruption warrants the student being thrown out of the class. Commiserating with the professor and acknowledging that it must be difficult to have such a student challenge his or her authority in class may open the door to being able to provide additional information about the disorder and the student, and making suggestions about ways to handle the behavior. Such a professor may end up feeling supported rather than angry at the student – the best possible outcome.

Course Expectations

Faculty members expect that college students possess a high degree of cognitive and intellectual sophistication. In addition, certain basic expectations form the core requirements for individual courses. The syllabus of a course gives deadlines for assignments, sets out curricular expectations, and provides a snapshot of what the course and the professor are about. Students must use the syllabus and talk to other students to discern if courses and professors are right for them.

Students with AS may have difficulty doing this and, therefore, need direction from a DS professional or a mentor. Course expectations cannot be changed, but accommodations can be made that retain the essential elements of the course while leveling the playing field for the student.

Typical College Course Demands
- Flexible problem solving
- Synthetic and categorical thinking
- Sequential thinking
- Use of logic
- Abstract skills
- Ability to draw inferences
- Capacity for insight
- Generating alternate solutions

Faculty members sometimes think that accommodations are intended to alter their expectations for the student receiving the adjustments. As discussed in the accommodations section above, this is a misunderstanding. Every effort must be made to assure faculty that accommodations are never intended to alter the fundamental expectations of a course, in terms of assignments, examinations, grading systems, penalties, and so forth.

Some of the accommodations in the table below are familiar to most professors, whereas others may be less familiar. At the beginning of the semester, it is useful to go over the unfamiliar adjustments first with the student and then with the professor so that the latter can better understand the nature of the accommodation and the benefit the student may derive from it (such as the extra sensory feedback to the writing instrument provided by the sandpaper or the enhanced organization of in-class essays when using a word processor).

Common Exam Accommodations
- Papers instead of exams (to be used sparingly)
- Breaks during exams
- Distraction-free setting
- Extended time
- Use of computer (possibly voice input)
- No scantron forms
- Sensory modifications (if necessary)
- Sandpaper under test form

Group projects. Group activities are common in many classes and labs. Students with AS may be at a disadvantage in group work for reasons discussed earlier. However, these activities often represent a core feature of a course or program, and as such are not subject to modification. Faculty are in the best position to evaluate the need for group projects in their classes, and no adjustments should be recommended by the student and/ or DS without discussing it at length with a faculty member. A point person in DS (or perhaps the counseling center) should be identified for the faculty member to use as a resource.

Every effort must be made to assure faculty that accommodations are never intended to alter the fundamental expectations of a course, in terms of assignments, examinations, grading systems, penalties, and so forth.

For the student with AS who is having trouble with the group dynamic in a required activity, we often recommend setting up a meeting with the faculty member to ask that he or she be more observant of the group or even hand-select group members or lab partners. Prior to this meeting, the student with AS should be asked to give permission for disclosure. Even if students refuse to permit the nature of their disability to be discussed, most are amenable to sharing that they have a social skills problem. Such admission could lead to helpful suggestions, such as taking a head count at regular group meetings to be sure the student with AS is attending or having the entire group schedule meetings with the teaching assistant or faculty member to clarify the work assignments and division of labor.

Group members should also be encouraged to share with faculty any impediments to the work of the group that may be addressed directly with the student with AS. The nature of the student's disability may never be shared with the group members without the student's permission, but DS staff can encourage the student to consider disclosing it himself or herself. We acknowledge that this is time consuming; however, such interventions result in a much more positive experience for all students involved.

Potential Group Work Problems
- Choosing partners
- Dividing tasks
- Managing group goals and timelines
- Working in close proximity to others
- Social skills
- Managing conflict
- Being taken advantage of

The "2-Card Strategy" for Faculty

Some students who are very bright sometimes have problems containing their enthusiasm for a course. This can be manifested in the student interrupting, correcting a professor, or monopolizing a lecture.

The 2-card system may be adapted as a classroom intervention to assist the professor in maintaining control of the student's interruptions. In a nutshell, it involves two laminated cards prepared by DS and reviewed with the student and the faculty member for use throughout the semester. Cards can be blank or can have some instructions typed on them.

The student begins class with the cards on his desk. Each time the student speaks in class, she must give a card to the professor. When both cards are gone, all other comments the student would like to make must be held until after the class or the professor's office hours. Cards are picked up from the professor immediately after each class so they can be reused.

We have found this simple strategy to help by giving students a visual and tactile clue regarding how many comments they make. Students who are very bright and have much to say but don't realize they are monopolizing class time need a way to control this behavior; otherwise, they can be brought up on conduct charges for disrupting the educational environment. The card system can be one step in avoiding this unfortunate circumstance.

Support and Train Faculty

Remind faculty to ...

- Use syllabus statements to remind students of how to request accommodations such as "If you have a documented disability and need accommodations in this class, please see me no later than this week to arrange those accommodations. You must be registered with DS and have approved accommodations. This can be done in person or by email; again my email is _____ "
- Refer student to DS before starting a judicial process
- Work with deans, department heads, and DS to identify course standards and accommodations
- Consider using universal design strategies to make accommodations that assist students with disabilities but are helpful for all students
- Review the faculty fact sheet (see Appendix F)
- Try to understand behaviors often associated with AS (underlying symptoms) included on the fact sheet

To many professors, students with AS appear to present a contradiction. Their level of intelligence can be equal to their level of difficult behaviors. Nevertheless, most faculty feel that the intellect that students with AS bring to the classroom far outweighs the difficulty in most cases.

Many professors establish long-lasting relationships with students on the spectrum once they realize their talents and insight into a topic. In addition, many faculty can relate to the single-mindedness of the student and can resonate with their own pursuit of their academic interests. A dedicated and (occasionally) obsessive student can be mentored to become a diligent lab or research assistant who will be a benefit and a credit to the professor who has taken the time to nurture such a relationship. This leads us to the next chapter on employment transition.

CHAPTER 10

Preparing Students to Enter the World of Work

We have discussed the importance of forging relationships with various offices across campus involved in student life and academic affairs. With this level of campus-wide understanding, the student will be in a good position to graduate and to enter the world of work. Many argue that this is the ultimate goal of higher education.

In this chapter we will discuss how the student may be prepared to move from the world of school to the world of work, including working with the office of Career Services, finding on-campus jobs and/or internships, and preparing to work after graduation.

Most DS offices focus on supporting students so they are successfully integrated into the academic and co-curricular fabric of university life. The matter of successful employment after graduation is typically not addressed in much depth, if at all, by DS staff. Instead, it is usually left in the hands of the campus Career Services office. Career Service offices, typically under-prepared to support students with significant needs in general, are often flummoxed when faced with working with students on the autism spectrum, many of whom have few job-readiness skills. As a consequence, these students frequently encounter painful rejection after rejection from large numbers of job interviews. If they are fortunate to be hired, many face a troubled relationship with their employers.

Preparing students on the autism spectrum for successful employment can be more time and labor intensive than for other populations of students with disabilities. Whether this work is done by the DS office or the Career Services office, or jointly, is a decision that needs to be made at the institutional level. Further, the timeframe for helping students on the spectrum acquire job readiness skills is rooted in the degree of the severity of their disability.

Transitioning to Work

College students' thoughts generally turn toward the search for full-time employment during their final academic year. However, the student with AS should begin preparing for the world of work much earlier, ideally during the sophomore year of studies. Disabilities professionals should engage in discussions to learn what the student knows and understands about work and use this information as a starting point for expanding the student's knowledge base.

Many college students on the spectrum have not had an opportunity to explore work or volunteer opportunities. Others may have had summer jobs or part-time jobs with varying degrees of success. Students should be drawn into discussion about their work experiences. In particular, focus discussions on the type of work environment(s) the students were exposed to, their responsibilities, the specific types of tasks in which they were engaged, and whether or not they enjoyed them.

It is important to try to get a sense of how successful students think they were at their jobs and why they feel their jobs were or were not successful experiences. Explore through discussion their relationships with coworkers and managers whom they liked/got along with and those whom they disliked/had difficulties with. When possible, parents can be consulted about the successes and challenges the students faced during their work experiences. Discussions with parents can also provide valuable information about students' work experiences and the degree of success or failure the students had experienced. Equally important, discussions with parents can provide valuable insights into how accurately students can interpret their work experiences and the level of understanding they have about any challenges they may have

... the student with AS should begin preparing for the world of work much earlier, ideally during the sophomore year of studies.

experienced both with the job itself and interpersonally. Beginning this work early on in the student's academic career affords the student time to develop and test out job readiness skills in the protected environment of the college setting through participation in summer jobs, internships, and work-study positions.

We suggest that students with AS become clients of their state vocational rehabilitation agency, whenever possible, to further expand the range of supports available to them. This national network of statewide programs was created to provide individuals having medical challenges and/or disabilities the education, training, and job placement services to enhance their employability. This will also afford an opportunity to develop a partnership between disabilities services staff and the vocational rehabilitation agency on behalf of the student.

Some students may already have registered with their state vocational rehabilitation agency as part of their IEP or 504 transition plan during their senior year of high school. In these cases, partnering with students' vocational rehabilitation counselors to jointly develop job readiness skills can be an ideal arrangement, leading to a smooth transition to appropriate employment placement following graduation.

177

In the vast majority of situations, however, this type of transition planning has not taken place in high school, often delaying the student becoming a registered client due to complications associated with lengthy waiting lists and the necessity of registering with the vocational rehabilitation agency in the student's state of legal residency. A comprehensive contact list of vocational rehabilitation agencies may be found at http://www.workworld. org/wwwebhelp/state_vocational_rehabilitation_vr_agencies.htm. Interested students and staff should also look at two resources prepared by Temple Grandin, a highly successful individual with high-functioning autism (Grandin, 2007; Grandin & Duffy, 2008).

Learning Style

Prior to determining a good fit for a job, it is important to investigate the student's ideal learning style, addressed in Chapters 3 and 5. Does the student learn best by explanation? If so, verbal instruction coupled with a written protocol might be the ideal vehicle to use in assisting the student to learn the job and the work culture. Tip sheets provided in Appendix G provide examples of written protocols prepared to reinforce verbal instructions provided as part of job training.

If the student learns best by being shown what to do, demonstrations coupled with numbered sample pages best serve the student. Perhaps the use of a flow chart or grid table is ideal for ensuring that the student learns the job and the work culture. The process of identifying the various skills and needs of the AS student, along with the student becoming more self-aware and developing the skills that enable him to be a productive and well-integrated employee, requires time and patience. These should not be goals in and of themselves, but should provide a baseline, with the ultimate goal of enabling the student to independently apply the steps and procedures identified in each work setting he may encounter.

Working with a Mentor

As in other areas of life, high-functioning students benefit from the support and guidance of a mentor who can translate the work environment and help them adjust to new and different experiences on the job. Higher functioning students generally are able to adapt and function well when they have a supportive and understanding coworker or supervisor to help "translate." At the very least, identify someone in the job site who can be the "go-to" person to answer questions the student may have either about her immediate responsibilities or about the office in general. Ideally, this should be someone who is willing to assume this responsibility and will do so with care, understanding, and patience.

Higher functioning students generally are able to adapt and function well when they have a supportive and understanding coworker or supervisor to help "translate."

In some instances, it is advisable to assign a mentor from outside the office to guide a student who does not easily pick up on even the more obvious cues around the office and who is, therefore, more likely to make major gaffes. The ideal situation is one in which the mentor is able to spend the initial day or two with the student as he learns his new job – to provide both support to the student and guidance to the immediate supervisor. The mentor should then maintain telephone contact with both the student and the supervisor or "go-to" person for several days to ensure that the student is adjusting to the work environment. Such contact also helps to reduce stress that the student may be experiencing from feeling overwhelmed by the sheer volume of new things to learn or by the challenge of having to be flexible.

Periodic check-in calls over the first weeks help to contain any difficult situations that might arise. In cases where students require a great deal of support, the use of a mentor minimizes the sometimes time-intensive effort required on the part of supervisors and coworkers to train and integrate the student into the work routine.

Given the pivotal role of mentors in the student's transition and integration into the work environment as well as his performance of the job responsibilities, sensitive, skilled mentors are key to the success of the students developing the workplace skills that will enable them to enter the workforce. The focus should be not only the acquisition of general workplace skills and the specific job skills of each placement, but also the development of transferable skills and tools that will enable and empower the student to navigate the world of work independently.

Graduate students in programs such as counseling, psychology, speech and language pathology, social work, college student personnel, special education, and rehabilitation are particularly well suited to serve as mentors. These graduate students can work either through internships, practica, graduate assistantships, or part-time workers to be trained as mentors and familiarize themselves with their student mentees, their knowledge bases, their strengths and weaknesses, and their developmental needs.

On-Campus Jobs

While the ultimate goal is to help the student fit into the job environment, a precursor is helping her understand that there are a wide variety of job cultures, ranging from the very formal to the very informal, but that some standards cut across all work cultures. To reinforce this notion, identify a variety of offices on campus that clearly reflect different work cultures and combinations of work cultures. In developing a list, think in terms of offices and departments that range from the more formal (such as the development/

fundraising office, president's office) to the more informal (recreation center, buildings and grounds office). Consider offices that have little contact with the "customer," such as the accounts payable department, juxtaposed with those having a primary responsibility of working with the customer, such as the dining hall or cashier's office. The following offices on campus might be considered for the possibilities they might offer.

Department	Formal	Informal	Much Public Contact	Limited Public Contact
Affirmative Action	X			X
Alumni Affairs office	X		X	
Audiovisual department		X	X	
Bookstore		X	X	
Cashiers' office		X	X	
Computer center		X	X	
Custodial services		X		X
Development office	X			X
Food services		X		X
Health center		X	X	
Human Resources	X			X
Library		X	X	
Mail services		X		X
President's or provost's office	X		X	
Public Safety		X		X
Registrar's office		X	X	
Recreation center or athletics department		X	X	
ROTC		X		

Consider also differences that might exist among academic departments, including the following departments:

- Biology, Chemistry, or Physics and their labs
- Theatre
- Engineering
- Nursing or Physical Therapy
- Social Work
- Psychology

In the process of identifying offices that are polar opposites, analyze the differences and similarities between them as well as among the pairings. Focus on the physical design of the offices: Do employees have private offices or do they share an office with several other coworkers? Do they work in cubicles, or are they situated in a wide-open area? Is the office quiet except perhaps for the sound of the telephone, or is the office visually or auditorally busy, distracting, and noisy?

It is also important to focus on the similarities among the offices for this is key in helping the AS student to better understand the world of work and will form the foundation upon that to build the student knowledge base about work environments in general.

Disabilities professionals or career counselors can develop an educational unit (see Appendix G) that will broaden the student's awareness of the various types of work environments he is likely to find. In so doing, it is important to identify standards that generally hold true regardless of the culture or type of department. The following are examples of some standards that typically apply and are important fundamental principles for students to learn and integrate.

Good Work Habits

- Arrive to work on time
- Know and observe the company's policy concerning illness-related absences
- Know and observe the company's policy about eating at one's desk
- Observe the company's dress code and adopt it
- Meet deadlines
- Do not make personal phone calls
- Do not play computer games
- Know who you must address more formally

How to Address People		
Who	How	Exceptions
Secretary	Linda	–
Bookkeeper	Don	–
Advisors	First Name	When referring to them in a phone call or with a student, refer to them by last name (Ms. Burns, Mr. Collins)
Assistant Director	Mr. Carmen	Can refer to him by his first name (Bill) when talking with an office worker
Director	Dean Welch	–

In developing the educational unit, we suggest DS providers identify a liaison at each of the offices that have been noted as representing key cultures that students should recognize and work with these liaisons. The first module should consist of experiences ranging from several visits to the offices to identify, analyze, compare, and contrast the types of work cultures to providing hands-on experiences in the form of volunteer work at several offices that reflect different types of work environments and cultures. Worksheets like the templates above, created by the student for each of the offices, can guide the student through a series of questions that directs her attention to the points that are important to the student's professional development.

As the student rotates among the offices, encourage him to discuss the key characteristics of each office. Engage the student to draw parallels, identify differences, and create a grid to reflect the key characteristics and personal implications. The goal of such an exercise is to provide the student with a personalized tool he can use for future job analysis, leading to better acculturation and smoother integration into the job.

While an introduction to the range and variety of work settings and cultures is a valuable approach to providing baseline information, its primary purpose is to develop a knowledge base from which the student can work with a tutor or professional to build awareness of increasingly more subtle issues. The goal is to arm the student with knowledge, tools, and skills that he can apply

The goal of such an exercise is to provide the student with a personalized tool he can use for future job analysis, leading to better acculturation and smoother integration into the job.

at each work setting in which he finds himself, with the interim goal being identification of appropriate behaviors in each new job setting and the ultimate goal being successful survival in the work world after graduation.

To that end, the individually designed educational units should begin at students' most basic levels of understanding about working and build progressively to create a solid foundation of information about the work culture and the skills necessary for the students to become successful in a variety of work environments. As students rotate through their office placements, their mentors should be sure to reinforce what they have learned through concrete discussions and case studies. The curriculum should bring students through levels of increasing sophistication in their understanding of work sites and make clear to them what they need to focus on in their own personal development to better adapt to the work environments in which they find themselves.

Success in this effort is measured by how well students can independently apply what they have learned in their educational units to the unfamiliar and novel work setting. Whether the student is naïve about work and requires introduction to the very basic aspects of being integrated to the world of work, whether the student has had a dozen unsuccessful interviews with little hope of success without change, or whether the student has had a succession of terminations from employment, the educational units must be designed to address his individual needs and assist him in acquiring the skills he needs to become a successful employee.

Fitting In

Once the student has gained a level of comfortable familiarity with identifying and analyzing the various types of work cultures, she is ready to expand her knowledge base. The second module in an employment educational unit should focus in greater detail on the department's culture, guiding the student to examine the overall "look" and "feel" of the office, including such variables as proper dress and hygiene, workplace behavior, computer use, and so on. See sample tip sheet on fitting in included in Appendix G.

Office attire. How are people attired? Does any of the staff wear jeans, sandals, flip-flops, or T-shirts with slogans? If so, who among the staff dress in this fashion? On a college campus this type of attire, if observed, might be restricted to student workers. On the other hand, some offices on college campuses have established dress codes that do not permit casual dress of this type. If the men wear sports jackets and ties, do they remove their jackets when they work at their desks? If so, do they put on their jackets when they go to office meetings and when others come into the office to meet with them, or only when they leave the office? Are the women wearing skirts or pants? Do they wear suits? When wearing skirts are they barelegged or do they wear nylons? Are open-toed shoes worn? These are all examples of questions students should be able to answer based on observation and inquiry.

Grooming and hygiene. Some students may need to focus additional time on grooming and hygiene. Unless they observe otherwise, male students should assume that they must be clean shaven when they visit, volunteer, or work in their campus job sites. Female students should be neatly attired, consistent with the office culture (socks and athletic shoes versus nylons and shoes,

Some students may need to focus additional time on grooming and hygiene.

for example). Inform students needing guidance on personal hygiene that they should shower, wash their hair, and use deodorant preferably every day but certainly on days that they will be at the work site. Their goal should be to look like everyone else on staff to fit in.

Office comportment. The student who needs assistance with the basics such as greeting staff upon her arrival and informing staff when she is leaving or taking a break should develop a tip sheet, and, if necessary, engage in role-playing. Use a worksheet to guide the student to an examination of general office comportment, taking time to observe how people interact with one another in the office. Do they sit quietly on their own and work independently, interacting only when necessary to continue their work? Do they engage in any small talk? If so, does this occur all the time or only at certain times of the day, such as first thing in the morning, at coffee breaks, or upon returning to the office after lunch? How long does the small talk last, a minute or 2, or 5 to 10 minutes? Is it different for different times of day? Does everyone engage in it, or is it always the same person(s)? How do those engaged in personal conversation respond when a superior or "customer" arrives?

Telephone etiquette. Whether or not the student will be answering office telephones, it is important that he be familiar with the office culture concerning use of the telephones, particularly if there is a possibility that he might be called upon to fill in to cover the telephones (see Appendix G). In addition to providing an outline of how to put a call on hold, transfer a call, and the appropriate office greeting for a new call, provide him with a list of staff and their telephone extensions as well as the common questions that generally come in and the correct responses.

This orientation should also include instructions on how to respond to callers when the student has reached the limits of his information and does not know how to answer an inquiry. Follow this up with several practice calls to ensure that the student is clear on the process. Additionally, provide the student with information about any office policies concerning personal use of telephones – both office phones and cell phones – during work hours.

Computer use. It is important to make it clear to students that playing computer games at work is not acceptable. For some students with AS the pull to play computer games is strong. For those who have difficulty detaching from playing games, interruption of this activity may result in angry outbursts, which, in turn, can have long-range implications with coworkers or supervisors. Along the same lines, students must understand that going into someone else's workspace and using his or her computer without permission violates basic office etiquette.

> *... students must understand that going into someone else's workspace and using his or her computer without permission violates basic office etiquette.*

New vocabulary. Most offices use terminology that is particular to their line of work and is pivotal in communicating with one another and accomplishing the work of the office. This can mystify some individuals with AS and limit their ability to easily integrate into a new position. Such terminology generally revolves around certain forms and how to process them, where things are located in the office, other departments with which they commonly interact, and the roles of certain individuals.

In helping the student become oriented to her new work environment, the student and mentor should meet with the student's supervisor to develop a list of common vocabulary, titles, and terms used by office staff, the definitions, and any additional comments that may be necessary to guide the student in her use of the terms. The student should be encouraged to add to the list until she has captured the most commonly used language. Assist her in developing approaches and questions she can use in her efforts to identify office terminology, as well as "go to" people in the office to whom she can turn, if she becomes stymied.

Office routines. Details can overwhelm a new member of an office. Some of these details are touched on as part of office orientation. Other items are covered even more informally. The student should develop a checklist of topics, with help, to ensure that he can ease himself into the established office routines. The following are some of the more common office routines.

- *Time sheets.* Part-time workers usually must complete some form of time sheet, as do individuals in certain trades and occupations. Should the student be volunteering, visiting, or working at an on-campus office, it is good practice to have him get into the habit of completing a time sheet. This will reinforce a common work practice and give him a better understanding of the nature of the employer-employee relationship that as an employee, one's employer "owns" one's time while one is at work. Ideally, it will also lead him to anticipate and inquire about this practice in other work settings.

- *Lunch hours.* Given that every office develops its own version of a lunch hour routine, whether it is to close its doors and put up an "out to lunch" sign, post a rotating lunch schedule that details when staff take their lunch, or stagger staff lunches, help the student to recognize the need to be aware that she may be part of the lunch hour planning process of any office with that he or she may be affiliated, and that disappearing for a lunch break without telling anyone is frowned upon.

- *Breaks.* Work venues and cultures are quite varied, so it can be difficult to generate a standard to assist a student in determining how to conduct himself regarding the taking of breaks. A good rule of thumb would be for the student to inquire after office protocol on this topic.

Doors. Though subtle, there is a "language" of doors, and at some point students should turn their attention to understanding the office culture regarding doors. We have provided a worksheet on dealing with doors in Appendix G.

- Does staff with private offices keep their doors open or closed?
- Does the office culture dictate keeping doors open under certain circumstances and closed in others, such as is likely to happen in a counseling center, when eating lunch at one's desk, or when one needs to focus on work uninterrupted?
- What does it mean if doors are half-closed? If it becomes necessary to speak with someone who is behind closed doors, are there times when one absolutely does not interrupt?
- Are some interruptions acceptable or necessary (such as those from particular individuals such as the president's office, public safety office, the dean)?
- If interruptions are acceptable, how does one handle the interruption: via telephone call, tap on the door, or instant messaging system?

Transitioning from the Educational Module to the Internship/Job

The true test of students' integration of job readiness skills lies in their ability to appropriately apply the strategies they have learned through their work in the various job settings around campus to the internship, practicum, or other real-work setting. Even before they can do so, however, they must secure a practicum or internship – and this requires competing with other students by conducting a convincing interview for the position. This is frequently where many otherwise competent students on the spectrum are screened out, unable to competitively present themselves and their abilities because of poor social skills. At this point the student must begin working on developing good interviewing and marketing skills by working with the career services department on campus.

Interview Training

Career services personnel may find their biggest challenges lie in helping students with AS find ways to sell their skills and talents to prospective employers, considering their socially awkward and idiosyncratic behavior. Some students may need intensive work on interviewing skills and, despite their best efforts, may still not be able to do an adequate job of presenting themselves.

Career services personnel may find their biggest challenges lie in helping students with AS find ways to sell their skills and talents to prospective employers, considering their socially awkward and idiosyncratic behavior.

In such cases, in addition to working with students on the typical areas, work with them to develop scripts on index cards for use during interviews. Scripts should cover the range of experiences encountered during a job interview, including meeting the interviewer, the type of questions that are typically asked, and the cues that the interview is ended.

The use of portfolios as a jumping-off point for discussion is a great way to steer interviews toward a discussion of students' strengths and talents in an effort to move the interviewer's attention toward students' accomplishments and away from their social awkwardness. Programs such as Engineering, Business, and Music, as well as those involving research, lend themselves to the use of portfolios for students who have been engaged in projects and research.

In preparation for an interview, students should research the job and the agency to identify points of nexus between themselves, the job, and the agency. Working with Career Services staff, students should find ways to express the reasons they are a good match for the position and their interest in the position. Again, the student should prepare scripts for these and other aspects of the interview, as identified by the Career Services counselor. Together, the student and counselor should invest abundant work on role-playing, rehearsing, and possibly videotaping practice interviews, comparing students' interviews with examples of successful interviews. Their work should also focus on contingency plans, to prepare the student with a "Plan B" or "Plan C" when the interview does not follow the expected plan.

Disclosure to Employers

Whether students disclose their disability during the interview is an important consideration. When students' social skills are significantly weak and their insights about handling themselves in unfamiliar situations are poor, disclosure could mean the difference between being accepted for a position or internship and being rejected by helping the potential employer to shift his/her attention to assessing the background skills the student brings to the position rather than focusing on her social awkwardness as reflective of her competence as an employee.

In these cases, career counselors, together with DS staff, can work with students to help them develop an effective and comfortable way for them to self-disclose. The student can either sign the disclosure/release of information form already in use by the DS office or can use a form specifically designed for the purpose of sharing information with an interviewer (see sample in Appendix G).

Understanding the Organizational Chart

It is important at some point to give the student some perspective regarding what part she plays in the overall operation of the department. Once she becomes relatively familiar with the office, its culture, and her own responsibilities in the office, a review of the office organizational chart can be useful, particularly for students who think more pictorially. In reviewing the organizational chart, include not only information about the reporting structure but also information that helps the student better understand how each staff person's role contributes to the overall mission of the office.

It is important at some point to give the student some perspective regarding what part she plays in the overall operation of the department.

Additional information about individual staff members can assist the student with interpersonal relationships. Comments such as "gets upset if Thursday's report is received after 11:00," "don't call by first name," "likes trains," or "always back from break late – careful" can help the student navigate her way through her days at work. At the same time, because the organizational chart and comments provide concrete information that provides a level of consistency for the student, it can also serve to reduce some of the anxiety she may feel on a daily basis.

At some point, a second organizational chart showing the relationship of the office to the other units in the agency or company can give the student a further sense of the overall operation. Once again, additional comments about other units and the staff of those units, including information about other workers with whom the student interacts as part of her job, will assist the student in seeing how the work that she does fits into the mission of the organization.

Getting Things Done

As mentioned earlier, one of the big challenges for individuals with AS is organizing their time to maximize productivity. Jobs with built-in structure, therefore, are often recommended for students who are facing their first jobs or who still struggle to develop structure independently. If the student tends to have difficulty with task initiation or staying on task, he should work with mentors to develop templates to guide him through his days. Common "to do" forms or day-at-a-time appointment calendars with the day broken into hours or even smaller time slots are helpful by providing a concrete structure for both the student who tends to hyper-focus on some tasks to the exclusion of others and the student who tends to have difficulty staying on task because his attention wanders. Such tools also provide immediate feedback on how productive or unproductive they have been.

... one of the big challenges for individuals with AS is organizing their time to maximize productivity.

We introduced a number of strategies in Chapter 3 to assist with time and project management in the academic environment. These same tools should be applied in the work setting to assist students in managing their work. Working with their mentors, students should begin by breaking their projects down step by step. Several helpful tools for managing time and projects may be found at the following sites:

- http://www.addplanner.com/index2.html
- http://www.actionagendas.com/
- www.homework-organizer.com

Two other areas to focus on with the student within the work setting are handling of stress and/or anger and social skills. Tolerance of inappropriate management of stress and anger is much lower in the work environment than it is in the educational environment, and the same can be said of poor social skills. These two issues are frequently primary reasons why individuals with AS are laid off or fired. For this reason, students and their mentors generally need to devote time to anger/stress management. Students and their mentors might find it helpful to use one of the dialogue simulations to assist students in improving their social skills and conversations. One such simulation, Social Animals Inc., may be found at http://www.socialanimals.com.

We have followed students with AS and other autism spectrum diagnoses through college, from the beginning transition to entry into the employment sector. We conclude by exploring where to go next.

CHAPTER 11

In Conclusion –
Where Have We Been and
Where Do We Go from Here?

It is the summer after Kevin's junior year. He is working for a landscaper at home while he rests up. It has been a long and sometimes bumpy road for him, filled with pretty predictable problems in the residence hall (he finally moved off campus last year), finding friends, navigating his classes and working with professors, deciding on a major (he declared modern European History), and learning to take care of his own personal and accommodation needs. Due to troubles early on, his GPA is 2.4, which is O.K., but not great. He had several close calls with trips to the emergency room and some near-misses with Judicial Affairs. He tried a few student groups but decided that after all he is not a joiner. He has worked hard to understand his AS and manage his own symptoms.

As he prepares to enter his senior year, Kevin has held one supervised on-campus job, observed on a few other jobs, and participated in an internship. He knows he does not have the grades for graduate work and is thinking about finding a job after graduation.

Where Have We Been?

For many years, most students with AS have been outcasts on college campuses, feeling like they did not belong and had no way of joining. Students prone to feeling alienated and alone were often left out of the environment that arguably could fit them best. Students, parents, and higher education professionals have recognized this unfair and damaging situation and have worked to begin changing the environment for students with AS in higher education.

Where Do We Go from Here?

Our work has only begun. We must educate clinicians, K-12 educators, faculty, staff, and other students. The authors began to present individually and together on college campuses nearly a decade ago, and in that time we have seen growing understanding of how to work with students on the autism spectrum in higher education. We have come a long way, but additional improvements are urgently needed. The numbers of students with AS reaching college age will continue to climb. Our understanding of this disorder must broaden to the world outside of academia to ensure gainful employment and a fulfilled life for college graduates with AS. Campuses must be educated, not just a few faculty and the Residence Life staff, but the entire campus – from Public Safety to the dining halls, student activities to the health center. Everyone must be educated even with a brief training on students with AS, their unique understanding of the world, and how these individuals add to the campus, if only we will allow their participation.

One college president has said that students with AS are our next great thinkers – the visionaries who will make great scientific discoveries, whose "outside the box" style will result in great works of art and music. How can we allow this group to go under- or unserved?

Some students will require more services for success. As we write, campuses nationwide are developing an array of programs designed to support students on the spectrum. We discussed some of the models in the Introduction. Some are based on DS best-practice models whereas others resemble therapeutic treatment facilities with college as an add-on. Some are research-focused; others are offered at no cost while others cost families tens of thousands of dollars (plus tuition). Some are small and are only available to a few. Others are difficult for families to locate and access.

Campuses must be educated, not just a few faculty and the Residence Life staff, but the entire campus – from Public Safety to the dining halls, student activities to the health center.

The goal must be to develop affordable and widespread programs that can reach many students. The alternative is bright and frustrated youth who cannot complete a typical college curriculum and are faced with undesirable employment or state support. This is an unnecessary evil for our time and the educational progressiveness of our country. We must find ways to provide appropriate adult services and educational programming throughout the country.

Intrinsic vs. Extrinsic

One of our central themes has been that the successful integration and accommodation of college students with AS involves a dynamic interplay between the variables the student brings to campus (intrinsic) and the factors a given campus imposes on the student (extrinsic). (See Appendix E for a worksheet for coding intrinsic and extrinsic domains.)

Intrinsic Meets Extrinsic
- **Intrinsic (student) variables**
  - » Cognitive, behavioral, social functioning
  - » Prior experiences and attitudes
- **Extrinsic (institutional) variables**
  - » Academic, classroom, co-curricular
  - » Campus culture and history

To the extent that all of our programming focuses on teaching, training, and remediating the student, we neglect to address the factors that are immutable in the student. Like all of us, individuals with autism spectrum diagnoses change over time; however, by the time an adolescent has arrived on a college campus, the chances for remediation and change in some areas have passed (for example, pragmatic language or reading speed). Further, some individuals have undergone many years of intensive therapies, remediation, and other interventions all aimed towards effecting change – to fix or repair the individual. To continue to focus solely on changing the intrinsic factors within the student risks sending a continued message that pathology rests within the individual.

We believe that the focus must be shared between individual interventions and addressing the means by which the academic environments can be transformed to welcome and better adapt to the individual with an autism spectrum diagnosis. What follows are some suggestions for effecting this transformation.

Campus Training and Education

We have found that students on the spectrum do not always attend the creative programming, social groups, and trainings that are available (Wolf & Thierfeld Brown, 2007). We have offered special tutoring sessions, individual coaching, and social contacts only to find that students with AS have had enough of being different and want nothing to do with special services.

Instead, we believe that an integrated approach is best – one where the entire campus becomes important to the success of the student with AS. In order for this approach to be actualized, the campus as a whole needs to be prepared and properly trained to help students reach their highest potential. The more prepared and educated the campus is, the more successful students on the spectrum will be. Both faculty and staff are crucial in this training. As our overall higher education numbers begin to decline in the next decade due to demographic trends such as the tailing off of the baby boom, students

The more prepared and educated the campus is, the more successful students on the spectrum will be.

on the spectrum with their above-average to brilliant intellect will become an even more important factor.

In 2006 the authors were asked to meet with two Japanese faculty members to discuss students with AS in higher education. At the time, Japan had never accepted students on the spectrum into higher education. Due to the declining birth rate in Japan, the population of college-age students has drastically decreased in recent years. In response, Japanese colleges and universities are paying more attention to capable students with disabilities and are seeking training to better service students with AS. Although excluding students with disabilities from admission and participation solely on the basis of their disability is patently illegal in the United States, we know institutions have excluded students on the spectrum if they identify in the admissions process.

Going forward, as the pool of potential college students decreases and the number of students on the autism spectrum increases, a more inclusionary model will emerge. Although, in principle, we do not go along with the implied concept of admitting students to college based on supply and demand, we agree with the likely outcome that as more students on the spectrum are accepted at colleges and universities, those schools will become better trained to provide services, and the students will become more successful. We prefer that institutions of higher education understand more fully the potential of students with spectrum disorders and welcome them to their ranks based on their talents and potential rather than unfairly excluding them based on fears about the impact and costs of enrolling large numbers of students with disabilities. Only when this has been achieved will full inclusion be realized.

Program Development

Many of the services needed by students on the spectrum are above and beyond our obligations under the law. Some of these include special tutoring sessions, social programming, peer mentoring, and (especially) campus-wide training. Campuses have developed and delivered these services in the spirit of the law, because it is their institutional mission to do so, or for a fee on top of tuition.

Since the services are not designed for all students with disabilities, it is important to have a distinction in the fee-for-service programs. That is, students paying an extra fee get services beyond what the university is doing, by law, for other students with disabilities. These programs have existed for many years for students with learning disabilities and ADD. More and more of these programs for students on the spectrum are being started every year. We will not provide a list of programs, as it will be quickly outdated. There are several resources for finding these programs. One is www.collegeautismspectrum.com.

Changing the Culture for the Benefit of All

Working with faculty and staff to understand and appreciate the fascinating and wonderful aspects of students with AS is worth the effort. Students on the spectrum will add to your campus in countless ways. The brilliance of many students will add to the academic classroom, to research potential, and to relationships with faculty. The unique insight into the world that students on the spectrum bring to a campus culture will broaden the view of other college students and everyone in the campus community.

For the families of students on the spectrum, wider access to higher education will broaden the otherwise limited future of their son or daughter and help make them contributing members of society. To date, many families have had no viable options for their high-functioning children on the spectrum and could only look to a future in which their

Opening the access to higher education for this increasing population of young students is not only the right thing to do for the student, but for society as a whole.

sons or daughters would live with them and hold menial jobs all their lives, unable to function independently or to have a career that would allow them to live on their own. Opening the access to higher education for this increasing population of young students is not only the right thing to do for the student, but for society as a whole. We are looking at the difference between a student with a high school diploma and a student who may get an advanced degree and have a career.

The students with AS and their families need these changes and the access to a future that comes with them. The numbers of students on the autism spectrum who are going to college are increasing and will continue to increase over the next 10 years – the highest numbers of students on the spectrum are presently in elementary school (U.S. Dept of Education, 2006). We must provide more higher education opportunities and increased access to all levels of education in order to meet the needs of students on the spectrum and their families. It is the right thing for our colleges and universities, the right thing for the families and students, and the right thing for our society.

References

Abele, E. (2006). *Developing pragmatic language skills for social integration in the workplace.* Presentation by Elsa Abele, CCC, SLP, Boston University, abele@bu.edu.

Abell, F., Krams, M., Ashburner, J., Passingham, R., & Friston, K. (1999). The neuroanatomy of autism: A voxel based whole brain analysis of structural scans. *Journal of Cognitive Neuroscience, 10,* 1647-1651.

Action Agendas. *Custom student agendas.* http://www.actionagendas.com/.

ADD Planner. *The planner for people with ADD.* http://www.addplanner.com/index2.html.

Akshoomoff, N., Pierce, K., & Courchesne, E. (2002). The neuropathological basis of autism from a developmental perspective. *Development and Psychopathology, 14,* 613-634.

American Occupational Therapy Association. (2008). *Occupational therapy's role with autism.* http://www.aota.org/.

American Psychiatric Association. (1994). *Diagnostic and statistical manual of mental disorders, 4th edition.* Washington, DC: American Psychiatric Association.

Americans with Disabilities Act of 1990 (ADA, 1990), www.ada.gov.

Ashwood, P., & Van de Water, J. (2004). Is autism an autoimmune disorder? *Autoimmunity Reviews, 3,* 557-562.

Asperger, H. (1991 translation). Autistic psychopathy in childhood. In U. Frith (Ed.), *Autism and Asperger Syndrome* (pp. 37-92). Cambridge, MA: Cambridge University Press.

Attwood, T. (2007). *The complete guide to Asperger's syndrome.* London: Jessica Kingsley Press.

Ayres, A. (2005). *Sensory integration and the child: Understanding hidden sensory challenges.* Los Angeles: Western Psychological Systems.

Bailey, A., LeCouteur, A., Gottesman, U., Bolton, P., Simonoff, E., Yuzda, E., et al. (1995). Autism as a strongly genetic disorder: Evidence from a British twin study. *Psychological Medicine, 25,* 63-77.

Bailey, A., Palferman, S., Heavey, L., & LeCouteur, A. (1998). Autism: The phenotype in relatives. *Journal of Autism and Developmental Disorders, 28,* 381-404.

Barkley, R. A. (1997). Behavioral inhibition, sustained attention, and executive functions: Constructing a unified theory of ADHD. *Psychological Bulletin, 121,* 65-94.

Baron-Cohen, S. (1989). The autistic child's theory of mind – A case of specific developmental delay. *Journal of Child Psychology and Psychiatry and Allied Disciplines 30,* 285-297.

Baron-Cohen, S. (1999). *Mindblindness: An essay on autism and theory of mind.* Cambridge, MA: Massachusetts Institute of Technology Press.

Baron-Cohen, S. (2004). The cognitive neuroscience of autism. *Journal of Neurology, Neurosurgery, and Psychiatry, 75,* 945-948.

Baron-Cohen, S., Ring, H. A., Wheelwright, S., Bellmore, E. T., Braymer, M. J., Simmons, A., et al. (1999). Social intelligence in the normal and autistic bran: An fMRI study. *European Journal of Neuroscience, 11,* 1891-1898.

Baron-Cohen, S., Wheelwright, S., Robinson, J., & Woodbury-Smith, M. (2005). The adult Asperger assessment (AAA): A diagnostic model. *Journal of Autism and Developmental Disorders, 35,* 807-818.

References

Baron-Cohen, S., Wheelwright, S., Stott, C., Bolton, P., & Goodyear, I. (1997). Is there a link between engineering and autism? *Autism, 1,* 153-163.

Barton, J. J., Cherkasova, M. V., Hefter, R., Cox, T. A., O'Connor, M., & Manoach, D. (2004). Are patients with social developmental disorders prosopagnosic? Perceptual heterogeneity in the Asperger and socio-emotional processing disorders. *Brain, 127,* 1706-1716.

Barton, M., & Volkmar, F. (1998). How commonly are known medical conditions associated with autism? *Journal of Autism and Developmental Disorders, 28,* 273-278.

Bauman, M., & Kemper, T. L. (1994). Histoanatomic observations of the brain in early infantile autism. *Neurology, 35,* 866-874.

Berthier M. (1994). Corticocallosal anomalies in Asperger's syndrome. *American Journal of Roentgenography, 162,* 236-237.

Bettelheim, B. (1967). *The empty fortress: Infantile autism and the birth of the self.* London: Collier-Macmillan.

Bishop, D.V.M. (1989). Autism, Asperger's syndrome, and semantic-pragmatic disorders: Where are the boundaries? *British Journal of Disordered Communication, 24,* 107-121.

Bishop, D.V.M., & Norbury, C. F. (2002). Exploring the borderlands of autistic disorders and specific language impairment: A study using standardized diagnostic instruments. *Journal of Child Psychology and Psychiatry, 43,* 917-929.

Bishop, D.V.M., & Norbury, C. F. (2005). Executive functions in children with communication impairments, in relation to autistic symptomatology 2: Response inhibition. *Autism, 9,* 29-43.

Blakemore, S. J., Tavassoli, R., Calo, S., Thomas, R. M., Catmur, C., Frith, U., et al. (2006). Tactile sensitivity in Asperger syndrome. *Brain and Cognition, 61,* 5-13.

Bolton, P., Macdonald, H. M., Pickles, A., Rios, P., Goode, S., Crowson, M., et al. (1994). A case control family study of autism. *Journal of Child Psychology and Psychiatry, 35,* 877-900.

Bolton, P., Murphy, M., Macdonald, H., Whitlock, B., Pickles, A., & Rutter, M. (1997). Obstetric complications in autism: Consequences or cases of the condition? *Journal of the American Academy of Child and Adolescent Psychiatry, 36,* 272-281.

Boucher, J., & Lewis, V. (1992). Unfamiliar face recognition in relatively able autistic children. *Journal of Child Psychology and Psychiatry, 33,* 843-859.

California Health and Human Services Agency, Department of Developmental Services. (1999). *Changes in the population of persons with autism and pervasive developmental disorders in California's developmental services system: 1987 through 1998: A report to the legislature, March 1, 1999.* Sacramento: California Health and Human Services Agency.

Carpenter, M., Nagell, K., & Tomasello, M. (1998). Social cognition, joint attention and communicative competence from 9 to 15 months of age. *Monographs of Social Research and Child Development, 63,* 1-143.

Carper, R. A., Moses, O., Tigue, Z. D., & Courchesne, E. (2002). Cerebral lobes in autism: Early hyperplasia and abnormal age effects. *NeuroImage, 16,* 1038-1051.

Centers for Disease Control and Prevention. (1999). Notice to readers: Thimerosal in vaccines: A joint statement of the American Academy of Pediatrics and the Public Health Service. *Morbidity and Mortality Weekly Report, 48,* 563-565.

Centers for Disease Control and Prevention. (2000). *Prevalence of autism in Brick Township, New Jersey, 1998 community report.* Atlanta, GA: Centers for Disease Control and Prevention, www.cdc.gov.

Centers for Disease Control and Prevention. (2007). *Prevalence of autism spectrum disorders – Autism and developmental disabilities monitoring network, 14 sites, United States 2002.* Atlanta, GA: Centers for Disease Control and Prevention, www.cdc.gov.

Chakrabarti, S., & Fombonne, E. (2001). Pervasive developmental disorders in preschool children. *Journal of the American Medical Association, 285,* 3093-3099.

Channon, S., Charman, T., Heap, J., Crawford, S., & Rios, S. (2001). Real-life type problem solving in Asperger's syndrome. *Journal of Autism and Developmental Disorders, 31,* 461-469.

Charman, T. (2003). Why is joint attention a pivotal skill in autism? *Philosophical Transactions of the Royal Society of London Series B-Biological Sciences, 358,* 315-324.

Coplan, J. (2000). Counseling parents regarding prognosis in autistic spectrum disorder. *Pediatrics, 105,* 65-67.

Courchesne, E., Karns, C. M., Davis, H. R., Ziccardi, R., & Carper, R. A. (2001). Unusual brain growth patterns in early life of patients with autistic disorder. *Neurology, 57,* 245-254.

Croen, L., Grether, J., Hoogstrate, J., & Selvin, S. (2002). The changing prevalence of autism in California. *Journal of Autism and Developmental Disabilities, 32,* 207-215.

Croen, L. A., Grether, J. K, Yoshida, C. K., Oduli, R., & Van de Water, J. (2005). Maternal autoimmune diseases, asthma, allergies and childhood autism. *Archives of Pediatric and Adolescent Medicine, 159,* 151-157.

Damasio, A. R., & Mauer, R. G. (1978). A neurological model for childhood autism. *Archives of Neurology, 35,* 777-786.

Dawson, G., Finley, C., Philips, S., & Galpert, L. (1986). Hemispheric specialization and the language abilities of autistic children. *Child Development, 57,* 1440-1453.

Dawson, G., Meltzoff, A., Osterling, J., & Rinaldi, J. (1998). Neuropsychological correlates of early symptoms of autism. *Child Development, 69,* 1276-1285.

Dawson, G., Webb, S., Schellenberg, G. D., Dager, S., Friedman, S., Aylward, E., et al. (2002). Defining the broader phenotype of autism: Genetic, brain, and behavioral perspectives. *Developmental Psychopathology, 14,* 581-611.

Debbaudt, D. (2006). *Autism spectrum disorders and juvenile justice professionals.* Briefing Document for the Illinois Juvenile Justice Association Conference.

Debbaudt, D., & Rothman, D. (2001, April). Contact with individuals with autism: Effective resolutions. *The FBI Law Enforcement Bulletin.* http://www.jbi.gov/publications/lib/2001/April01/lib/pdf.

deBruin, E. I., Ferdinand, R. G., Meester, S., & De Nijs, P. F. (2007). High rates of psychiatric co-morbidity in PDD-NOS. *Journal of Autism and Developmental Disorders, 37,* 877-886.

DeStafano, F., Karapurka Bhasin, T., Thompson, W. W., Yeargin-Allsopp, M., & Boyle, C. (2004). Age at first measles-mumps-rubella vaccination in children with autism and school-matched control subjects: A population based study in metropolitan Atlanta. *Pediatrics, 113,* 259-266.

DiCicco-Bloom, W., Lord, C., Zwaigenbaum, L., Courchesne, E., Dager, S. R., Schmitz, C., et al. (2006). The developmental neurobiology of autism spectrum disorder. *The Journal of Neuroscience, 26,* 6897-6906.

Doyle, B. T. (2004). *And justice for all: Unless you have autism: What the legal system needs to know about people with autism spectrum disorders.* www.barbaradoyle.com.

Dunn, W., Myles, B. S., & Orr, S. (2002). Sensory processing issues associated with Asperger syndrome: A preliminary investigation. *American Journal of Occupational Therapy, 56,* 97-102.

Evers, M., Novotny, S., & Hollander, E. (2003). Autism and environmental toxins. *Medical Psychiatry, 24,* 175-198.

Federal Educational Rights and Privacy Act (FERPA), http://www.ed.gov/policy/gen/guid/fpco/ferpa/index.html.

Findling, R. L. (2005). Pharmacologic treatment of behavioral symptoms in autism and pervasive developmental disorders. *Journal of Clinical Psychiatry, 66,* 26-31.

References

Fitzgerald, M. (2007). Suicide and Asperger's Syndrome. *Crisis, 28,* 1-3.

Folstein, S. E., Gilman, S. E., Landa, R., Hein, J., & Santangelo, L. S. (1999). Predictors of cognitive test patterns in autistic families. *Journal of Child Psychology and Psychiatry, 40,* 1117-1128.

Folstein, S., & Rutter, M. (1977). Infantile autism: A genetic study of 21 twin pairs. *Journal of Child Psychology and Psychiatry, 18,* 297-321.

Fombonne, E. (2003). Epidemiological surveys of autism and other pervasive developmental disorders: An update. *Journal of Autism and Developmental Disorders, 33,* 365-382.

Fombonne, E., & Chakrabarti, S. (2001). No evidence for a new variant of measles-mumps-rubella-induced autism. *Pediatrics, 108,* 1-8.

Frith, U. (1991). Asperger and his syndrome. In U. Frith (Ed.), *Autism and Asperger Syndrome* (pp. 1-36). Cambridge, MA: Cambridge University Press.

Frith, U. (2001). Mind blindness and the brain in autism. *Neuron, 32,* 969-979.

Firth, U. (2003). *Autism: Explaining the enigma* (2nd ed.). Oxford: Blackwell.

Frith, U. (2004). Emanuel lecture: Confusions and controversies about Asperger Syndrome. *Journal of Child Psychology and Psychiatry, 45,* 672-686.

Geier, M. R., & Geier, D. A. (2003). Neurodevelopmental disorders after thimerosal-containing vaccines: A brief communication. *Experimental Biological Medicine, 228,* 660-664.

Ghaziuddin, M., Ghaziuddin N., & Greden, J. (2002). Depression in persons with autism: Implications for research and clinical care. *Journal of Autism and Developmental Disorders, 32,* 299-306.

Gillberg, C. (1992). Autism and autistic-like conditions: Subclasses among disorders of empathy. *The Journal of Child Psychology and Psychiatry and Allied Disciplines, 33,* 813-842.

Gillberg, C., & Billstedt, E. (2000). Autism and Asperger syndrome: Coexistence with other clinical disorders. *Acta Psychiatrica Scandinavica, 102,* 321-330.

Gillberg, C., & Coleman, M. (1996). Autism and medical disorders: A review of the literature. *Developmental Medicine and Child Neurology, 38,* 191-202.

Gillberg, C., & Wing, L. (1999). Autism: Not an extremely rare disorder. *Acta Psychiatrica Scandinavica, 99,* 399-406.

Glasson, E. J., Bower, C., Petterson, B., de Klerk, N., Chancy, G., & Hallmayer, J. F. (2004). Perinatal factors and the development of autism. *Archives of General Psychiatry, 61,* 618-627.

Goldman, L. R., & Koduru, S. (2000). Chemicals in the environment and developmental toxicity in children: A public health and policy perspective. *Environmental and Health Perspectives, 108,* 443-448.

Grandin, T. (2007). *Making the transition from the world of school into the world of work.* Center for The Study of Autism, www.autism.org.

Grandin, T., & Duffy, K. (2008). *Careers for individuals with Asperger Syndrome and high-functioning autism.* Shawnee Mission, KS: Autism Asperger Publishing Co.

Green, J., Gilchrist, A., Burton, D., & Cox, A. (2000). Social and psychiatric functioning in adolescents with Asperger syndrome compared with conduct disorder. *Journal of Autism and Developmental Disorders, 30,* 297-293.

Gunter, H. L., Ghaziuddin, M., & Ellis, H. D. (2002). Asperger syndrome: Tests of right hemisphere functioning and inter-hemispheric communication. *Journal of Autism and Developmental Disorders, 32,* 263-281.

References

Happe, F., Booth, R., Charlton, R., & Hughes, C. (2006). Executive function deficits in autism spectrum disorders and attention deficit/hyperactivity disorder: Examining profiles across domains and ages. *Brain and Cognition, 61,* 25-39.

Herbert, M. R. (2003). Autism: A brain disorder or a disorder that affects the brain? *Clinical Neuropsychiatry, 2,* 354-379.

Hill, E. L. (2004). Executive function in autism. *Trends in Cognitive Science, 8,* 26-32.

Holtmann, M., Bolte, S., & Poustka, F. (2007). Autism spectrum disorders: Sex differences in autistic behavior domains and coexisting psychopathology. *Developmental Medicine and Child Neurology, 49,* 361-366.

Homework Organizer, www.homework-organizer.com.

Howlin, O. (2005). The effectiveness of interventions for children with autism. *Journal of Neuronal Transmission, 69,* 101-119.

Institutes of Medicine. (2004). *Immunization safety review: Vaccines and autism.* Washington, DC: The National Academies Press.

Johnson, D. J., & Myklebust, H. R. (1971). *Learning disabilities: Educational principles and practices.* New York: Grune & Stratton, Inc.

Joseph, R. M., McGrath, L. M., & Tager-Flusberg, H. (2005a). Executive dysfunction and its relation to language ability in verbal school-age children with autism. *Developmental Neuropsychology, 27,* 361-378.

Joseph, R. M., Steele, S. D., Meyer, E., & Tager-Flusberg, H. (2005b). Self-ordered pointing in children with autism: Failure to use verbal mediation in the service of working memory. *Neuropsychologia, 43,* 1400-1411.

Joseph, R. M., & Tager-Flusberg, H. (2004). The relationship of theory of mind and executive functions to symptom type and severity in children with autism. *Developmental Psychopathology, 16,* 137-155.

Joseph, R. M., Tager-Flusberg, H., & Lord, C. (2002). Cognitive profiles and social-communicative functioning in children with autism spectrum disorder. *Journal of Child Psychology and Psychiatry and Allied Disciplines, 43,* 807-821.

Kanner, L. (1943). Autistic disturbances of affective contact. *Nervous Child, 2,* 217-250.

Kinnealey, M., Oliver, B., & Wilbarger, P. (1995). A phenomenological study of sensory defensiveness in adults. *American Journal of Occupational Therapy, 49,* 444-451.

Kleinhans, N., & Akshoomoff, N. (2005). Executive functions in autism and Asperger's disorder: Flexibility, fluency, and inhibition. *Developmental Neuropsychology, 27,* 379-401.

Klin, A., Danovitch, J. H., Merz, A. B., Dohrmann, E. H., & Volkmar, F. R. (2007). Circumscribed interests in higher functioning individuals with autism spectrum disorders: An exploratory study. *Research and Practice for Persons with Severe Disabilities, 32,* 89-100.

Klin, A., Jones, W., Schultz, R., & Volkmar, F. (2003). The enactive mind, or from actions to cognition: Lessons from autism. *Philosophical Transactions of the Royal Society Series B, 358,* 345-360.

Klin, A., Jones, W., Schultz, R., Volkmar, F., & Cohen, D. (2002). Defining and quantifying the social phenotype in autism. *American Journal of Psychiatry, 159,* 895-908.

Klin, A., McPartland, J., & Volkmar, F. R. (2005). Asperger syndrome. In F. R. Volkmar, R. Paul, A. Klin, & D. Cohen (Eds.), *Handbook of autism and pervasive developmental disorders: Diagnosis, development, neurobiology, and behavior* (pp. 88-125). Hoboken, NJ: John Wiley & Sons, Inc.

Klin, A., Saulnier, C., Sparrow, S., Cicchetti, D., Volkmar, F., & Lord, C. (2007). Social and communication abilities and disabilities in higher functioning individuals with autism spectrum disorders: The Vineland and the ADOS. *Journal of Autism and Developmental Disorders, 37,* 748-759.

Klin, A., Sparrow, S. S., de Bildt, A., Cicchetti, D. V., & Volkmar, F. R. (1999). A normed study of face recognition in autism and related disorders. *Journal of Autism and Developmental Disorders, 29,* 497-507.

Klin, A., Volkmar, F. R., Sparrow, S. S., Cicchetti, D. V., & Rourke, B. P. (1995). Validity and neuropsychological characterization of Asperger's syndrome: Convergence with nonverbal learning disabilities syndrome. *Journal of Child Psychology and Psychiatry, 36,* 1127-1140.

Lavoie, R. (1994). *Social competence and the child with learning disabilities.* Downloaded January 15, 2009, from www. ricklavoie.com

Leary, M. R., & Hill, D. A. (1996). Moving on: Autism and movement disturbance. *Mental Retardation, 34,* 39-53.

London, E., & Etzel, R. (2000). The environment as an etiological factor in autism: A new direction for research. *Environmental Health Perspective, 108,* 401-404.

Lord, C., & Risi, S. (2000). Diagnosis of autism spectrum disorders in young children. In A.M. Wetherby, & B. M. Prizant (Eds.). *Autism spectrum disorders: A transactional developmental perspective* (pp. 11-30). New York: Paul H. Brookes, Co.

Lord, C., Rutter, M., Dilavore, P., & Risi, S. (2001). *Autism Diagnostic Observation Schedule (ADOS).* Los Angeles: Western Psychological Services.

Lotter, V. (1966). Epidemiology of autistic conditions in young children: I. Prevalence. *Social Psychiatry, 1,* 124-137.

Macurdy, A., & Geetter, E. (2008). Legal issues for adults with learning disabilities in higher education and employment. In L. E. Wolf, H. Schreiber, & J. Wasserstein (Eds.), *Current issues in adult learning disorders* (pp. 415-432). New York: Psychology Press, Taylor & Francis.

Maestro, S., Muratori, F., Barbieri, F., Casella, C., Cattaneo, V., Cavallaro, M. C., et al. (2001). Early behavioral development in autistic children: The first 2 years of life through home movies. *Psychopathology, 34,* 147-152.

Manoach, D. S., Lindgren, K. A., & Barton, J. J. S. (2004). Deficient saccadic inhibition in Asperger's disorder and the social-emotional processing disorder. *Journal of Neurology, Neurosurgery, & Psychiatry, 75,* 1719-1726.

Manoach, D., Sandson, T., & Weintraub, S. (1995). The developmental social-emotional processing disorder is associated with right hemisphere abnormalities. *Neuropsychiatry, Neuropsychology, and Behavioral Neurology, 8,* 99-105.

McAlonan, G. N., Daly, E., Kumari, V. et al. (2002). Brain anatomy and sensorimotor gating in Asperger's syndrome. *Brain, 127,* 1594-1606.

McKelvy, J. R., Lambert, R., Mottron, L., & Shevell, M. I. (1995). Right hemisphere dysfunction in Asperger's syndrome. *Journal of Child Neurology, 10,* 310-314.

Minshew, N. J. (2001). The core deficit in autism and autism spectrum disorders. *Journal of Developmental and Learning Disorders, 5,* 107-118.

Money, J., Bobrow, N. A., & Clark, F. C. (1971). Autism and autoimmune disease: A family study. *Journal of Autism and Childhood Schizophrenia, 1,* 146-160.

Muhle, R., Trentacoste, S. V., & Rapin, I. (2007). The genetics of autism. *American Academy of Pediatrics, 113,* 472-486.

Muris, P., Steerneman, P., Merckelbach, H., Holdrinet, I., & Meesters, C. (1998). Comorbid anxiety symptoms in children with pervasive developmental disorders. *Journal of Anxiety Disorders, 12,* 387-393.

Murphy, D. G., Critchley, H. D., Schmitz, N., McAlonan, G., van Amerlsvoort, R., Robertson, D., et al. (2002). Asperger syndrome: A proton magnetic resonance spectroscopy study of brain. *Archives of General Psychiatry, 59,* 885-891.

Myles, B. S. (2003). Behavioral forms of stress management for individuals with Asperger syndrome. *Child and Adolescent Psychiatric Clinics of North America, 12,* 123-141.

National Research Council. (2001). *Educating children with autism.* Washington, DC: Committee on Educational Interventions for Children with Autism, Division of Behavioral and Social Sciences and Education.

Nayate, A., Bradshaw, J. L., & Rinehart, N. J. (2005). Autism and Asperger's disorder: Are they movement disorders involving the cerebellum and/or the basal ganglia? *Brain Research Bulletin, 67,* 327-334.

Ozonoff, S. (1997). Components of executive functioning in autism and other disorders. In J. Russell (Ed.), *Autism as an executive disorder* (pp. 179-211). New York: Oxford University Press.

Ozonoff, S., Pennington, B., & Rogers, S. J. (1991). Executive functioning deficits in high-functioning autistic individuals: Relationship to theory of mind. *Journal of Child Psychology and Psychiatry, 32,* 1081-1085.

Ozonoff, S., South, M., & Miller, J. N. (2000). DSM-IV-defined Asperger syndrome: Cognitive, behavioral and early history differentiation from high-functioning autism. *Autism, 4,* 29-46.

Piven, J. (2001). The broad autism phenotype: A complementary strategy for molecular genetic studies of autism. *American Journal of Medical Genetics, 105,* 34-35.

Piven, J., Arndt, S., Bailey, J., & Andreasen, N. (1996). Regional brain enlargement in autism: A magnetic resonance imaging study. *Journal of the American Academy of Child and Adolescent Psychiatry, 35,* 530-536.

Piven, J., Palmer, P., Jacobi, D., Childress, D., & Arndt, S. (1997). Broader autism phenotype: Evidence from a family history study of multiple-incidence autism families. *American Journal of Psychiatry, 154,* 185-190.

Piven, J., Palmer, P., Landa, R., Santangelo, S., Jacobi, D., & Childress, D. (1997). Personality and language characteristics in parents from multiple-incidence autism families, *American Journal of Medical Genetics, 74,* 398-411.

Prior, M. (2003). Is there an increase in the prevalence of autism spectrum disorders? *Journal of Pediatric and Child Health, 39,* 81-82.

Quigley, E. M., & Hurly, D. B. (2000). Autism and the gastrointestinal tract. *American Journal of Gastroenterology, 95,* 2154-2155.

Rajendran, G., & Mitchell, P. (2007). Cognitive theories of autism. *Developmental Review, 27,* 224-260.

Rapin, I., & Allen, D. (1983). Developmental language disorders: Nosological considerations. In U. Kirk (Ed.), *Neuropsychology of language, reading and spelling* (pp. 155-184). New York: Academic Press.

Redcay, E., & Courchesne, E. (2005). When is the brain enlarged in autism: A meta-analysis of all brain size reports. *Biological Psychiatry, 58,* 1-9.

Rehabilitation Act Section 504 (1973). http://www.hhs.gov/ocr/504.html.

Rehabilitation Act Section 508 (1973), http://www.hhs.gov/ocr/508.html.

Reichelt, K. L., Scott, H., & Ekrem, J. (1990). Gluten, milk proteins, and autism: The results of dietary intervention on behavior and peptide secretion. *Journal of Applied Nutrition, 42,* 1-11.

Rodier, P. M. (1998). Neuroteratology of autism. In W. Slikker & L. W. Chang (Eds.), *Handbook of developmental neurotoxicology* (pp. 661-672). San Diego, CA: Academic Press.

Rogers, S. J., & Ozonoff, S. (2005). What do we know about sensory dysfunction in autism? A critical review of the empirical evidence. *Journal of Child Psychology and Psychiatry, 46,* 1255-1268.

Rosenn, D. W. (1999). What is Asperger's disorder? *Harvard Mental Health Letter, 16,* 4-8.

References

Rourke, B. P. (1987). Syndrome of nonverbal learning disabilities: The final common pathway of white matter disease/dysfunction? *Clinical Neuropsychology, 1,* 209-234.

Russell, J. (1997). How executive disorders can bring about an inadequate theory of mind. In J. Russell (Ed.), *Autism as an executive disorder* (pp. 256-304). New York: Oxford University Press.

Rutter, M. (2005a). Aetiology of autism: Findings and questions. *Journal of Intellectual Disability Research, 49,* 231-238.

Rutter, M. (2005b). Incidence of autism spectrum disorders: Changes over time and their meaning. *Acta Paediatrica, 94,* 2-15.

Schechter, R. C., & Grether, J. K. (2008). Continuing increase in autism reported in California's developmental services system: Mercury in retrograde. *Archives of General Psychiatry, 65,* 19-24.

Schopler, E., Mesibov, G. B., & Kunce, L. J. (Eds.). (1998). *Asperger syndrome or high functioning autism?* New York: Plenum Press.

Schuler, A. L., & Wolfberg, P. J. (2000). Promoting peer play and socialization: The art of scaffolding. In A. Wetherby & B. M. Prizant (Eds.), *Transactional foundations of language intervention* (pp. 251-277). Baltimore: Brookes Publishing.

Schwartz-Watts, D. M. (2005). Asperger's disorder and murder. *Journal of the American Academy of Psychiatry and the Law, 33,* 390-393.

Shallice, T. (2001). Theory of mind and the prefrontal cortex. *Brain, 24,* 247-248.

Shattuck, P. T. (2006). The contribution of diagnostic substitution to the growing administrative prevalence of autism in U.S. special education. *Pediatrics, 117,* 1028-1037.

Shields, J. (1991). Semantic-pragmatic disorder: A right hemisphere syndrome? *British Journal of Disorders of Communication, 26,* 383-392.

Silberman, S. (2001, December). The geek syndrome. *Wired, 9,* 11.

Southeastern Community College v. Davis, 442 US 397, 423 (1979).

Sparks, B. F., Friedman, S. D., Shaw, D. W. W., Aylward, E. H., Echelard, D., Artru, A. A., et al. (2002). Brain structural abnormalities in young children with autism spectrum disorder. *Neurology, 59,* 184-192.

Spiral Foundation. (2006). *Signs and symptoms of sensory processing disorder,* www.spiralfoundation.org.

Stokes, M., Nauton, N., & Kaur, A. (2007). Stalking and social and romantic functioning among adolescents and adults with autism spectrum disorder. *Journal of Autism and Developmental Disorders, 37,* 1969-1986.

Stratton, K., Gable, A., & McCormick, M. (Eds.). (2001a). *Immunization safety review: Measles-mumps-rubella vaccine and autism.* Washington, DC: National Academy Press.

Stratton, K., Gable, A., & McCormick, M. (Eds.) (2001b). *Immunization safety review: Thimerosal-containing vaccinations and neurodevelopmental disorders.* Washington, DC: National Academy Press.

Stuss, D. R. (2007). New approaches to prefrontal lobe testing. In J. L. Cummings & B. L. Miller (Eds.), *The human frontal lobes: Functions & disorders* (pp. 292-305). New York: The Guilford Press.

Szatmari, O., Bryson, S. E., Boyle, M. H., Streiner, D. L., & Duku, E. (2003). Predictors of outcome among high functioning children with autism and Asperger syndrome. *Journal of Child Psychology and Psychiatry, 44,* 520-528.

Tager-Flusberg, H. (1999). A psychological approach to understanding the social and language impairments in autism. *International Review of Psychiatry, 11,* 325-334.

Tager-Flusberg, H., & Joseph, R. M. (2003). Identifying neurocognitive phenotypes in autism. *Philosophical Transactions of the Royal Society of London, 358,* 303-314.

References

Tan, A. (2007). Meeting the needs of employers. *Graduan*, 109-111.

Tanguay, P. (2000). Pervasive developmental disorders: A 10 year review. *Journal of the American Academy of Child and Adolescent Psychiatry, 39*, 1079-1095.

Tanguay, P., Robertson, J., & Derrick, A. (1998). A dimensional classification of autism spectrum disorder by social communication domains. *Journal of the American Academy of Child and Adolescent Psychiatry, 37*, 271-277.

Tani, P., Lindberg, N., Nieminen-von Wendt, T., von Wendt, L., Alanko, L., Appelberg, B., et al. (2003). Insomnia is a frequent finding in adults with Asperger syndrome. *Biomedical Central: Psychiatry, 3*, 12-22.

Tantam, D. (1991). Asperger syndrome in adulthood. In U. Frith (Ed.), *Autism and Asperger Syndrome* (pp. 147-183). Cambridge, MA: Cambridge University Press.

Tantam, D. (2000). Psychological disorder in adolescents and adults with Asperger Syndrome. *Autism, 4*, 47-62.

Tantam, D., Holmes, D., & Cordess, C. (1993). Nonverbal expression in autism of Asperger type. *Journal of Autism and Developmental Disorders, 23*, 111-133.

Taylor, B., Miller, E., Farrington, C. P., Petropoulos, M. C., Favot Mayaud, I., Li, J., et al. (1999). Autism and measles, mumps and rubella vaccine: No epidemiological evidence for a causal association. *Lancet, 353*, 2026-2029.

Thierfeld Brown, L., & Wolf, L. E. (in press). Transition to higher education for students with autism spectrum disorders. In A. Klin, F. Volkmar, & S. Sparrow (Eds.), *Asperger Syndrome* (2nd ed.). New York: Guilford Press.

Towbin, K. E. (2003). Strategies for pharmacological treatment of high functioning autism and Asperger syndrome. *Child and Adolescent Psychiatric Clinics of North America, 12*, 23-45.

Tracing the origins of autism. (2006). *Environmental Health Perspectives, 114*, 7.

Tsatsanis, K. D., & Rourke, B.P. (2008). Syndrome of nonverbal learning disabilities in adults. In L. Wolf, H. Schreiber, & J. Wasserstein (Eds.), *Adult learning disorders: Contemporary issues* (pp. 159-190). London: Taylor & Francis.

U.S. Bureau of Labor Statistics. (2004). *Occupations with largest job growth 2004-2014.* http://www.bls.gov/opub/ted/2005/dec/wk3/art04.htm.

U.S. Department of Education. (2006). *Table 1-9. Children and students served under IDEA, Part B, in the U.S. and outlying areas by age group, year and disability category: Fall 1996 through fall 2005.* https://www.ideadata.org/tables29th/ar_1-9.htm.

Voeller, K. (1986). Right hemisphere deficit in children. *American Journal of Psychiatry, 143,* 1004-1009.

Volkmar, F. M., Klin, A., Schultz, R. T., Rubin, E., & Bronen, R. (1995). Clinical case conference: Asperger's disorder. *American Journal of Psychiatry, 157,* 262-267.

Wakefield, A. J. (1999). MMR vaccinations and autism. *Lancet, 354,* 949-950.

Wakefield, A. J. (2002). The gut-brain axis in childhood developmental disorders. *Journal of Pediatric Gastroenterology and Nutrition, 34,* 14-17.

Walker, D., Thompson, A., Zwaigenbaum, L., Goldberg, J., Bryson, S. E., Mahoney, W. J., et al. (2004). Specifying PDD-NOS: A comparison of PDD-NOS, Asperger syndrome, and autism. *Journal of the American Academy of Child and Adolescent Psychiatry, 43,* 172-180.

Weintraub, S., & Mesulam, M. (1983). Developmental learning disabilities of the right hemisphere: Emotional, interpersonal, and cognitive components. *Archives of Neurology, 40,* 463-468.

Wetherby, A. M., & Prizant, B. M. (Eds.). (2004). *Autism spectrum disorders: A transactional developmental perspective.* New York: Paul H. Brookes, Co.

References

Williams, D. (1996). *Autism: An inside-out approach. An innovative look at the 'mechanics' of 'autism' and its developmental 'cousins.'* London: Jessica Kingsley Publishers.

Williams, D. L., Goldstein, G., Kojkowski, N., & Minshew, N. J. (2007). Do individuals with high functioning autism have the IQ profile associated with nonverbal learning disability? *Research in Autism Spectrum Disorders, 2,* 353-361.

Wing, L. (1981). Asperger's syndrome: A clinical account. *Psychological Medicine, 11,* 115-130.

Wolf, L. E., & Kaplan, E. (2008). Executive functioning and self-regulation in young adults: Implications for neurodevelopmental learning disorders. In L. E. Wolf, H. Schreiber, & J. Wasserstein (Eds.), *Adult learning disorders: Contemporary issues* (pp. 219-246). New York: Psychology Press Taylor and Francis.

Wolf, L. E., Thierfeld Brown, Bork, R., & Shore, S. (2004, July). *Students with Asperger's Syndrome in higher education.* Presentation at the Association of Higher Education and Disabilities Annual Conference, Miami Beach, FL.

Wolf, L. E., & Thierfeld Brown, J. (2007, October). *Strategic education for students with Asperger Syndrome in higher education.* Presentation at the California Association for Postsecondary Education and Disability, Ventura Beach, CA.

Wolf, L. E., & Thierfeld Brown, J. (2008). *Strategic education for students with Asperger syndrome* (SEADS). Submitted for publication.

Wolf, L. E., Thierfeld Brown, J., & Bork, R. (2001). *Asperger's syndrome in college students.* Presentation at the conference of the Association for Higher Education and Disability, Portland, Oregon.

Wolf, L. E., & Wasserstein, J. (2001). Adult ADHD: Concluding thoughts. *Annals of the New York Academy of Sciences, 931,* 396-408.

223

Wolff, S., & Chick, J. (1980). Schizoid personality in childhood: A controlled follow-up study. *Psychological Medicine, 10,* 85-100.

Workforce2.org. *Job search, resumes & job interview guide.* http://www.workforce2.org/qualities-employers-look-for.htm.

World Health Organization. (1992). *International statistical classification of diseases and related health problems (ICD-10th revision).* Geneva, Switzerland: Author.

Wrightslaw, http://www.wrightslaw.com.

Wu, J. Y., Kuban, K. C., Allred, E., Shapiro, F., & Darras, B. T. (2005). Association of Duchene muscular dystrophy with autism spectrum disorder. *Journal of Child Neurology, 20,* 790-795.

Wynne v. Tufts Univ. School of Medicine, 932 F.2d 19, 26 (1st Cir. 1991).

Yeargin-Allsopp, M., Rice, C., Larapurkar, T., Doernberg, N., Boyle, C., & Murphy, C. (2003). Prevalence of autism in a U.S. metropolitan area. *Journal of the American Medical Association, 289,* 49-55.

Zilbovicius, M., Garreau, B., Samson, Y., Remy, P., Barthelemy, C., Syrota, A., et al. (1995). Delayed maturation of the frontal cortex in childhood autism. *American Journal of Psychiatry, 152,* 248-252.

Zwaigenbaum, L., Szatmari, P., Jones, M. B., Bryson, S. E., MacLean, J. E., Mahoney, W., et al. (2002). Pregnancy and birth complications in autism and liability to the broader autism phenotype. *Journal of the American Academy of Child and Adolescent Psychiatry, 41,* 572-579.

Appendices

Some Applied Clinical and Cognitive Science

Lorraine E. Wolf, Ph.D.

Cognitive Problems and AS

There are many theories of cognitive disability in AS; however, three have come to dominate the field. These include theory of mind (Baron-Cohen, 1999), central coherence (Frith, 2001), and executive functioning (Ozonoff, Pennington, & Rogers, 1991).

Theory of mind. Some authors describe the core deficit in autism spectrum disorders (ASD) as involving theory of mind, or the ability to appreciate that the contents of someone else's mind are different from one's own. This "interpersonal understanding" (Klin et al., 2007), "mentalizing" (Baron-Cohen, 1999, 2004), or "intuitive social knowledge" (Tanguay, Robertson, & Derrick, 1998) means having the ability to tell what other people are thinking or feeling and use that knowledge to predict or understand their behavior. Some believe that this is the true foundation of social discourse (Klin et al., 2007) and that the social difficulties in ASD stem from a failure to develop this skill. Klin proposes that, due to this basic deficit, the child with an ASD is not cued into the social world from the outset. Unlike the neurotypical individual, the AS brain is not wired to process and interpret social situations automatically (Klin, Jones, Schultz, & Volkmar, 2003; Rajendran & Mitchell, 2007). This may also be construed as not being able to put oneself in others' shoes, or a lack of empathy. Such difficulties might underlie the problems individuals with AS have in complex social situations, where the behavior of others is unpredictable (Rajendran & Mitchell, 2007). The person with AS may try to work out the interaction in a literal fashion, as he or she cannot look beyond the obvious in understanding what is going on.

Theory of mind can be directly tested by laboratory experiments that simulate social situations. For example, some studies have shown that individuals with AS do not infer the mental states of others by looking at pictures or by hearing tapes (Baron-Cohen et al., 1997, 1999). Other studies have shown that individuals with AS do well on such tasks (Klin, Jones, Schultz, Volkmar, & Cohen, 2002). The ability to perform on theory of mind tasks varies with age, intelligence, and severity of symptoms (Channon, Charman, Heap, Crawford, & Rios, 2001).

Some authors have proposed that executive function deficits may underlie difficulties in theory of mind (Shallice, 2001; Stuss, 2007). While deficits in executive functioning as well as theory of mind are often found in individuals with ASD, this is not always the case (Dawson, Meltzoff, Osterling, & Rinaldi, 1998). (Executive functioning will be discussed further below.)

Tager-Flusberg and colleagues have proposed that there are two components to theory of mind: one comprised of "social perception" and the other comprised of "social cognition" (Tager-Flusberg & Joseph, 2003). Tager-Flusberg (1999) proposes that individuals with classical autism are impaired in both areas, but those with AS are only impaired in social perception. In other words,

228

they know what to do in social situations but don't really "get" it. A model that encompasses different components of theory of mind might explain some of the inconsistencies in the research findings. Because studies have not shown that theory of mind is specific or universal in AS, it is unlikely that this can account for all of the core cognitive and social difficulties that are seen (Ozonoff, South, & Miller, 2000; Rajendran & Mitchell, 2007).

Central coherence. This theory may capture the often noted inability of the person with AS to successfully integrate large streams of information. Many studies have demonstrated that AS involves widespread deficits in integration and synthesis of sensory and other information (Baron-Cohen, 2004; Manoach, Sandson, & Weintraub, 1995; McAlonan et al., 2002). Rosenn (1999) hypothesized that this accounts for the rigidity seen in persons with AS. A rigid processing style and preference for sameness lessens the amount of novel information that must be integrated, thus minimizing anxiety.

Most individuals with AS tend to be highly attuned to details but miss the big picture because they do not put the pieces together faithfully. In other words, they miss the forest for the trees. They may process information in a piecemeal fashion, processing details rather than integrating them into a whole. This can especially affect facial processing (Klin, Sparrow, deBildt, Cicchetti, & Vollkmar, 1999). Psychologists refer to this as "gestalt processing," or the ability to integrate perceptual details into meaningful constructs (Baron-Cohen, 2004; Rajendran & Mitchell, 2007). Gestalt processing also encompasses the ability to process salient information against a background of irrelevant "noise" (e.g., picking up someone calling your name at a noisy party). Many individuals with AS have difficulty in this realm as well and may complain that the lecture hall is a cacophony of noise.

Executive dysfunction. Others have characterized the neurocognitive deficit in AS as one in that involves executive dysfunction (Hill, 2004; Ozonoff, 1997), which may manifest as a faulty internal organizational system. We stress executive function (EF) in our discussion below, not because we believe it is the best cognitive model of AS, but because deficits in EF are so central to the college difficulties in students with AS. By corollary, EF deficits are not impossible to accommodate and remediate. Indeed, doing so can greatly impact the success level of the student

The term "executive function" is often used to describe a set of behaviors attributed to systems in the frontal and subcortical regions of the brain (see Wolf & Kaplan, 2008; Wolf & Wasserstein, 2001, for reviews). Tasks associated with the executive system include self-reflection and control, inhibition, planning, flexibility, and delay of gratification (Stuss, 2007; also see Wolf & Kaplan, 2008, for review). In other words, EF permits the individual to adopt a more mature, forward-thinking stance and disengage from immediate concerns and rewards (Barkley, 1997; also see Wolf &Wasserstein, 2001, for reviews).

In addition to the familiar cognitive executive processes such as planning and shifting, a parallel system exists to regulate affect, motivation, and social-emotional functioning (Stuss, 2007; also see Wolf & Kaplan, 2008, for review). This system operates with cognitive EF and is thought to be involved in prioritizing and setting goals, adjusting behavior in accordance with intrinsic goals (adapting and shifting), emotional regulation, and self-awareness (Stuss, 2007). Finally, the regulatory system is intimately bound with language functioning.

To successfully navigate the world, adults use language to mediate rule-governed behavior. For example, we use verbal

230

self-reminding to stay on task, use inner speech to keep us motivated, and use "self-talk" to maintain response rules and goals in memory. This allows us to understand social rules and mores and use them to guide behavior, such as reminding oneself that a conversation with a boss calls for different behavior than one with a classmate in the residence hall. This ability to use language to guide regulatory and executive systems in ongoing behavior develops gradually over the life span, as the child learns to internalize the rules of the adult world and use self-directed speech in the service of self-regulation.

AS and EF. Executive dysfunction may account for some of the inflexibility seen in persons with AS, especially in social and language functioning. Deficits in impulse control, attention control, planning, shifting, and inhibition have been noted in individuals with AS (Manoach, Lindgren, & Barton, 2004; McAlonan et al., 2002). One study found that children with ASD did not use language to develop rules to guide behavior (Joseph et al., 2005a, 2005b). In other words, they did not use self-talk to regulate their behavior.

Taken together, these studies suggest that AS may be characterized by selective deficits in EF, including poor performance on complex verbal tasks that require switching and initiation of efficient strategies (Kleinhans & Akshoomoff, 2005), and failure to use language to guide behavior when tasks are novel or complex (Hill, 2004). Thus, regulatory problems in AS may involve both executive functioning (poor integration and synthesis, rigidity, missing the bigger picture, deficits in planning, shifting, inhibiting, and prioritizing) and self-regulation (taking another's perspective, social agency, initiation and self-direction, and motivation).

Developmental Course of Symptoms

Early Course

The course and presentation of AS varies considerably with age. While in retrospect some babies who are later diagnosed with ASD are described as being fussy and easily overstimulated, there are no good early predictors of which babies or toddlers might later be diagnosed with an ASD. Some parents report that there was little spontaneous smiling or eye contact, and that the infant was not responsive to social approaches (turns away or cries). Sleep and eating have been described as problematic (Lord & Risi, 2000). Studies of early family movies are ongoing (Maestro et al., 2001) and may eventually find such early markers. Early patterns may be characterized by a general lack of normal developmental signs, such as lack of reciprocal play, joint attention, or interest in peers (Carpenter, Nagell, & Tomosello, 1998; Charman, 2003; Lord & Risi, 2000).

Compared to other autistic diagnoses, AS tends to be diagnosed somewhat later, usually at about age 10 or 11 (Frith, 2004). Parents of youngsters with classical autism typically notice symptoms by about 18 months of age; however, parents of children later diagnosed as AS often do not recognize symptoms before age 3 (Chakrabarti & Fombonne, 2001; Frith, 2004). It has been speculated that early symptoms do not alarm some parents who may share some autistic traits with their children and thus do not see the behaviors as abnormal (Frith, 2004). Further, good language skills in a young child may lead parents and pediatricians away from a diagnosis on the autism spectrum, whereas challenging behaviors or learning problems may be misdiagnosed as an attention deficit disorder or learning disability. Due to increased awareness of atypical symptoms, this may be changing.

Early childhood symptoms may include precocious language, delayed echolalia (repeating phrases memorized from TV shows or conversations), highly systematized interests (lining up cars or toys), adherence to rituals or special interests, repetitive play, and lack of pretend play. There may be little or no interest in playing with other children. On the other hand, some children may be described as overly imaginative or gifted intellectually, especially if their play is fantasy- and language-based rather than pretend. Motor clumsiness or immaturity such as abnormal reflexes, poor gait or balance, and delayed walking may predate social and language symptoms (Leary & Hill, 1996; see also Nayate et al., 2005, for a review). Perseverative behaviors such as hand flapping, staring, or spinning objects may be present, although this tends to diminish somewhat with age. Poor attention to faces, including those of parents and caregivers, may be present (Dawson et al., 1998; Klin et al., 1999). By corollary, there may be no variation in facial expression and use of gesture to communicate on the part of the child. Such early disturbances of social skills and social cognition are thought to be an early defining symptom (Baron-Cohen et al., 1999).

There may also be early sensory problems, including easy startling to loud sounds, aversion to smells, or resistance to touch (stroking or even hugging). Some children present with severe sensory integration difficulties that make daily care such as bathing, hair washing, or toilet training intolerable to them. Symptoms may wax and wane depending on the context, increasing in unfamiliar or stimulating environments (such as birthday parties, family celebrations, restaurants, or the circus) and decreasing in familiar environments like home or daycare. This variability in presentation often confuses caregivers and extended family members, who see such behaviors as willful evidence of a spoiled child rather than someone who is overwhelmed by his or her sensory and social environments.

Early School Years

Compared to the general absence of some normal signs in young children, older children with ASD may be best characterized as having an excess of certain features (such as overly sensitive, repetitive language, or obsessional play) (Attwood, 2007). Poor frustration tolerance and peer difficulties increase with age as children begin to enter the school environment. They may become more rigid and anxious as their environments demand greater flexibility.

In middle school, social and peer conflicts may become prominent, and children may become victims of bullies, socially marginalized, or withdrawn. Further, school demands for organization and independent learning becomes challenging for the child with AS and executive dysfunction.

Children with good early reading skills may not be picked up for early diagnosis, whereas those with challenging behaviors may be better recognized. Aspects related to nonverbal learning disability may appear around age 10, and social difficulties plus increasing academic demands may result in oppositional or defiant behavior. These factors may drive the comprehensive evaluation, which ultimately makes the correct diagnosis.

High School

Many adults with AS recall high school as the worst time in their lives. Social pressures, peer demands, emphasis on physical appearance and clothes, clubs, cliques, and dating are so much part of the landscape of high school. Adolescents with AS may be socially outcast or rejected although they may crave friends and dates. However, some do well with one or two longtime friends.

In addition, there is less adult supervision in class and at home, which may result in more opportunities for being bullied or victimized.

The lack of structure coupled with increasing academic demands may bring academic deficits into focus for the first time. Difficulties in planning, time management, and other executive skills may derail academic efforts in high school students. Attention problems may be prominent as well (Attwood, 2007). Students may become depressed and withdrawn at this point, and suicide is not uncommon in adolescents with AS. Psychiatric difficulties may be more prominent in boys at this age (Holtmann, Bolte, & Poustka, 2007). Insomnia is common, which can attribute to emotional distress and poor overall functioning in adolescents and adults with AS (Tani et al., 2003).

College Students
Many students with AS describe college as a vast improvement over high school. College-age students are more tolerant of individual differences, and students can usually find others who share their common interests. Nonetheless, certain unique behaviors are commonly seen in this age group.

Difficulties in communication, poor eye contact, and unusual gestures are among the first characteristics that mark the young adult with AS as different. He or she may not answer questions when directly addressed and typically does not engage in social small talk. This might appear as odd or off-putting to a new college roommate or floor mate casually inquiring who this person is and what he or she is interested in.

Adults with AS are often described as self-absorbed or selfish, demonstrating a disregard for others (although typically they want friends and spouses) (Frith, 2004). The individual with AS may not appear to be listening to a conversational partner and appear bored, rude, and aloof. Further, the use of stilted or outmoded phrases or parroting back what was asked appears odd or different to other young people. Alternately, the student with AS may stare or stand too close, appearing threatening or scary.

This young person may misunderstand cues signaling when a conversation is over and when he or she should leave. Misreading social signals marks one as odd or different. The inability to communicate reciprocally, including being able to stop talking about one's special interests and inquiring about somebody else's interests, may result in social rejection. Repeated experiences of this kind are demoralizing and, when coupled with stress in unfamiliar situations, confusion, and overload, may cause serious depression. Not surprisingly, therefore, depression and chronic anxiety are common symptoms in adolescents and young adults with AS (Ghaziuddin et al., 2002; Green, Gilchrist, Burton, & Cox, 2000; Holtmann et al., 2007).

Because of deficits in theory of mind, it is often difficult for the young adult with AS to put himself in another's shoes, to empathize with somebody else's experiences, take another's perspective, share, or cooperate fully. It is this quality that others perceive as selfishness or coldness (Frith, 2004; Tantam, 1991). When this is coupled with an obsessive interest or preoccupation with one particular area, the ability to empathize and participate in reciprocal friendship becomes challenging. Indeed, this failure of empathy restricts the degree to which a young person with AS can develop meaningful social relationships.

Assessment and AS

Most children with ASD are referred to specialists by age 2 or 3, but often it is later depending on the severity of symptoms and how they change during development. Typically, difficulties in language development (even sometimes a loss of previous language milestones) or relatedness (disinterest in cooperative play patterns) are causes for assessment in younger children. In older children, learning problems and oppositional behavior are common causes for assessment. In teens, depression, anxiety, social isolation, and lack of motivation are common referral reasons.

A multidisciplinary assessment approach is often critical for the child's success. The child or adolescent team should optimally include a neuropsychologist, a speech-language pathologist, an occupational therapist, and academic specialists. A behavioral neurologist, psychiatrist, and/or developmental pediatrician may also be consulted. Severe autistic disorders are rarely missed, but less severe ones, such as AS, are often misdiagnosed. Involving a team of specialists early helps to obtain an accurate diagnosis. The earlier a treatment plan is put in place and the more comprehensive it is, the better the prognosis.

Methods of Assessment and What They Tell Us
Each of the various assessments that individuals with AS may undergo contributes separately to understanding the wide-ranging manifestations of the condition. We suggest that the DS professional pay attention to all evaluations presented, as each can add considerably to an understanding of the student. We will briefly discuss some of these evaluations below.

Speech and language. Assessment in this area is more commonly conducted on younger students than on young adults. It may be particularly useful when pragmatic and language deficits are present. This type of assessment may lead directly to recommendations for social language or conversational remediation. Many speech-language pathologists have considerable experience in diagnosing conditions which may either accompany or resemble AS, such as pragmatic language deficits and hyperlexia.

A comprehensive speech and language assessment will test hearing and thoroughly assess both expressive and receptive language, including word and sound reception, vocabulary, grammatical understanding and use, level of language organization, organization of discourse and conversational capacity, as well as pragmatic and paralinguistic aspects of speech. Important information may be derived, including the level and nature of pragmatic difficulties and language organization, both of which can seriously impede college learning. Difficulties in language processing may warrant accommodations such as note takers, clarification of oral directions, or written instructions. Many speech-language professionals possess expertise in remediation of EF deficits in children and adults, and their assistance should be sought when appropriate.

Occupational therapy (OT). OT evaluations are more common in younger individuals with AS. Many OTs are specially trained in the evaluation of young children with AS-like conditions such as sensory integration dysfunction and motor dyspraxia (American Occupational Association, 2008). A thorough OT evaluation will elaborate on any sensory or motor difficulties present, leading to recommendations for intervention. Particularly useful is the construction of a "sensory diet," or an elaboration of the sorts of sensory sensitivities an individual may possess, along with recommendations for adjustments that can lessen their impact. These might include substituting incandescent bulbs for fluorescent lights, eliminating perfume in the classroom, or moving a lecture to a quieter environment.

Psychoeducational assessment. This type of assessment is geared towards evaluating and diagnosing learning disabilities. As such, it is typically limited to assessment of intelligence and academic ability based upon the IQ-achievement discrepancy model that governs eligibility for special education for students with LD. Since college students with AS are not usually classically learning disabled, this limited assessment is often not useful (unless it is the only measure of intelligence or academic function available).

Deep analysis of the learning profile may accompany higher quality psychoeducational assessments, which may be useful in understanding particular academic weaknesses (such as ability to decode unfamiliar versus familiar words). Psychoeducational assessments typically do not assess any co-existing disorders such as psychiatric or medical conditions (Gillberg & Billstedt, 2000) and are rarely able to accurately diagnose AS.

Psychological assessment. This typically encompasses assessment of intelligence and personality. The former is assessed with traditional IQ tests, the latter with rating scales, interviews, and projective tests such as the Rorschach. This type of evaluation is designed to elucidate the emotional and psychological functioning of the individual. In some cases, a clinical psychiatric diagnosis will be made. In others, the assessment will highlight areas of conflict but stop short of formal diagnosis. We do not find this assessment particularly useful in documentation of AS, unless the psychologist is formally trained in this differential diagnosis and unless the assessment contains instruments that might highlight features of AS (such as some of the standardized rating scales to be discussed below).

Neuropsychological assessment. This is our preferred mode of documentation. Neuropsychologists possess advanced training in evaluating brain-behavior disorders. As such, these professionals are best able to integrate developmental, medical, family history, clinical (psychiatric), and objective test data in (a) establishing a diagnosis of AS or (b) documenting the areas of functional impairment in an individual diagnosed by another professional. For example, the neuropsychologist will be able to tease out processing deficits that might be due to AS but also might be complicated by co-existing sleep disorder and depression.

A thorough neuropsychological assessment will include measures of intelligence and academic achievement, as well as individual tests of attention, perception, sensory processing, motor functioning and motor planning, language and verbal skills, nonverbal and spatial skills, memory, complex problem solving, and executive functioning. Results will be analyzed against the background of a very detailed personal, family, medical, and psychiatric history. The findings will often lead to recommendations for various medical and non-medical interventions as well as thorough recommendations for academic accommodations.

Psychiatric assessment. Conducted by a medical professional, this type of assessment typically comprises a combination of interviews, history, and rating scales. Many standardized rating scales such as the Autism Diagnostic Schedule (Lord, Rutter, Dilavore, & Risi, 2001) and the Adult Asperger Assessment (Baron-Cohen, Wheelwright, Robinson, & Woodbury-Smith, 2005) are available for use in adults. It is difficult to find adult psychiatrists familiar with making a diagnosis of AS in many communities, especially those without access to large medical centers with research and training facilities. In our area, some young persons wait up to three years to see one of the several renowned psychiatrists specializing in this kind of assessment. Ideally, this will change with more psychiatrists receiving training in identifying and treating adults with AS spectrum disorders.

In addition to diagnosing AS, psychiatric assessment may be particularly useful for identifying and treating associated psychiatric and emotional conditions, such as anxiety or panic disorders, depression, suicidality, and OCD. We strongly suggest that all adults with AS diagnoses be evaluated by a psychiatrist if they are at an emotionally vulnerable transition point, or if there is strong personal or family history of severe symptoms of depression or anxiety.

Treatment and Interventions

Most individuals with AS have or continue to receive a combination of treatments. One guiding principle is that early and intensive intervention is the most effective (Howlin, 2005). Thus, we see college students who have had 15 years or more of intensive and varied interventions that have optimally changed with their needs. We will briefly outline some of the common interventions that young adults with AS may have had in the past, as well as some current treatment practices.

Medications

Adolescents and adults with AS may be prescribed medications for symptom control. This is especially the case if prominent behavioral disturbances are present (such as aggression or self-injury), prominent anxiety symptoms, or depression. Many young adults with AS are treated with antidepressant medications, stimulants, or other attention-enhancing medications, anti-anxiety medications, or even antipsychotics (Findling, 2005; Towbin, 2003).

Educational Intervention

Along with formal and informal education plans, many students have worked with cognitive remediation specialists or strategy tutors to improve their academic fluency and organization. These have often been provided by the school district; however, once the child reaches college age, this sort of service may come at extra expense to the family. The needs of the student with AS for educational coaching can overwhelm the resources of the DS office or college tutoring services, and community resources should be sought where possible.

If a student has been accustomed to this sort of individual attention, we suggest that all efforts be made to keep it in place through key transition points. Cognitive and regulatory strategies (including time management, organizing, breaking assignments down, tracking, feedback, etc.) should be addressed early and continue beyond the initial transition to college. Strategy tutoring should proceed with the awareness that students with AS may not be able to use strategies flexibly or know when to shift among different strategies they have been taught due to their executive and other cognitive deficits.

Psychotherapies

Because of its high demand for interpersonal contact and revelation, young adults with AS may not be particularly good candidates for insight-oriented psychotherapy. However, considerable benefit may be derived from cognitive and/or behavioral treatment to reduce symptoms (Myles, 2003). Strategies for stress reduction and stress management may be beneficial, particularly if they can be taught in a programmatic or scripted fashion. Many students with AS have also benefited from social skills training with a therapist, in that they learned to model social behaviors, and learn scripts for particular interactions. We suggest that counseling centers on campus be targeted for training so as to better recognize and respond to the therapeutic needs of students with AS.

Adjunctive Services

In earlier years and sometimes into college, many students with AS have benefited from adjunctive services, such as speech and language therapy, and occupational and physical therapy. Pragmatic language groups are often useful through the teen years (Abele, 2006) in that participants learn modes of social communication and how to monitor their language behavior in a supportive group. This may continue as social coaching in the young adult.

While effective in reducing sensory sensitivities and aversions in young children (American Occupational Association, 2008), there is no evidence that sensory integration therapy by an OT is effective in adults. However, it may be useful for a young adult to be assessed to develop a "sensory diet" that teaches the individual how to recognize sensory overload and how to cope with sensitivities. Occupational therapy for fine- and gross-motor deficits, handwriting, and motor planning similarly can be very effective in children but to date few studies have examined its effectiveness in adults (Kinnealey, Oliver, & Wilbarger, 1995).

Alternative Treatments

Alternative treatments include dietary restrictions (such as casein- and gluten-free diets), vitamin and mineral supplements, detoxification and chelation, EEG neurofeedback, Irlen lenses, auditory integration therapy, and vision therapy. Most alternative treatments claim to be based on theories of underlying cause (e.g., detoxification of heavy metals in the body by chelation or improving brain wave integration by auditory retraining). Many websites and practitioners make great claims as to their success. Families of children with disabilities are especially vulnerable to claims suggesting that their children will be cured. Unfortunately, it is not often possible to differentiate between alterative treatments that may hold promise and others that are unfounded.

We are not aware of alterative treatments for AS that have been subjected to the rigors of scientific study and publication in the peer review literature. Most insurance companies do not consider these medically proven interventions, and some professional organizations (such as the American Speech and Hearing Association and the American Academy of Ophthalmology) disavow claims to treatment validity. (It should be noted that many feel sensory integration therapy also falls into this category.) Many alternative treatments appear to be harmless; however, some may be less benign.

It is not our intent to advocate for or against any particular treatment regimen. As with all treatments, we advocate a cautious approach and suggest that families and others do their own research, ask for professional assistance in interpreting the scientific and nonscientific literatures, and seek the advice of medical and other professionals before undertaking any intervention of this type.

Some Basic Science

Lorraine E. Wolf, Ph.D.

Etiology

It is now well accepted that AS is a genetic neurodevelopmental disorder. Although rare, similar symptoms have been known to occur in other medical conditions, such as Fragile X, tuberous sclerosis, and Duchene's muscular dystrophy (Wu, Kuban, Allred, Shapiro, & Darras, 2005; see Rutter, 2005b, for a review). A major problem in interpreting the literature is that until 1994, there was no diagnostic standard for AS. Therefore, it is difficult to interpret earlier studies, which may have included subjects who would not meet the current diagnostic criteria.

Genetic hypotheses. Many lines of evidence point to genetic factors in the etiology of AS. Like all genetic neurodevelopmental disorders, there appears to be a complex interaction between genetic susceptibility (an autism susceptibility gene, or more likely multiple genes) and some (as yet unknown) environmental factor (Ashwood & Van de Water, 2004; Bailey et al., 1995; London & Etzel, 2000). Asperger Syndrome has been referred to as the "geek syndrome" (Silberman, 2001), as spikes of AS are seen especially in regions heavily populated by people in the high-tech industry in the Northeast and Silicon Valley. It was asserted that these individuals may carry a lesser variant of autism and are passing this along to their offspring.

Because of these groupings, some researchers attribute the increase in incidence to a phenomenon known as "assortative mating," or the notion that like is attracted to like (spectrum folks marry spectrum folks; see Baron-Cohen, 1997, 2005). It has been speculated that individuals with AS of both genders whose oddness or solitary nature otherwise may have precluded marriage and child rearing are now working together in high-tech industries and producing offspring with a greater incidence of autism (Silberman, 2001). Indeed, the fathers and grandfathers (both maternal and paternal) of individuals with AS are twice as likely to be employed as engineers (Baron-Cohen et al., 1997), lending some support to this hypothesis.

Twin studies reveal that individuals with ASD share common genes. Thus, identical twins (with the same genetic material) are much more likely to develop an ASD if one member of the twin pair is affected (Bailey et al., 1995; Folstein & Rutter, 1977). The risk of autism in identical twins may be as high as 92% (either classical autism or a milder variant) compared to 10% in fraternal twin pairs (Bailey et al., 1995; Folstein & Rutter, 1977). The fact that one member of the twin pair is not autistic indicates that the condition is not directly inherited but that there is an interaction with some other factor in the environment.

The non-autistic twin often has a mild form of cognitive impairment, including social and communication deficits. Siblings, including fraternal twins, of individuals with ASD also have a rate of autism that is much greater than that of the general population (reviewed in Dawson et al., 2002). Further, the non-autistic siblings of individuals with autism may have a milder version of the disorder, often described as the "broader autism phenotype" (Piven, 2001; Piven et al., 1997a, 1997b). Thus, autistic traits may be present in the unaffected relatives of autistic individuals. Again, as in other genetic neurodevelopmental disorders such as schizophrenia, it is possible that it is this broader autism phenotype that is inherited, with the secondary environmental hit producing autism in susceptible individuals (London & Etzel, 2000).

Piven and colleagues (1997, 2001) have demonstrated that parents in families with multiple autistic offspring have a characteristic personality type, including aloofness, rigidity, and anxiety; few close friends; deficits in pragmatic language, trouble understanding nonverbal cues; and difficulty with planning and shifting among different cognitive set (Piven 2001; Piven et al., 1997b). Thus, Piven has characterized the broader autism phenotype as involving four factors: (a) communication deficits, (b) cognitive deficits, (c) anxious and rigid behaviors, and (d) social deficits. This supports other research (Folstein, Gilman, Landa, Hein, & Santangelo, 1999) that characterized the autism phenotype as a combination of social reticence, pragmatic language difficulty, and resistance to change. An early history of language disorder or delay, decreased verbal fluency, repetitive behaviors, depression, and anxiety has been shown in parents and siblings as well (Bailey, Palferman, Heavey, & LeCouteur, 1998; Bolton et al., 1994).

Autistic traits may thus be present in the unaffected relatives (twins, siblings, parents, grandparents) of the autistic individual. These include difficulties with facial recognition, social motivation, imitative motions, memory, executive functioning (including planning and flexibility), and language (specifically phonological processing, or the processing of individual word sounds) (Bolton et al., 1994; Dawson et al., 2002). It is important to note that not all studies have demonstrated this, perhaps because of differences in study design (interviewing family members about other family members versus direct assessment) (Piven, 2001). It has also been speculated that the presence of mild autistic features in the parents of autistic individuals underlies outdated and damaging hypotheses that emotional rejection and coldness in the mother (the refrigerator mother) produced autism (Bettelheim, 1967).

Traits that cluster in families provide many clues about the underlying genetic mechanisms involved. Candidate genes have been found on multiple chromosomes. Some research has proposed that the interaction of multiple genes that affect different features of autism spectrum disorders may combine to produce the full picture of autism (Dawson et al., 2002; Muhle, Trentacoste, & Rapin, 2007). This may account for the variability in symptoms in AS.

Nongenetic hypothesis. Not everyone believes that AS is a genetic disorder. Some of the nongenetic theories have attracted a lot of media and governmental attention. Some areas are well studied from a scientific perspective, while others are much less rigorously researched. Nongenetic theories coalesce around environmental influences, citing several causes, including an abnormal immune response, diet and food allergies, diagnostic over-identification, vaccinations, or exposure to thimerisol or mercury poisoning (Bolton et al., 1997; Croen et al., 2002; Evers, Novotny, & Hollander, 2003; Geier & Geier, 2003). It is important to point out that environmental risk factors, even if present, do not preclude the possibility of genetic risk as well. In other words, environmental risk factors may operate on a genetically susceptible individual. It is even possible that different external risk factors can affect different individuals differently.

Perinatal complications. Obstetrical complications have been reported in some studies. Mothers of autistic children have been reported to have a higher rate of such complications as advanced maternal age, bleeding, intrauterine infections, and fetal distress to name a few (Glasson et al., 2004; Rutter, 2005a). Interestingly, more birth complications are found with individuals who are lower functioning than those who are higher functioning (Glasson et al., 2004). However, some have speculated that the birth complications themselves are the response to a genetically abnormal pregnancy and thus are not causally related to development of autism (Bolton et al., 1997; Rutter, 2005a; Zwaigenbaum et al., 2002).

Medical conditions. Less commonly, autism diagnoses can be related to a known medical condition such as Duchene's muscular dystrophy, Fragile X, or a metabolic disorder (Gillberg, 1992; Gillberg & Coleman, 1996; Rutter, 2005a). Medical etiologies are reported to be more common in individuals with classical autism and mental retardation than in diagnoses such as AS (Barton & Volkmar, 1998). It is likely that only a small number of cases of autism are related to medical diagnosis, however (Rutter, 2005a).

Autoimmune reaction. Some studies have suggested an autoimmune reaction against the developing nervous system in individuals with ASD (Ashwood & Van de Water, 2004). High frequencies of autoimmune diseases (such as thyroid disorder and lupus) have been reported in the families (especially the mothers) of individuals with ASD (Money, Bobrow, & Clark, 1971). Some have proposed that maternal antibodies attack the developing central nervous system (Croen et al., 2005). However, not all studies show increased rates of autoimmune disorders in the first-degree relatives of individuals with ASD (Micali et al., 2004), and it is unlikely that material autoimmune disease confers much risk for development of autism (Croen, Grether, Hoshida, Oduli, & Van de Water, 2005).

In addition to familiar clusters of autoimmune disorders, individuals with ASD often have immune dysregulation, including antibodies targeted against proteins in their own brains (reviewed in Ashwood & Van de Water, 2004; Quigley & Hurly, 2000). While the immune system plays a role in early brain development and can cause developmental changes (Ashwood & Van der Water, 2004), the relationship between autoimmunity and autism is far from clear (Tracing the Origins of Autism, 2006). It is possible that antibodies are actually a marker for nonspecific brain abnormality rather than a causal factor in development of autism (Ashwood & Van de Water, 2004).

Autoimmune reactions have also been hypothesized to affect the intestinal tract in individuals with ASD. Thus, autoimmune colitis and other intestinal disorders are common in ASD (Reichelt, Scott, & Ekrem, 1990; Rutter, 2005b). Antibodies to intestinal cells have been found, leading some to speculate that abnormal immune systems cause autism (Wakefield, 1999, 2002). It has been suggested that environmental toxins may provoke an immune response and thus influence brain development (Ashwood & Van der Water, 2004). It has also been suggested that an autoimmune gastrointestinal condition permits the entrance of environmental or other toxins into the bloodstream, which then disrupt brain development (Wakefield, 1999). This hypothesis has not been supported, however (see Rutter, 2005b, for a review).

Autoimmune theories have been invoked in the well-publicized (but unfounded) link between autism and vaccinations, especially the presence of thimerisol (a heavy metal related to mercury) in some vaccination preparations. Thimerisol has been shown to affect the immune system and brain development in mice and to produce an autistic-like behavior. We will discuss this further below.

250

Environmental toxins. It is well understood that multiple chemicals permeate our world that have the potential to damage the developing brain. For example, we know that heavy metals (lead, mercury), pesticides, PCBs, and certain drugs are potentially neurotoxic. Children's brains are more susceptible to toxins than those of adults, and developing brains are more vulnerable still (Evers, Novotny, & Hollander, 2003; Tracing the Origins of Autism, 2006). The possible effect of environmental toxins in the etiology of autism has raised much alarm (often unfounded). For example, one study (CDC, 2000; Goldman & Koduru, 2000) found a high rate of autism diagnoses in one industrialized area with many superfund sites but failed to find any association with environmental contaminants.

Some studies have focused on the toxic effects of medications administered during pregnancy. It has been shown that thalidomide (Stromland, Nordin, Miller, Akerstrom, & Gillberg, 1994) and other drugs, including valproic acid (an anticonvulsant), may produce autistic-like conditions (Tracing the Origins of Autism, 2006). It is possible that toxins influence brain development through their effects on the immune system or that the toxins directly damage the developing brain. It is also possible that a small subgroup of genetically vulnerable children is sensitive to different types of toxic exposures (Tracing the Origins of Autism, 2006). To date, no studies have documented any specific toxic risk factor for autism. This important area needs additional rigorous study.

Vaccinations. One of the potential toxins that has generated a great deal of press is thimerisol, a derivative of ethyl mercury, which is used as a preservative in some vaccination preparations (Rutter, 2005b). Since ethyl mercury is a known neurotoxin, some have concluded that thimerisol given in multiple doses to children through the battery of vaccinations they receive in the first three years of life must be a culprit in the development of autistic symptoms.

Most studies, however, fail to find an association between thimerisol and autism (see Rutter, 2005b, for a review; also see Institutes of Medicine, 2004). Thus, we would expect that if there were a direct relationship between the two, rates of autism would decline in countries that have eliminated thimerisol (Rutter, 2005b). However, no such relationship has been found (Rutter, 2005b). As a precaution, the American Academy of Pediatrics recommended delimitation of thimerisol from vaccinations in the United States (CDC, 1999). Again, we would expect a decrease in the rates of autism following this step. However, the opposite was recently reported. The rate of autism continued to climb even after removal of thimerisol from most vaccinations in the United States (Schecheter & Grether, 2008).

Other fears about vaccinations and autism have coalesced around the reported link between autism and the measles-mumps-rubella (MMR) vaccination (DeStafano et al., 2004). This was compounded by the findings of Wakefield (1999), who reported acute development of autistic behaviors within weeks of being administered the MMR vaccination. Wakefield proposed that the presence of colitis allowed toxins into the bloodstream, which affected the brain acutely (a subsequent study revised this to a delayed effect; see Rutter, 2005b). This hypothesis has generated considerable concern among parent advocacy groups, some researchers, and the online community and has brought the issue to the awareness of the federal government, in the United States and abroad. Indeed, the United States has begun vaccination injury hearings to address the claims by many parents that routinely administered vaccinations resulted in their child's autism.

Despite these fears, considerable bodies of research have found no relationship between the MMR vaccination and autism (Fombonne & Chakrabarti, 2001; Rutter, 2005b; Taylor et al., 1999). At the request of Congress, the CDC, the Institutes of Medicine, and a panel of experts reviewed the existing studies and found no evidence to support this link (Rutter, 2005; Stratton, Gable, & McCormick, 2001a, 2001b). Even so, Sir Michael Rutter, one of the world's authorities on autism, cautions that there may be a link that is not understood in the etiology of autism for a small number of individuals (Rutter, 2005b).

Brain abnormalities. Brain abnormalities in ASD have been demonstrated through neuroanatomical studies, brain imaging studies, and studies of brain function. Not all studies have detected brain abnormality in ASD, and when present most report such abnormalities to be subtle overall, rather than dramatic as in brain injury. In addition, changes are found in the structure of brain cells in some areas of the brain, suggesting that the brain changes are of very early neurodevelopmental origin (perhaps in the first months of pregnancy) (Rodier, 1998). This has important implications for some speculation about the causes of autism by suggesting that the developmental brain changes far predate exposure to such factors as toxins, vaccinations, mercury, and the like.

It is unlikely that brain changes are restricted to a single brain region. Rather, multiple brain regions have been found to be affected, including the frontal lobes, the cerebellum, right hemisphere structures, and limbic structures (underlying emotional behavior and some aspects of memory). Very exciting new research indicates the existence of "mirror neurons," which typically are active when we imitate someone, may be abnormal in ASD, perhaps underlying some of the deficits in empathy (DiCicco-Bloom et al., 2006). Baron-Cohen has also hypothesized dysfunction in limbic-frontal lobe circuitry affecting social and emotional behavior (Baron-Cohen et al., 1999). Let us review some basic brain facts to ground further discussion.

Brain facts. The human cortex is comprised of two hemispheres, the right and the left, and four lobes (frontal, temporal, parietal, and occipital), which are involved in sensory and information processing, language, memory, and complex higher functioning. The cortex is connected to important motor and emotional centers in the middle (medial) and lower (subcortical) sections of the brain and in the brainstem by networks of grey matter (cell bodies and structures) and white matter (nerve fibers) tracts. At the back of the brain lies the cerebellum, which is important in producing skilled motor patterns, synchrony, and sequencing of movement and thought.

The brain is comprised of gray matter (nerve cells or neurons) and white matter (nerve fibers). Nerve cells contain the important biological machinery to produce nerve signals (including neurochemical, neurotransmitters, and nerve endings). Nerve signals are transmitted between neurons via white matter fibers. These nerve fibers are wrapped in an insulating material called myelin, which serves to increase the speed of nerve signaling. It is the white color of myelin that gives white matter its name. White matter facilitates communication both within and between hemispheres, thus serving an important integrative function. The right hemisphere of the brain contains a larger proportion of white matter than gray matter compared to the left hemisphere. White matter is thought to be more susceptible to damage by disease, development, or injury than gray matter. Thus, the right hemisphere may be more vulnerable to white matter damage than the left hemisphere.

The left hemisphere of the brain is thought to be specialized for rapidly processing sequentially ordered information. This makes it ideal for such activities as language processing and for controlling complex motor patterns. The left hemisphere is thought to play a large role in processing details.

The right hemisphere of the brain is thought to be involved in the processing of spatial information due to its preference for nonlinear information. In other words, it is specialized for processing information simultaneously as opposed to the left hemisphere's specialization for rapid sequential processing. The right hemisphere appears to serve an integrative role between and across cognitive domains and sensory modalities. It is thought to be involved in constructing brain maps of the body and of space and to play a large role in attention and novel problem solving. Further, it is specialized to process nonlinguistic information, such as music, faces, rhythms, patterns, and emotions. Thus, it is specialized to put together the big picture (or to construct gestalts).

Brain development and size. Normal brain development is characterized by an initial overgrowth followed by systematic pruning. Children with AS have been shown to have enlarged heads and big brains as infants and toddlers (Akshoomoff, Pierce, & Courchesne, 2002), although this enlargement has been found to be age dependent (Piven, Arndt, Bailey, & Andreasen, 1996; Redcay & Courchesne, 2005). Many (but not all) studies have found that head circumference is normal at birth; however, circumference may increase as much as 10% by age 4-5. Typically, this normalizes by about age 6-7, although some individuals with AS continue to show head enlargement (Redcay & Courchesne, 2005). This reflects regional increase in both white and grey matter in the cerebral cortex and cerebellum (Courchesne, Karns, Davis, Ziccardi, & Carper, 2001; DiCicco-Bloom, et al., 2006; Herbert, 2003).

Some (but not all) studies document that overall brain weight is increased in children with ASD that appears to normalize with age (Bauman & Kemper, 1994; Sparks et al., 2002). Brain growth dysregulation appears to occur especially in the frontal lobes and cerebellar areas. Following accelerated early growth (Dawson et al., 2002), there is an arrest in development of grey and white matter. There may be restricted pruning in the frontal lobe (Frith, 2003) as well as a slower rate of frontal lobe white matter development (Carper, Moses, Tigue, & Courchesne, 2002). Decreased volume in the frontal lobes, subcortical movement regions, and the cerebellum has been associated with the movement disorders seen in ASD (Courchesne et al., 2001; McAlonan et al., 2002). Others have demonstrated volume differences in the cerebellum and medial temporal lobe (Sparks et al., 2002). Courchesne and colleagues (2001) hypothesized that fronto-cerebellar circuitry underlying social processing is often disrupted during the first years of life in AS.

The development of other brain regions has been implicated; however, research findings have been inconsistent on this point. Debate continues over whether increased prefrontal white matter disrupts inter-regional communication (Herbert, 2003) and whether cerebellar changes (such as smaller white matter tracts) affect the synchrony and timing of skilled motor movements (Damasio & Mauer, 1978; Nayate et al., 2005). It is believed that in AS there are connectivity problems between brain regions, but once again, the studies on this are confounded by diagnostic and sample variables.

Frontal lobe hypotheses. Studies of adults with AS have demonstrated abnormalities in neuron structure in the frontal lobes. These abnormalities were related to the severity of obsessional behaviors and symptoms (Murphy et al., 2002). Decreased volume in the frontal lobes has been demonstrated (Abell, Krams, Ashburner, Passingham, & Friston, 1999; McAlonan et al., 2002) (although brain changes are also observed elsewhere, see below). Other studies have demonstrated decreased brain maturation (Zilbovicius et al., 1995) and anatomical changes in the frontal lobes (Piven et al., 1996). This may result in decreased conductivity between the frontal lobes and other brain regions. Frontal lobe abnormalities in AS have been corroborated by neuropsychological studies indicating deficits on tests associated with frontal lobe and systems (see Hill, 2004, for a review) such as set shifting, inhibition, and perseveration. Moreover, the parents and siblings of individuals with autism spectrum disorders have been shown to have neuropsychological deficits in these areas.

Not all agree that the cortical frontal lobes per se are the site of disruption. Some authors have posited that brain defects differentially affect the middle and subcortical areas of the brain, including the underside of the frontal lobe, the temporal lobe (affecting memory and limbic emotional regions), and related subcortical areas (Damasio & Maurer, 1978). A recent study implicated defects in the medial temporal limbic circuits affecting gating of sensorimotor information (McAlonan et al., 2002). Finally, studies have shown decreased volume in the medial temporal lobe (Abell et al., 1999) and cerebellum (McAlonan et al., 2002).

Right-hemisphere hypotheses. Other authors have implicated the right hemisphere in children and adults with ASD (Gunter, Ghaziuddin, & Ellis, 2002; Volkmar, Klin, Schultz, Rubin, & Bronen, 1995). Developmental abnormalities in the right hemisphere have been demonstrated (McKelvy, Lambert, Mottron, & Shevell, 1995), including white matter deficits and abnormalities (Berthier, 1994). Many studies have found abnormalities in the brain regions thought to be involved in empathy and social behavior (see review in Dawson et al., 2002).

The right hemisphere is especially skilled at perceiving and interpreting faces. The human face contains a multitude of signals that cue us to the emotions, intent, and relationship to others. Typically developing infants pay a great deal of attention to faces, particularly the eyes and mouth regions. Because processing of human faces has such an important social and developmental function, specific brain regions have evolved that are specialized for handling this information.

Brain studies have shown decreased activation in right hemisphere areas involved in processing human faces in children and adults with ASD (Klin et al., 2002). Thus, it has been speculated that abnormal development of these regions underlies the early development of autism. Dawson and colleagues (2002) proposed that youngsters with ASD do not pay attention to faces because they have learned that processing of faces is not inherently rewarding to them. Further, they speculated that this faulty processing is caused by a basic defect in brain regions associated with face processing. It has been hypothesized that this is the underpinning of the social problems that define these disorders, seriously compromising the young child's ability to understand and relate to other people (Dawson et al., 1998; Klin et al., 2002).

Children and adults with autism spectrum diagnoses have been shown to have an abnormal pattern of focus on human faces (Boucher & Lewis, 1992; Klin et al., 2002). They may pay more attention to the lower face than the eye region (Joseph, Tager-Flusberg, & Lord, 2002; Klin et al., 2002). Yet, the lower face and mouth do not contain as much critical information for understanding emotion and motivation as do the eyes.

An innovative study mapping eye movement while subjects viewed an emotionally charged movie scene (from *Who's Afraid of Virginia Woolf*) revealed that high-functioning adults with ASD did not search faces for the reactions of others and, therefore, did not appreciate the subtle details and emotional overtone of the social interaction (Klin et al., 2002, 2007). It is thought that they paid more attention to the physical cues, treating the characters as objects rather than individuals (Klin et al., 2002).

The Borders of Autism

A number of other diagnoses are often thought to be related to or be on the borders of autism, referred to as "cousins" (Williams, 1996). This includes diagnoses such as high-functioning autism, nonverbal learning disability, semantic pragmatic language disorder, schizoid personality disorder, sensory integration dysfunction, developmental right-hemisphere disorder, hyperlexia, and social-emotional learning disability. There is controversy about whether these are genetically and biologically related conditions or merely disorders that resemble ASD. It is these disorders that make interpretation of many earlier studies difficult, as there is no way of knowing which subjects may or may not have been included.

Most of the "cousins" share with AS superficially well-developed language, notable social and interpersonal difficulties, and cognitive and behavioral peculiarities. Some impairment in reciprocal social interaction is commonly affected, as is nonverbal communication. Most "cousins" share that the members of these groups are perceived as eccentric, odd, or peculiar.

AS is grouped with several other disorders in the Pervasive Developmental Disorders (PDD) category of the DSM-IV (APA, 1994). We will thus divide our discussion into the disorders that appear in the formal nomenclatures ("autistic cousins") and those that do not ("non-autistic cousins").

Autistic Cousins
- *Pervasive developmental disorder-not otherwise specified (PPD-NOS).* This category of PDD may also be referred to as "atypical autism." The criteria in the DSM are vague and comprise a very heterogeneous group of chil-

dren (Walker et al., 2004). Some feel that this category is larger than AS, due to the looseness of the diagnostic criteria (Walker et al., 2004).

A diagnosis of PDD-NOS is usually assigned in cases where the individual does not meet the full criteria for one of the more specific PDDs. For example, this diagnosis may be used if a child does not show repetitive behaviors in the setting of social or communicative deficits. It may also be used in cases where the onset of symptoms is late, or the symptoms are not typical. PDD-NOS may also be assigned when symptoms are subclinical, or mild.

Many believe that the PDD-NOS label is the mildest of the PDD diagnosis; however, several studies have demonstrated that individuals with PDD-NOS may be quite debilitated by comorbid psychiatric symptomatology (deBruin et al., 2007; Muris et al., 1998), including disruptive behavior disorders (such as AD/HD), anxiety disorder, and mood disorders. As PDD diagnoses are acceptable by many school districts and insurance companies, they are often assigned where services are necessary but the full diagnostic criteria for autism cannot be ascertained.

- *High-functioning autism (HFA).* HFA may best be viewed as an autistic disorder with adequate language and higher IQ than classical autism. Deficits are seen in the three domains discussed above, albeit milder in presentation.

Questions often arise as to the degree of overlap between AS and HFA. Indeed, entire books have been devoted to this inquiry (Schopler et al., 1998). The differences between AS and HFA are unclear, and some authors propose that there is no meaningful difference. Some believe that HFA is AS with lower IQ. Baron-Cohen (2004) asserted that the differences between lower and higher functioning individuals with autism is dependent upon intelligence rather than core differences between conditions.

The degree of early language delay and functional language ability may differentiate between the two conditions. In the early descriptions of Asperger and Kanner, children with AS were described as having better language abilities, more prominent motor difficulties, and later age of onset than the children described by Kanner (Wing, 1981). This distinction has been borne out by more recent studies comparing individuals with AS and those with HFA. Thus, the individuals with HFA had lower verbal IQ scores, more language delay, better fine- and gross-motor functioning, and more impaired social and communicative skills than those with AS (Volkmar et al., 1995).

Some studies have indicated that HFA is characterized by relatively preserved nonverbal skills in the setting of language impairment (recall that AS may be characterized by the opposite pattern). Children with HFA may have significant language delay along with prominent social, behavioral, and other cognitive deficits, whereas children with AS may only have more subtle deficits in pragmatic or social language. While the neuropsychological cluster seen in HFA is suggestive of a left-hemisphere-mediated language disorder (Klin et al., 1995), no conclusive neuroanatomical studies have proven this hypothesis.

Social and behavioral deficits may not differ between the groups. Further, differences may be more prominent in children than in adults. Indeed, by adulthood, AS and HFA are functionally quite similar. Many individuals choose to identify as AS due to higher recognition of that disorder. We do not believe that there are any programming differences to be made at the higher education level, with the caveat that each person and his individual strengths and weaknesses always be evaluated on an individual basis.

Non-Autistic Cousins

A range of other syndromes appears to be related to autism, and the differences between them are often unclear. None of these conditions appears in the DSM. Indeed, part of the difference may lie in the credentials and training of the person making the diagnosis. Some individuals are diagnosed by psychiatrists, others by neuropsychologists, still others by occupational therapists or speech pathologists. The overlap between these disorders (and possibly the other AS cousins) also reflects the lack of diagnostic consensus in the field about how to characterize children with social deficits (Barton et al., 2004).

- *Nonverbal learning disability (NLD).* The resemblance between AS and NLD was mentioned previously. Nonverbal learning disability is a nonspecific neuropsychological profile, not a diagnosis. This lack of specificity limits the interpretation and generalized nature of most studies.

  Nonverbal learning disability as characterized by Rourke (1987) is a neuropsychological and cognitive disorder whose primary disturbance is in the processing of nonverbal information and novelty. This leads to secondary difficulties in social and emotional functioning, including restricted interests. Like individuals with AS, there is a reliance on rote and restricted behaviors (Tsatsanis & Rourke, 2008). These authors posit that the NLD profile is the consequence of early damage to fibers communicating with the right hemisphere. However, the etiology of NLD is questionable. Some individuals manifest the profile as a result of neurodevelopmental differences, some as secondary to psychiatric illness, yet others as secondary to medical compromise. Finally, in some it is acquired. Acquired NLD includes traumatic brain injury, brain tumor, treatment for pediatric cancers, and some medical illnesses. Developmental, familial NLD is probably an autism cousin.

The resemblance between NLD and AS is evident in the earliest descriptions of the NLD syndrome. Johnson and Mykelbust (1971) identified difficulty decoding nonverbal cues, such as a lifted eyebrow, a frown, or a disapproving tone of voice; social interaction; sense of time and space; and visual-motor processing in the context of good reading, spelling, and poor math. Rourke (1987) also identified deficits in nonverbal and novel problem solving, reading comprehension, math, social perception, visual spatial perception, visual motor skills, motor planning and coordination abilities in the context of good superficial language. Strengths were seen in rote memory, long-term knowledge, decoding, simple motor performance, spelling, and verbosity (Tsatsanis & Rourke, 2008). Like Mykelbust, Rourke hypothesized that the NLD profile is attributable to a dysfunctional right hemisphere, leading to difficulties in processing novelty, tactile and motor deficits (especially left-sided), decreased visual spatial processing, and decreased processing of nonverbal cues.

The core of NLD thus includes motor deficits (fine-motor, gross-motor, and psychomotor), deficits in visual-perceptual-organization skills, nonverbal communication, attention deficits, and self-regulation. This closely resembles deficits seen in many individuals with AS. Motor deficits include poorer balance and coordination, clumsiness, difficulty making finer movements, such as holding a pen or tying a knot, and poor handwriting. Visual perceptual organizational deficits include attention to detail, visual memory, spatial orientation, face recognition, and re-visualizing.

Like AS, nonverbal communication deficits include a stiff and stereotyped demeanor that appears formal and pedantic. Deficits in social language and communication are common. Vocabulary, grammar, and syntax (the linguistic aspects of speech) are intact while paralinguistic aspects (pragmatics and prosody) are impaired in both expressive and receptive language systems. Cognitive deficits also include poor neurointegration, with a focus on details rather than wholes. Processing preferences are for sequential information, rather than simultaneous information. This means that information is processed in the order in which it is presented, in a linear fashion. Self-regulation and executive deficits, including working memory, response inhibition, task shifting and planning, motivation, and social emotional regulation, are common.

Similar to AS, these core deficits appear typically in behavior, academic, social, and emotional domains. In terms of behavior, like AS, individuals are socially maladroit, rigid, and inflexible, with poor frustration tolerance. They prefer rules and routine and may have severe tantrums when expectations or circumstances are changed without forewarning. Thus, they are poorly modulated in their behavior and may appear rude or aloof.

However, not all individuals with NLD appear autistic. Many have well-preserved social and interpersonal skills. When present, the social deficits in NLD parallel those seen in AS. Because of poor processing of nonverbal cues in space and in language, individuals misunderstand others and misjudge situations. Facial recognition is typically impaired. Thus, the important behavioral and language cues by which most people regulate their social interactions are missed.

The neurocognitive profiles of NLD and AS overlap. Both disorders share verbal strengths and nonverbal weaknesses, as well as social deficits, which can lead to social rejection and isolation (Klin, Volkmar, Sparrow, Cicchetti, & Rourke, 1995; Williams, Goldstein, Kojkowski, & Minshew, 2007). Many individuals with AS have the NLD profile on testing. Thus, a neuropsychological pattern consistent with NLD may distinguish AS from HFA (Klin et al., 1995). The neuropsychological pattern in AS is suggestive of right-hemisphere dysfunction, while the neuropsychological profile of HFA, on the other hand, is suggestive of left-hemisphere dysfunction (Dawson, Finley, Philips, & Galpert, 1986).

- *Developmental right-hemisphere learning disability.*
  This diagnosis is sometimes found in neurological assessments by a physician (neurologist or developmental
  pediatrician), whereas NLD is more often diagnosed by
  neuropsychologists. Neither diagnosis is codified in the
  DSM-IV. In 1983 Weintraub and Mesulam described a
  group of adolescents who strongly resembled what we
  now call NLD or possibly AS. These subjects had high
  IQs, spoke articulately with excellent vocabulary, and had
  notable visual spatial deficit and sensory and motor deficits, suggesting right-hemisphere dysfunction (Voeller,
  1986). Further, they were described as awkward and shy,
  with academic deficits especially in math (Weintraub &
  Mesulam, 1983). Interestingly, the parents were found to
  have similar personality features. It is unclear whether
  this might be a separate syndrome from NLD.

- *Social-emotional processing disorder.* This category
  (Manoach, Sandson, & Weintraub, 1995) sometimes appears in research studies, most often as a combination of
  subjects with a variety of similar conditions such as NLD,
  AS, and developmental right-hemisphere learning disability. Generally, subjects share nonverbal weaknesses
  and social deficits. Again, it is not clear that any of these
  are separate syndromes.

- *Semantic pragmatic disorder (SPD).* The diagnosis of
  semantic pragmatic disorder (or pragmatic language deficit) is most commonly made by speech-language pathologists and is considered by most to be a language disorder.
  Semantic pragmatic disorder was originally defined by
  Rapin and Allen (1983) to describe a group of children

with mild autistic-like traits and difficulty processing the meaning of language rather than the linguistic code itself. Children with pragmatic language deficits show fluent speech with intact basic grammar, but have restricted communication skills. These children may take everything literally and often memorize words and phrases rather than decoding their meaning. They may parrot entire phrases, including regional accents and intonations, sounding robotic or pseudo-mature (Rapin & Allen, 1983). Referred to as "delayed echolalia," it may persist in adults.

Individuals with SPD may be more likely to initiate than to respond to conversation (Bishop & Norbury, 2002, 2005). While linguistic awareness is often well developed, difficulties may be evident in applying grammatical rules in conversation (semantics). There may be difficulties producing complete grammatical sentences. On the other hand, the pragmatic difficulties may occur when applying often well-developed linguistic skills in social interactions. Interestingly, children with SPD may show language characteristics similar to those with right-hemisphere brain damage, such as verbosity and poor understanding of jokes and humor (Shields, 1991). Despite some surface similarity, not all children with pragmatic language disorders share features related to autism (Bishop, 1989).

- *Schizoid personality disorder.* This diagnosis appears in the DSM-IV under Adult Personality Disorders. Originally thought to be related to schizophrenia, we now understand that individuals with this diagnosis might lie on the autism spectrum. The definition of schizoid personality disorder includes a pervasive pattern of detachment from social relationships and a restricted range of expression of emotions and interpersonal settings. This pattern begins by early adulthood and is present in a variety of contexts (APA, 1994).

Unlike AS, individuals with schizoid personality disorder do not seem to be drawn to interpersonal contact (including family). They prefer mechanical or abstract tasks and may be insensitive to social cues and social pressures (APA, 1994; Wolff & Chick, 1980). Interestingly, according to DSM-IV, a diagnosis of a PPD such as AS cannot be assigned if an individual has been diagnosed with a schizoid personality disorder (APA, 1994) although it might be exceedingly difficult to clinically and historically differentiate between the two.

The DSM asserts that schizoid personality disorder may be diagnosed in children, and indeed the label of schizoid disorder of childhood has long been applied to unusual, solitary children (Wolff & Chick, 1980). While an association with AS is clear, this diagnosis is rarely applied in modern psychiatric or educational settings.

- *Hyperlexia.* Like SPD, hyperlexia is most often described by speech-language pathologists and occasionally by educational psychologists. Clinical descriptions of children with hyperlexia appear on websites, but it is not a standard diagnosis. Hyperlexic children show mild behavioral symptoms similar to AS (albeit with less behavioral rigidity and psychiatric comorbidities); however, the condition is defined by an early development of select reading skills. Children may show excellent core processing of sound-letter relationships and basic word recognition, with restricted reading comprehension. Many children who are diagnosed with NLD or AS demonstrate excellent early reading skills, perhaps leading to diagnostic confusion. Alternately, hyperlexia may be a very mild autism variant.

- *Sensory integration dysfunction.* Sensory integration dysfunction (now also known as sensory processing disorder) is a core trait in many individuals with AS, although it can also be diagnosed in individuals who do not have autism. It is not a clinical diagnosis in DSM, and symptoms may be found in many other neurodevelopmental and learning disorders (Ayres, 2005). Sensory integration dysfunction is based on the premise that in addition to the five special senses (hearing, sight, taste, touch, smell), other systems assist in coordinating the special senses. These include the proprioceptive system, which permits us to know where our bodies are in space, and the vestibular sense, which allows us to balance and move in a coordinate fashion. Together, the senses and the parallel systems enable us to navigate the sensory environment and to regulate behavior (Ayres, 2005). Some individuals have difficulty integrating these senses and may have impairments in attention and behavior, eating, self-regulation, social functioning, motor coordination, and learning, as a result (Ayres, 2005; also see Spiral Foundation, 2006). Sensory dysfunction has been shown to persist into adulthood (Kinnealy, Oliver, & Wilbarger, 1995). As a diagnosis, sensory processing disorder is most often assessed by occupational therapists and applied to children who have abnormal responses to sensory, motor, and tactile stimulation. Many of these children show extreme responses to environmental stimuli, called "sensory defensiveness." For example, some find light touch painful and prefer deep sensations. They may find certain textures intolerable and prefer to wear the same well-worn clothes every day. Temple Grandin describes this eloquently and even invented a "squeeze machine" that delivered deep pressure she found calming (www.grandin.com/inc/intro-squeeze.html). Others have strong reactions to certain sounds, smells, or light patterns. Sensory defensive behaviors can include withdrawal, flight, or avoidance but also extreme reactions, such as hitting or running away (Blakemore et al., 2006).

Some individuals who are diagnosed with sensory integration dysfunction show interpersonal and behavioral patterns similar to those seen in AS. Indeed, many children with sensory symptoms are assigned a diagnosis of PDD-NOS. Other children with a sensory integration disorder would not qualify for a PDD diagnosis and achieve good results with intensive treatment and support. For that reason, it is unclear where the diagnostic boundaries of a description of a common symptom in AS and a separate diagnosis lie.

Getting to Know Your Student

- **Sample Intake Questionnaire for Students (general information)**
- **My Areas of Difficulty Checklist (signs and symptoms)**
- **My Stress Tolerance (stress reactions and behaviors)**
- **Stress Thermometer**
- **20 Questions Stress Test**

Sample Intake Questionnaire for Students

In an effort to anticipate your needs at college, please complete this form to the best of your ability prior to our appointment. Feel free to ask your parents or other people who know you well to assist. Please provide as much information as possible, so that we can get a better understanding of how we can help you be successful in college. Please bring a copy of the form with you, and also mail or fax to:

[Put campus contact information here]

General Information:

Today's date: _____

Your full name: _____

Your age: _____

Your birthday: _____

Your home address (street, city, state, zip code): _____

Your phone: _____

Your e-mail: _____

Parent contact information (name, address, phone, email): _____

Do we have your permission to contact your parents? _____

(If yes, ask student to sign appropriate release form)

Did anyone help with this form? _____

Who? _____

Educational Background:

Where did you go to high school? _____

Year graduated? _____

Diploma or GED? _____

ACT or SAT Scores: Verbal, Quantitative, Writing_____

Advanced Placement courses and test scores: _____

Were you in special education? _____

      If so please describe services received

      and for how long _____

Guidance counselor name, address, and phone number_____

Do we have your permission to speak with this individual? _____

[If yes, ask student to complete appropriate release] _____

Other colleges you attended

      College or program (name and address)_____

      Dates attended_____

      Degrees or certificates received _____

Current School Information:

College or university attending: _____

      City and state: _____

Student ID number: _____

School or degree program:_____

Current major:_____

Year (circle one): High School Freshman   Sophomore   Junior

Senior Grad Professional Nonmatriculated

Academic standing (circle one):

      Good

      Academic Warning

      Probation

      Suspension

Academic advisor's name: _____

Advisor's phone/e-mail: _____

Do we have your permission to speak with this individual? _____

[If yes, ask student to complete appropriate release]

Campus Life Information:

On-Campus Residents

Do you live on campus now? If so, we would like to know where

and with whom: _____

Name of residence hall: _____

Single room?_____

Suite? How many suite mates? _____

With roommate? _____ How many? _____

How are you getting along with your roommate(s)?_____

Off-Campus Residents

With parents at home? _____

With other family member?_____ With whom? _____

Off campus apartment? Shared or alone?_____

Other (such as group home)_____

Please tell us about your lifestyle and habits (privacy needs, personal space needs, neatness, etc.). _____

_____

_____

_____

_____

Are you having any difficulties with your living arrangements? ___

Appendix C

Dining:

Are you on a meal plan? _____ Which one? _____

Do you know where the dining halls are for your residence? _____

Please tell us about your food preferences or needs. _____

_____

_____

_____

Do you follow any specific diet? _____

Do you have strong food likes and dislikes? _____

Student Activities:

Are you a member of any groups on campus? _____

If so, which ones? _____

What is your role in these groups? _____

Would you like help in locating groups and activities? _____

Tutoring:

Do you have tutors for your academic subjects? If so, which sub-

jects and from where? _____

Do you need help in locating tutors? _____

Do you use academic support centers on campus? _____

       Which ones? _____

Would you like help in locating appropriate resources? _____

Judicial or Disciplinary Actions:

Are you involved in any judicial actions now or in the past? _____

Are you aware of any situations that make you uncomfortable such as bullying or drug use that you would like to discuss with someone? _____

Personal Care:

Have you located the laundry rooms? _____

Do you know how to use the machines? _____

Are you comfortable with the washroom facilities in your residence? _____

Do you know where the public phones are for your hall? _____

Do you know your important phone numbers? _____

       Doctor? _____

       Parents? _____

Transportation:

How do you plan to get to and around campus? _____

Do you get lost easily? _____

Will you need help? _____

Walk:

Do you know the route between your residence and the academic buildings? _____

Are you O.K. walking at night? _____

Bicycle:

Do you know where the bike racks are on campus or in your residence hall? _____

Do you have a chain and lock? _____

Appendix C

Car:

Do you have a car? _____

A driver's license? _____

A carpool? _____

Public Transportation:

Bus? _____

Subway/train? _____

Campus shuttle? _____

Are you familiar with the local public transportation system? ____

Health and Disability Information:

Please tell us about your main disability _____

_____

_____

_____

When you were first diagnosed with this condition? _____

When was your latest assessment? _____

By whom? _____ (Please attach reports)

Please describe your condition and how it affects you

At home? _____

At work? _____

At school? _____

With friends? _____

Do you have any other health issues or medical conditions? ____

Have you ever seen a medical doctor about this or another condition? _____

Have you been treated for a psychological disorder such as anxiety or depression? If yes, please provide details _____

_____

_____

_____

_____

Diagnosis? Treatment plan? Medications? Duration of treatment? Continuing symptoms? _____

Name of physician or therapist (name, address, phone)

_____

_____

Do we have permission to speak with this individual? _____
[If yes, ask student to sign appropriate release]
Medications taken _____
Side effects _____
Do you have a current prescription?_____
Do you know how to take your medications?_____

Would you like to understand more about your conditions and how they affect you? _____
Have you used accommodations in school in the past? If so, please list them below

_____

_____

_____

Will you be requesting any accommodators at this school? If so, please list them

_____

_____

_____

Please make sure you or your parents sent all current documentation of your disability to the Office of Disability Services at the following address:

[Mailing address here]

Personal Strengths, Weaknesses and Goals:

My best subjects and skills are:_____

My areas of special interest and talent are: _____

My goals for this semester are: _____

My long range goals are: _____

I really need a lot of help with: _____

_____

_____

_____

From Wolf, L. E., & Thierfeld Brown, J. (2008). Strategic education for students with Asperger Syndrome (SEADS). Program materials in development. Adapted with permission from L. Legere, A. Sullivan Soydan, & L. E. Wolf (Eds.), *Boston University Office of Disability Services: Supported education intern manual.* Copyright 2004, Trustees of Boston University.

My Areas of Difficulty Checklist

The following is a list of some areas of difficulty experienced by
many students with ASD. It is helpful to identify problems so that we
can better understand you and make the best recommendations for
you. Please check all of the statements that apply to you.

Learning & Memory

- ☐ New assignments are confusing
- ☐ I can't make decisions
- ☐ I don't have enough energy to start things
- ☐ I only like to study things that are interesting to me
- ☐ I have difficulty remembering instructions unless I
  write them down
- ☐ I get overwhelmed in class or when studying
- ☐ Sometimes my mind goes blank during exams
- ☐ I have a lot of memory problems
- ☐ I have trouble taking notes in class
- ☐ I don't have good study habits

Attention and Organization

- ☐ Sometimes I can't concentrate
- ☐ Little things get me distracted
- ☐ I have trouble getting started on things
- ☐ My room and notes are really disorganized
- ☐ I need to move around when I have to sit still
- ☐ I never plan my work in advance
- ☐ I don't have enough time to do everything I need to
- ☐ Deadlines make me panicky
- ☐ I start a lot of projects that I don't finish
- ☐ I only like to do one thing at a time

Communication Skills

- ☐ Sometimes I speak too softly
- ☐ I hate small talk like at parties
- ☐ I don't answer questions or say one or two words
- ☐ It is hard to listen to and understand people
- ☐ I don't like to look people in the eyes
- ☐ Sometimes I talk too loud or too high
- ☐ I am very hard to interrupt
- ☐ I only talk about things that interest me
- ☐ Some people say my voice sounds funny
- ☐ I sometimes stand too close when talking to others
- ☐ It is hard for me to start or join a conversation
- ☐ I'm boring to talk to

Behavior

- ☐ I start many things before thinking
- ☐ I need to fidget or pace
- ☐ People sometimes look at me funny
- ☐ I like to do things the same way every time
- ☐ Sometimes my behaviors seem unusual to others.
- ☐ I spend too much time online instead of studying.
- ☐ I can't relax because I am so stressed.
- ☐ I need to have something in my hands to stay focused
- ☐ I have the same idea over and over again
- ☐ I get upset when things unexpectedly change

Interpersonal Skills

- ☐ I don't like to talk to kids at school
- ☐ I don't know how to act when people come up to me
- ☐ Making friends seems really difficult to me
- ☐ I don't know how to ask someone for a date
- ☐ I just don't understand what makes other people tick
- ☐ I don't have any friends at school
- ☐ Group projects are awful – I prefer to work by myself
- ☐ It is difficult for me to ask for help.
- ☐ I tend to stay away from people at school
- ☐ I have always been rejected at school
- ☐ I like to eat by myself
- ☐ All the activity in school gets me too stimulated

Sensory

- ☐ Sometimes voices get too loud for my ears
- ☐ Being too close to other people makes me jumpy
- ☐ I only like to wear certain clothes
- ☐ I am very sensitive to heat or cold
- ☐ Things that rotate are fascinating to me
- ☐ I need to look at things to understand them
- ☐ I get lost and don't remember how to get around places
- ☐ Being touched by someone is really uncomfortable
- ☐ I get stressed in noisy places
- ☐ I avoid people who wear certain perfumes
- ☐ I wish I had a private bathroom

Appendix C

Emotions

- ☐ I feel too nervous to stay in school
- ☐ I get really afraid of people, places, or activities
- ☐ People tell me I over react to little things
- ☐ I am too afraid to talk to my teachers
- ☐ Even when I get good grades, I worry about failing
- ☐ I get down or blue a lot
- ☐ I cry all the time
- ☐ I get panic attacks
- ☐ I need to be alone
- ☐ Sometimes I get over-excited

Wellness and Self-Care

- ☐ I don't take the medicines my doctor prescribes
- ☐ At times, I don't eat very well
- ☐ I don't sleep as much as I need
- ☐ I sleep too much
- ☐ I forget things like laundry or showers
- ☐ I don't exercise or do any physical fitness activities
- ☐ Sometimes I work long hours and don't take any breaks
- ☐ I don't know how to get to a doctor when I am sick
- ☐ When I see a doctor I don't know what to tell them
- ☐ I forget to clean my room
- ☐ I don't know where or how to get my medications

Campus Resource Needs

☐ I don't know how to get accommodations

☐ I can't get a meeting with an academic advisor

☐ I don't have a quiet place to study

☐ I can't find a tutor or academic coach

☐ I have problems with my financial aid

☐ I have housing problems

☐ I don't have a local doctor or therapist

☐ I don't have transportation to school

☐ I don't have enough money for books and supplies

From Wolf, L. E., & Thierfeld Brown, J. (2008). Strategic education for students with Asperger Syndrome (SEADS). Program materials in development. Adapted with permission from L. Legere, A. Sullivan Soydan, & L. E. Wolf (Eds.), *Boston University Office of Disability Services: Supported education intern manual.* Copyright 2004, Trustees of Boston University.

My Stress Tolerance

Everyone has their own individual level of comfort, and different things affect us all differently. Some people get easily stressed or annoyed, and others don't react much. We are interested in learning about situations where you might get stressed or nervous and what tings have helped you deal with these reactions.

Please tell us about particular situations that stress you out.

Please tell us how you react or what do you do to cope when you get very:

Fearful

Angry

Frustrated

Confused

Do you use fidgets, comfort objects, or repetitive behaviors to reduce your stress or anxiety? If so, please describe.

Please use the Stress Thermometer (see page 286) to rate the following examples of day-to-day changes you may encounter as a student, based on your ability to manage the stress it may cause you.

Please also tell us more about specific things you might do in each of those situations.

Stress Thermometer

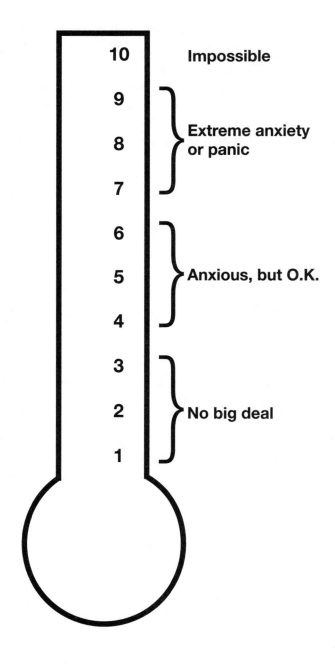

20 Questions Stress Test

		Rating	How would I cope?
1	The seat you usually sit in is taken when you get to class.		
2	The professor has left a note on the classroom door explaining that class will be held in an alternative building today.		
3	You are called upon in class to discuss a reading or answer a question.		
4	The bookstore does not have the book you need when you arrive to purchase it.		
5	Your professor announces a pop quiz when you enter the room.		
6	Your roommate has eaten something that was in the refrigerator that belonged to you.		
7	The bus you are riding forgets to stop at your stop to let you off.		
8	You must walk through a very crowded hallway every time you need to get to your classroom or dorm room.		
9	The professor wants to see you about your paper.		
10	Your roommate has left dirty clothes on your side of the room.		
11	Your roommate has left a note on the door explaining that he/she has a guest and you can't come in.		
12	Your RA tells you there have been complaints about you.		
13	They are out of the only foods you like when you get to the dining hall.		
14	The electricity goes off in your residence hall during a storm.		
15	You are locked out of your room because you forgot to bring your keycard.		
16	You misplaced your book bag with all of your homework in it.		
17	The student down the hall turns up his stereo full blast after you have gone to bed.		
18	There are no stalls available when you planned to take a shower.		
19	The fire alarm goes off unexpectedly.		
20	You need to choose a lab partner.		

©2005. Lisa King, co-director, Higher Education and Autism Spectrum Disorders Inc.; www.collegeautismspectrum.com. Used with permission.

APPENDIX D
SAMPLE FORMS AND TOOLS:

Identifying Student Needs and Resources

- **Identifying My Academic Strengths and Weaknesses**
- **Student Accommodations Needs**
- **My Campus Resource Assessment**
- **My Resource Planning Worksheet**
- **My Daily Schedule (time management tool)**
- **Assignment and Grade Tracking Form (self-monitoring tool)**
- **Pre- and Post-Semester Checklist (self-monitoring tool)**

Identifying My Academic Strengths and Weaknesses

Academic Domain	Activity	Strength	Needs Help
Registration	Knowing what to take		
	Choosing classes		
	Fitting my schedule		
	Behavior in classes		
Accommodations	Identifying needs		
	Gathering documentation		
	Going to Disability Services		
	Disclosing to faculty		
	Asking for accommodations		
	Using my accommodations		
In Class	Being on time		
	Attending classes		
	Asking or answering questions		
	Taking notes		
	Asking for help		
	Sitting still		
	Paying attention		
	Sensory symptoms		
	Unusual behaviors		
	Interrupting		
Homework	Understanding homework		
	Gathering materials		
	Following instructions		
	Organizing and prioritizing		
	Scheduling time		
	Finding space		
	Finishing homework		
	Handing in homework		

Academic Domain	Activity	Strength	Needs Help
Studying	Making a study plan		
	Finding time to study		
	Finding study group or partner		
	Finding/managing study space		
	Handling distractions		
	Staying motivated		
Writing	Outlining		
	Researching		
	Composing		
	Editing (grammar, spelling, etc)		
	Clarifying topic (with professor)		
	Finding help		
	Finishing papers		
	Handing papers in		
	Needing it to be perfect		
Reading	Understanding text		
	Too much to read		
	Lose track of what reading		
	Integrating readings		
Dealing with Peers	Feeling shy		
	Introducing myself		
	Starting a conversation		
	Looking at people		
	Sitting next to people		
	Working in groups		
	Talking to peers		

Academic Domain	Activity	Strength	Needs Help
Dealing wth Peers	Finding people to dine with		
	Afraid of people		
	Scaring people		
	Tone of voice		
Dealing with Professors	Asking for meetings		
	Getting feedback		
	Disclosing disability		
	Asking for help		
	Asking for accommodations		
	Speaking on the phone		
	Clarifying assignments		
	Negotiating accommodations		
	Making eye contact		
	Speaking up for self		
	Planning for follow-up		
Residence Life	Sharing living space		
	Coordinating with roommates		
	Negotiating		
	Resolving conflicts		
	Noise		
	Managing belongings		
	Doing laundry		
	Personal hygiene		
Other	Seeking medical assistance		
	Navigating campus		

From Wolf, L. E., & Thierfeld Brown, J. (2008). Strategic education for students with Asperger Syndrome (SEADS). Program materials in development. Adapted with permission from L. Legere, A. Sullivan Soydan, & L. E. Wolf (Eds.), *Boston University Office of Disability Services: Supported education intern manual.* Copyright 2004, Trustees of Boston University.

Student Accommodations Needs

(To complete, please get information from
My Areas of Difficulty Checklist)

Problem Areas (see form)	Possible Accommodations
Learning and Memory	
Attention and Organization	
Communication Skills	
Behavior	
Interpersonal	
Sensory Skills	
Emotions	
Wellness and Self-Care	
Campus Resource Needs	

From Wolf, L. E., & Thierfeld Brown, J. (2008). Strategic education for students with Asperger Syndrome (SEADS). Program materials in development. Adapted with permission from L. Legere, A. Sullivan Soydan, & L. E. Wolf (Eds.), *Boston University Office of Disability Services: Supported education intern manual.* Copyright 2004, Trustees of Boston University.

My Campus Resource Assessment

Domain	Resources (list all that apply)	Yes	No
Accommodations			
Administrative Support			
Academic Support			
Career Goals			
Financial Aid			
Housing			
Health and Wellness			
Other			

From Wolf, L. E., & Thierfeld Brown, J. (2008). Strategic education for students with Asperger Syndrome (SEADS). Program materials in development. Adapted with permission from L. Legere, A. Sullivan Soydan, & L. E. Wolf (Eds.), *Boston University Office of Disability Services: Supported education intern manual.* Copyright 2004, Trustees of Boston University.

My Resource Planning Worksheet

For each resource need identified above, complete this information:

Office:_____

Name of contact person: _____

Address:_____

Phone number: _____

Date of appointment:_____

Purpose of appointment: _____

My Daily Schedule

My Daily Schedule	
8:00	
8:30	
9:00	
9:30	
10:00	
10:30	
11:00	
11:30	
12:00	
12:30	
1:00	
1:30	
2:00	
2:30	
3:00	
3:30	
4:00	
4:30	
5:00	
5:30	
6:00	
6:30	
7:00	
7:30	
8:00	
9:30	
10:00	
10:30	
11:00	

Assignment and Grade Tracking Worksheet

Class: _____

Professor: _____

Assignment: _____

Percent of grade: _____

Due date: _____

Estimated time to complete: _____

Resources or materials needed to complete: _____

      Do I have all of the above? _____

      If no, what do I need? _____

Start date: _____

Completion date: _____

Grade received: _____

Pre- and Post-Semester Status Checklist

Pre-Date: **Post-Date:**

1. ACADEMICS

- ☐ Contacting DS for an appointment ☐
- ☐ Discussing your disability or accommodations ☐
- ☐ Contacting professors ☐
- ☐ Using a syllabus and planner ☐
- ☐ Finding a tutor, writing center, resource centers ☐
- ☐ Setting up e-mail account ☐
- ☐ Accessing student accounts (financial aid, bills, transcripts) ☐

2. MEALS/EATING

- ☐ Using a meal plan (the types, rules, and times) ☐
- ☐ Where to eat during non-meals ☐
- ☐ Other places to purchase food ☐

3. HEALTH AND WELLNESS

- ☐ Getting physical exercise ☐
- ☐ Accessing health and dental services ☐
- ☐ Medical emergencies or just feeling under the weather ☐

4. MONEY/BUDGETING

- ☐ Using a campus card or I.D. ☐
- ☐ Using a credit card ☐
- ☐ Balancing a checkbook ☐

Pre- and Post-Semester Status Checklist (cont.)

Pre-Date: **Post-Date:**

5. LAUNDRY
☐ ☐   Knowing how to do laundry   ☐
    Operating the machine   ☐
    (coin operated, credit cards)
☐   Finding an acceptable Laundromat   ☐

6. RESTROOMS
☐   Sharing bathrooms   ☐
☐   Maintaining regular hygiene   ☐
☐   Finding restrooms across campus   ☐

7. TRANSPORTATION
☐   Knowing how to get to and   ☐
    from campus
☐   Developing class routes,   ☐
    navigating campus
☐   Locating campus maps   ☐

8. RESIDENCE HALL
☐   Using an alarm clock   ☐
☐   Getting help from an advisor or buddy   ☐
☐   Communicating with the   ☐
    residential advisor
☐   Participating in scheduled activities   ☐
☐   Responding to fire alarms/emergencies   ☐
☐   Locating clubs or hobbies

From Wolf, L. E., & Thierfeld Brown, J. (2008). Strategic education for students with Asperger Syndrome (SEADS). Program materials in development. Adapted with permission from L. Legere, A. Sullivan Soydan, & L. E. Wolf (Eds.), *Boston University Office of Disability Services: Supported education intern manual.* Copyright 2004, Trustees of Boston University.

APPENDIX E
SAMPLE FORMS AND TOOLS:

Disability Services Toolkit

- **Sample Confidential Release of Information Form**
- **Guidelines for Documentation of Autism Spectrum Disorders in Young Adults**
- **Ideas for Working with Students Who Have No Documentation**
- **Worksheet for Coding Intrinsic and Extrinsic Domains**

Sample Confidential
Release of Information Form

I (student name or legal guardian) _____
hereby give permission to [your name and institution here] to
(circle one) provide OR receive information about (circle one) (my
OR my minor child's) _____ treatment or evaluation
by the following person(s).

I understand this information is for the purpose of evaluating a
request for academic accommodations and/or services. I understand such material will be held in strict confidence and may not
be released without written authorization by myself.

_____

_____

_____

_____   _____
Student/Parent Signature   Date

_____   _____
Witness   Date

Guidelines for Documentation of Autism Spectrum Disorders in Young Adults

Documentation for all disabilities must include:

1. A clear statement of the disability including diagnosis and Prognosis.

2. Documentation for eligibility should be current, preferably within the last three years (the age of acceptable documentation is dependent upon the disabling condition, the current status of the student, and the student's request for accommodations).

3. A summary of evaluation procedures as well as diagnostic tests/evaluation results used to make the diagnosis.

4. Medical information should include a statement of the functional impact or limitations the disability has on learning and other major life activities.

5. Each recommended accommodation should be accompanied by an explanation of its relevance to the disability that is diagnosed as well as, supporting data from the evaluation.

6. Date of first meeting with student and date of most recent meeting with student.

Specific Disabilities:
All students who wish to receive academic adjustments need to provide all of the aforementioned information that must be specific to their disability; as well as the additional information specific to their disability, as outlined below:

Autism Spectrum Disorder

Students requesting accommodation on the basis of ASD must provide documentation from a professional who has undergone comprehensive training and has relevant experience diagnosing autism in children or adults (depending on student's age at diagnosis.

- Thorough history by a developmental pediatrician or a developmental medical doctor.

- Comprehensive neuropsychological examination, within the past three years, including a discussion of the individual's current functioning as it impacts the educational environment.

- Academic testing – standardized achievement tests, including scores; and a review of the academic record.

- Current social/emotional functioning if not in neuropsychological evaluation, then by separate evaluator.

- Integrated summary, including impact of symptoms on learning, ability to function in a residential college community, and executive functioning deficits as relevant to post secondary education.

- Clear identification of DSM-IV criteria

An interview including a description of the presenting problem(s) including any significant developmental, medical, psychosocial and employment; family history; and a discussion of dual diagnosis where indicated. A comprehensive summary/interview with both parents and a self-report is needed to get a view of the individual's present function and ability.

Prescribed medications, dosages and schedules that may influence the learning environment, including any possible side effects.

Developed by Thierfeld Brown, J., Monagle, K., & Wolf, L. E. (2004). Used with permission.

Ideas for Working with Students with Asperger Syndrome Who Have No Documentation

Some students will come to disability services with little or no documentation, or with documentation suggesting another disorder other than AS. Yet the provider suspects that the student in fact has AS or a related condition because:

- Students with Asperger Syndrome typically have very poor eye contact, little or no affect, a flat tone, or lack of modulation to their voice.

- Social skills are sorely lacking as is the ability to interpret nonverbal communication.

- Most students with this diagnosis intensely dislike change and avoid it when at all possible.

As a spectrum disorder, service providers will notice a wide variety in intensity of these symptoms.

If asked to make accommodations without the presence of documentation, or while awaiting documentation, service providers might consider:

- Extended time for tests
- Distraction-free environment for tests
- Note takers if distraction is a problem for the student
- Referral for social skills instruction through counseling or groups
- Individual work with students and/or faculty members to assist with understanding assignments
- Accommodation for work/assignments dependent on groups (usually accommodated with an assignment for the individual student)
- Often a single housing assignment is requested/suggested
- Psychoeducation for the student geared to have them accept referral for assessment of possible AS
- Written release to speak with parents and other care providers
- Referred for more complete assessment (if appropriate)

Worksheet for Coding Intrinsic and Extrinsic Domains

INTRINSIC

Domain	1. Cognitive	2. Behavioral	3. Interpersonal
E A. Academic			
X			
T			
R B. Behavioral			
I			
N			
S			
I C. Co-Curricular			
C			

From Wolf, L. E., & Thierfeld Brown, J. (submitted for publication). Strategic education for students with Asperger Syndrome. Adapted with permission from L. Legere, A. Sullivan Soydan, & L. E. Wolf (Eds.), *Boston University Office of Disability Services: Supported education intern manual.* Copyright 2004, Trustees of Boston University.

APPENDIX F
SAMPLE FORMS AND TOOLS:

Campus Training Tools

- **Tips for Training Campus Police**
- **Faculty Fact Sheet**
- **Faculty Guide for Working with Students with Asperger Syndrome**
- **Sample Faculty Letter for a Student Who Has Difficulty in a Class**
- **Tips for Training Residence Assistants**
- **Sample Social Autopsy After Stressful Student Situation**

Tips for Training Campus Police

- Training of the Campus Security force is essential to create a safe environment for students with AS.

- A general training and specifics about students on campus (with releases) is not only helpful, but necessary.

- Foremost concerns for students with AS that should be addressed in trainings include:

  - Being the target for bullies

  - Stalking

  - Losing possessions due to forgetfulness or as an easy target

  - General safety on campus due to lack of awareness of surroundings

  - Outbursts in residence halls or classrooms

Faculty Fact Sheet

Asperger Syndrome

Definition
"A neurodevelopmental disorder characterized by deficits in social relations, communications and repetitive or stereotyped behavior which affects the ability to comprehend and use the thoughts and feelings" (Attwood, 2007).

Asperger Syndrome is the high end of the autism spectrum, sometimes referred to as high-functioning autism.

Typical Symptoms
- ✔ Poor eye contact
- ✔ Inappropriate social interaction
- ✔ Unusually strong narrow interests
- ✔ Above average to superior intellect
- ✔ Lacks voice intonation
- ✔ Impulsive
- ✔ Very literal and concrete thinking patterns

Classroom Behaviors
Students may:
- ✔ Attempt to monopolize conversation
- ✔ Become tangential in answering questions
- ✔ Exhibit distracting behavior in long classes
- ✔ Engage in self-stimulating behavior (rocking, tapping, playing with "stress toys")
- ✔ Be argumentative

Strategies:
- ✔ Breaks during class, particularly for movement
- ✔ Redirect responses to bring student to point of answer

Faculty Guide for Working with Students with Asperger Syndrome

Asperger Syndrome is a developmental disorder that is characterized by deficits in social skills, communication, and unusual repetitive behaviors. It is sometimes referred to as "high-functioning autism." The core feature appears to be the individual's inability to understand the thoughts, feelings and motivations of other people and to use this understanding to regulate his or her own behaviors.

The following characteristics are typical in an individual with Asperger Syndrome. Due to the diversity and complexity of this disability, you may not see all of these characteristics in a given student. It is important to understand these characteristics, because they can result in behaviors that are easy to misinterpret. Often behaviors that seem odd or unusual or even rude are in fact unintentional symptoms of AS.

General Characteristics
- Frequent errors in interpreting others' body language, intentions or facial expressions
- Difficulty understanding the motives and perceptions of others
- Problems asking for help
- Motor clumsiness, unusual body movements and/or repetitive behavior
- Difficulty with the big picture, perseverate on the details (can't see the forest for the trees)
- Difficulties with transitions and changes in schedule
- Wants things "just so"
- Problems with organization (including initiating, planning, carrying out, and finishing tasks)
- Deficits in abstract thinking (concrete, focuses on irrelevant details, difficulty generalizing)

310

- Unusual sensitivity to touch, sounds, and visual details, may experience sensory overload

Functional Impact

Communication and Social Skills

- Difficulty in initiating and sustaining connected relationships
- Poor or unusual eye contact
- Problems understanding social rules (such as personal space)
- Impairment of two-way interaction (May seem to talk "at you" rather than "with you")
- Conversation and questions may be tangential or repetitive
- Restricted interests that may be unusual and sometimes become a rigid topic for social conversation
- Unusual speech intonation, volume, rhythm, and/or rate
- Literal understanding of language (difficulty interpreting words with double meaning, confused by metaphors and sarcasm)

Some Tips

- Don't use absolute words such as "always" or "never" unless that is exactly what you mean
- Supplement oral with written instructions when revising assignments, dates, etc.
- Contact Disability Services (Put contact name and phone number here)
- Use clear directives and establish rules if …
  » a student invades your space or imposes on your time
  » the student's classroom comments or conversational volume become inappropriate

Writing

- Information in papers may be redundant, returning to the same topic focus repeatedly
- Student may be able to state facts and details, but be greatly challenged by papers requiring
  - » taking another's point of view
  - » synthesizing information to arrive at a larger concept
  - » comparing and contrasting to arrive at the "big picture"
  - » using analogies, similes, or metaphors

Some Tips

- Use clear and detailed directives when referring to revisions that need to be made
- Listing or numbering changes on the paper will provide guidelines for student when working
- If modeling writing rules, write them on a separate sheet for future reference
- Keep directions simple and declarative
- Ask students to repeat directions in their own words to check comprehension

Example: (Student arrives at your office at 1:40). "We have 20 minutes to work together. At 2:00, I'm going to ask you to take my suggestions home and start making changes to your paper. Come to my office tomorrow afternoon at 3:00 and show me what you've done."

Some Considerations

Student may have sophisticated and impressive vocabulary and excellent rote memory but may have difficulty with high-level thinking and comprehension skills. They can give the impression that they understand, when in reality they may be repeating what they have heard or read. Many individuals with Aspergers Syndrome are visual learners. Pictures and graphs may be helpful to them.

Instructional Tips

- Clearly define course requirements, the dates of exams and when assignments are due. Provide advance notice of any changes.
- Teach to generalize and to consolidate information.
- Go for gist, meaning, and patterns. Don't get bogged down in details.
- Use scripts and teach strategies selectively.
- Make sure all expectations are direct and explicit. Don't require students to "read between the lines" to glean your intentions. Don't expect the student to automatically generalize instructions. Provide direct feedback to the student when you observe areas of academic difficulty.
- Encourage use of resources designed to help students with study skills, particularly organizational skills.
- Avoid idioms, double meaning, and sarcasm, unless you plan to explain your usage.
- If the student has poor handwriting, allow use of a computer if easier for the student.
- Use the student's preoccupying interest to help focus/motivate the student. Suggest ways to integrate this interest into the course, such as related paper topics.
- Make sure the setting for tests takes into consideration any sensitivity to sound, light, touch, etc.

Sample Faculty Letter for a Student Who Has Difficulty in a Class

Dear Professor,

I write to you at the request of Kevin, who is enrolled in your History 101 class. Kevin asked me to write to you regarding his status as a student with a disability in the hope that this will help you to better understand some difficulties he is having in your class. While we typically prefer that students act as their own advocates in this regard, in some cases the nature of the disability is such that additional assistance is beneficial.

Kevin has been working with the Student Disability Office since his first semester on campus. He recently met with me to discuss some issues that have come up in your class. It is our hope that providing you with a better understanding of Kevin may facilitate communication and enable him to develop a more productive relationship with you.

Kevin's disability is called Asperger Syndrome (AS), a neurobiological condition on the mildest end of the autistic spectrum. Autism spectrum disorders are a group of disorders that share a range of difficulties in three core domains: social, behavioral, and cognitive. Individuals with this condition are often highly intelligent and academically gifted. Young children are often called "little professors" based on their vast, sometimes arcane, knowledge base and their penchant for displaying this knowledge. Young adults with AS are often uniquely qualified to succeed in the intellectual atmosphere of higher education.

Despite high intelligence, the cognitive style of AS tends to be overly literal. Some students may "miss the forest for the trees" as they focus on details and struggle with integration across multiple domains. When faced with ambiguity, some may become rigid and perfectionistic. This has implications for understanding the intent of assignments and readings in a course such as yours.

314

People with AS usually struggle interpersonally. Although linguistically and verbally advanced, many find social communication and the give-and-take of conversation challenging. Moreover, many find it difficult to appreciate the perspective of others in conversations. Coupled with some cognitive inflexibility, this rigid communication style may give the appearance of arrogance or argumentativeness. This is far from the case.

The difficulties Kevin has described with your class strike me as clearly due to his AS. Although he has not asked for academic accommodations this semester, I would like to offer some suggestions that have been helpful to other professors in similar situations. As these are suggestions that do not lend themselves to prescribed accommodations, we are approaching this in a much more informal manner. It is my hope that you and Kevin can negotiate these suggestions.

Kevin would likely benefit from more clear and regular feedback regarding his interpretation of your assignments, preferably before he has devoted too much time to developing an essay (perhaps based on a misinterpretation). Perhaps providing him the opportunity to clarify assignments ahead of time and to hand in outlines or more frequent drafts would be feasible. If the writing is an in-class quiz or exam, a brief meeting to clarify the questions would be useful. Simply understanding that Kevin approaches assignments from a somewhat different perspective than most other students in your class may help you in comprehending his efforts.

Both Kevin and I greatly appreciate your efforts to further your understanding of his condition and to assist him in being more successful in your class. If I can be of any further assistance, do not hesitate to contact me directly. Thank you very much for your time and consideration.

Disability Service Provider

Tips for Training Residence Assistants

Note: This training exercise can also be used for faculty and staff by modifying the case studies as appropriate. If you are training faculty, use the Faculty Fact Sheet (which can be adapted for Residence Life staff and others). We have provided three scenarios that are based on 20-minute training. More scenarios can be developed to be as long as needed to fill a Residence Life staff training or faculty meeting. The training can be longer by adding examples and discussing specific issues on your campus. Of course, no discussion of specific students is allowed without their permission.

Trainer:

Defines Asperger Syndrome – A neurological disorder that affects the ability to understand and respond to others' thoughts and feelings.

Describes some typical behaviors of students with AS. See Chapter 2 and Appendices A and B.

Explains some issues specific to the residence hall and college living:
1. Roommates
2. Isolation
3. Sensory defensiveness
4. Lack of understanding of nonverbal communication
5. Hygiene
6. Friends
7. Intense interests

Trainer and Group:

Case Studies:

1. Kevin moves into his residence hall and has a single room. Students see him only leave to go to class or use the bathroom; otherwise his door is always closed. Students are getting concerned about him and approach the RA. How do you respond?

   The response to this scenario is very campus specific. We recommend someone checking in on the student and the director of the residence hall contacting DS to see if they know of the student. DS cannot disclose if the student is registered, but if he is, DS will contact the student. Your campus must follow its own protocol.

2. Kevin is very disturbed by the noise on his hall and keeps telling the RA that she must keep the other students quiet. The RA knows Kevin is not very social and does not want him further isolated by asking the students to be quiet when there are no quiet hours in this hall except during exams. How should the RA respond?

   Again, this is campus and residence hall specific. A good response for some campuses would be to suggest some other places for the student to study, a white noise machine to help with sleep, and earplugs to shut out the noise. In some cases, a transfer to a quieter residence hall is in order (if that is possible).

3. Kevin has not consented to disclose his disability to the RA or hall directors, but some issues have arisen that are putting him in jeopardy of being separated from housing. One of the RAs has a sibling with autism spectrum disorders and recognizes some of Kevin's traits. How should she respond?

   Training in student confidentiality is in order here so that Kevin's right to privacy is not violated. A good training exercise would include reviewing the campus confidentiality polices and relevant laws. With a little training, the sensitive RA can be a good resource for Kevin in the residence hall, but she needs to know what she can and cannot do in terms of disclosing his disability.

Sample Social "Autopsy"*
After a Stressful Student Situation

What happened: Economics class was moved for the day to another building; Kevin knew he would be late for class by the time he got to the other building.

Sensory Issues: As classes were starting and ending, the hallways and the walkways outside were crowded with people. The noises and pushing and shoving of so many people around him created sensory overload for Kevin, who usually got to classes early to avoid this problem.

Anxiety: Kevin's anxiety was peaking as he was getting later and later for class. He was on sensory overload and began rubbing his arms and his face (to deal with the feeling of so many people around him). His rubbing became more intense as he walked with his head down. By the time he reached the Business building to which his class had been moved, he was near a meltdown. Though on the edge, he remembered that the person from DS had walked him many times to this building and taken him to an office where one of his "safe people" was. He walked directly to Amanda's office but found that she was on the phone. She saw Kevin and quickly got off the phone and closed the door to her office.

Reviewing the Situation: Amanda asked what happened. Instead of answering directly, Kevin asked if he could have a few minutes by himself. Amanda left the room and Kevin attempted some calming techniques. He kept rubbing his arms and face,

---

* A social autopsy (Lavoie, 1994), in this context, refers to a review of a situation in which the student and a DS professional, mentor, or clinician process what happened in a step-by-step problem-solving mode for the purpose of dissecting and discussing what worked and what didn't work and how to ensure good outcomes in the future. See Lavoie (1994) for more specific information.

which were now very red. About five minutes later, Amanda came back and asked Kevin what happened. She praised him for remembering to come to her office if he felt close to a meltdown.

Kevin explained what happened and how he felt. Amanda felt comfortable (with her training from DS) getting the information and knowing the questions to ask. She then called her contact from DS who came over to help out now that Kevin was calm (but exhausted). The DS person came and talked to Kevin, told him she would arrange to get him notes from the class and made an appointment to debrief this situation later that afternoon. Then she walked Kevin part of the way to his residence hall, after they had decided he could not go to class. Kevin went to his DS appointment that afternoon. He would rather just sleep, but he did not want to feel the way he did earlier in the day and knew he had to figure out ways to make this better.

Employment Tools

- **Office Culture Worksheets**
- **Sample Tip Sheets:**
  - **– Fitting into the Workplace**
  - **– Phone Calls**
- **Dealing with Doors Worksheet**
- **Interviewing Worksheet**
- **Sample Disclosure Form for Employers**
- **Outline for Sample Educational Unit**

NOTE: The worksheets and tip sheets may be administered by DS or any individual preparing a student with AS to enter an internship or job well in advance of the first work day. Alternately, they may be administered by a supervisor of an employee with AS as part of ongoing training. All worksheets and tip sheets are intended to be used to stimulate discussion, repetition, and rehearsal with the student.

Office Culture Worksheets

Department _____

What does this department do?_____

What types of people come to the office?

Type	Many Visitors	Some Visitors
Administrators		
Faculty		
Guests		
Prospective students		
Staff from other officers		
Students		

Does the office consist of mostly private offices with doors?
☐ yes ☐ no

Does the office consist of mostly partitioned work area?
☐ yes ☐ no

Does the office conduct a lot of its business with staff working in an open area, accessible to many? ☐ yes ☐ no

Do the men wear ties or suits? ☐ yes ☐ no

Do the women wear pants suits or dresses? ☐ yes ☐ no

Do you observe that people call or come in often to conduct business? ☐ yes ☐ no

Do you believe this office is a formal office? ☐ yes ☐ no
Why or why not? _____
_____
_____

Do you believe this office is an informal office? ☐ yes ☐ no
Why or why not? _____
_____
_____

Jobsite Comparison Worksheet

Department	Formal	Informal	Much Public Contact	Limited Public Contact	What I Need to Do to Fit In

Office Attire Worksheet

Staff person	Jeans	Slacks/ khakis	Tie	Collared shirt	T-shirt	Flip-flops	Suit	Dress/ skirt	Athletic shoes	Dress shoes

Sample Tip Sheet

Fitting into the Workplace

1. Remember to greet people in the office when you arrive with a "good morning" or "good afternoon," as appropriate.

2. It is O.K. to engage in a brief chat about the weekend, the weather, or something interesting that occurred between the time you left work and your arrival, but then turn your attention to your work.

3. Be sure to check in with others before you take lunch or breaks if office coverage is a concern.

4. If office coverage is not a concern when staff takes breaks and you would like to join the rest of the staff, ask "Would you mind if I join you?"

5. Follow the discussion, and if you join in, practice good turn-taking and do not take over the conversation.

6. If others invite you to join them and you would prefer not to, thank them and tell them you have made other plans and perhaps you can join them on another day.

7. Be sure you are dressed appropriately.

8. Ask for help when you need it or are stuck.

9. If you see someone needs help with something that you can do, offer to help.

10. Meet your deadlines.

11. If someone is doing something that is annoying to you, work with your supervisor to see if there is some way to deal with it appropriately.

12. When leaving for the day, say "Goodbye" or "See you to-morrow."

Sample Tip Sheet

Phone Calls

1. Telephone calls should be answered by the fourth ring. If you are covering or responsible for the telephones, be sure you pick up the call in time.

2. Follow the proper office protocol when answering the telephone.

3. If you are helping someone when the telephone rings, say "excuse me for a moment" and answer the call.
   - If you know the answer and it is short, respond.
   - If you know the answer and it is long, say "please hold for a moment."
   - Do not keep the caller holding for more than half a minute. If your work with the person will take more than a minute, speak to the caller, take his/her name and telephone number, and say that someone will call back.
   - If you do not know the answer, ask "May I put you on hold for a moment, please?" and finish up with the person whom you have been helping.

4. All messages should be taken following departmental policy; if written, be sure to write the date and time of the call, and ask the caller to spell the name for you. After writing down the caller's telephone number, say "Let me repeat the number" and do so, to give the caller an opportunity to correct any errors.

5. Do not leave the message on the desk, but follow office policy on distributing messages

Dealing with Doors Worksheet

Who?	Door Open?		Interrupt?		Exceptions	How Do I Handle It?
	Y	N	Y	N		
Dean Welch	X		X		Don't interrupt when Dean Welch is either on the telephone or talking with someone in his office. If it is very important (check this out with the secretary, Linda, or another staff member first), it is O.K. to interrupt.	Tap lightly on door and say, "Excuse me, Dean Welch" and explain the reason for your interruption.
Dean Welch		X		X	Sometimes Dean Welch will leave instructions that he does not want to be disturbed except for certain calls, visitors, or circumstances. If uncertain, check with the secretary, Linda, or another staff member.	Tap lightly on door and say, "I'm sorry to disturb you, Dean Welch, but ..." and explain the reason for your interruption.
Dean Welch		X	X		Try to minimize the number of interruptions; ask Linda or another staff member for advice if you are not sure if you should interrupt.	If Dean Welch doesn't mind a few interruptions but needs to muffle noise from the office he sometimes closes his door half way. Tap lightly on door and say, "Excuse me, Dean Welch" and explain the reason for your interruption.

Dealing with Doors Worksheet (cont.)

Who?	Door Open?		Interrupt?		Exceptions	How Do I Handle It?
	Y	N	Y	N		
Mr. Carmone	X			X	Mr. Carmone rarely closes his door all the way. If his door is partway closed, this means he does not want to be disturbed except for certain calls, visitors, or circumstances. If uncertain, check with the secretary, Linda, or another staff member.	Tap lightly on door and say, "I'm sorry to disturb you, Mr. Carmone, but …" and explain the reason for your interruption.
Advisors				X	Advisors work in cubicles and have no doors.	Check the advisor's schedule; if s/he has an appointment, meeting, or is working with a student, don't interrupt. Take a message. If the person is very insistent, check with the secretary, Linda, or another staff member.

Interviewing Worksheet

Arriving for the Interview

When you arrive for your interview, look for the secretary or receptionist and say:

"Hello. My name is _____ and I have an appointment with Ms._____to interview for the _____ position."

When the secretary/receptionist responds, thank her.

Meeting the Interviewer

When you meet the interviewer, rise (if you have been seated) and shake hands. Say:

"Hello. I'm _____. Thank you for meeting with me."

Sit down after the interviewer sits.

At the End of the Interview

When you hear the interviewer thank you for coming for the interview, and she rises, the interview is over.

Rise, also, shake the interviewer's hand, and say:

Thank you, Mr/Ms _____.
I appreciate your taking the time to meet with me.

Sample Disclosure Form for Employers

Student Name _____

ID # _____

Address _____

_____

e-mail address _____

Telephone # _____ cell ☐ landline ☐

I authorize the Disability Resource Center and the Office of Career Services to disclose information that would facilitate or contribute to acceptance into internships, practica, participation in work-study employment programs, or participation in programs leading to full- or part-time employment.

Signed _____

Date _____

Outline for a Sample Educational Unit

I. Introduction
    A. Purpose and goals of the program
    B. How the program works
    C. The university as a laboratory

II. Establishing the foundation
    A. The six categories of job types

    B. Basic expectations of employees
        1. Attendance
        2. Understanding the modified office organization chart
        3. Getting work done and meeting deadlines
        4. Lunch time and breaks
        5. Proper use of computers
        6. Proper use of telephones

    C. Office culture
        1. Dressing appropriately
        2. Names and titles
        4. Developing office social skills
        5. Office policies and routines

III. Working with your mentor

IV. Module I: identifying campus job sites
    Module II: Visiting the first placement
        Learning the organizational chart
        The daily and weekly time management schedule
        Office vocabulary
        Getting along with others on the job
        Dealing with stress and anger

V. Modules III to VI: Rotation through the various campus jobs
        Discussion about lessons learned
        Identification of any additional weaknesses

VI. Module VII: Working with Career Services to develop job
    readiness skills
        Résumé writing
        Interviewing skills

Index

333

Index

APC

Autism Asperger Publishing Company
P.O. Box 23173
Shawnee Mission, Kansas 66283-0173
877-277-8254
www.asperger.net